The way companies deal with their environmental footprint, the social consequences of their activities, and the way they govern themselves are a mess. The impact of large corporations on democracy is also in urgent need of evaluation and repair. The financial world cannot continue to be a bystander of the myriad conflicts rocking societies. In these pages, Marcos Buscaglia offers a lucid and well-informed diagnosis of the situation and an original and provocative set of ideas and proposals. *Beyond the ESG Portfolio* will become an obligatory reference in the urgent debates about the future of democracy that are happening worldwide.

—Moises Naim, PhD
Distinguished Fellow, Carnegie Endowment for International Peace and author of *The Revenge of Power*

Is Wall Street unwittingly financing wannabe dictators and undermining democracy? To know the answer, and what to do about it, read Marcos Buscaglia's fascinating new book. An unusual mixture of politics, economics, finance, and detailed knowledge of how the world works, the book provides both sharp analysis and creative solutions. Strongly recommended reading for anyone interested in ensuring democracy remains in good health.

—Andres Velasco
Dean of the School of Public Policy at the London School of Economics and Political Science, and former Finance Minister of Chile

BEYOND THE
ESG PORTFOLIO

BEYOND THE ESG PORTFOLIO

HOW WALL STREET CAN HELP DEMOCRACIES SURVIVE

MARCOS BUSCAGLIA

New York   Chicago   San Francisco   Athens   London   Madrid
Mexico City   Milan   New Delhi   Singapore   Sydney   Toronto

1 2 3 4 5 6 7 8 9   LCR   28 27 26 25 24 23

ISBN   978-1-265-11560-9
MHID   1-265-11560-5

e-ISBN   978-265-11763-4
e-MHID   1-265-11763-2

This publication is designed to provide accurate and authoritative information in regard to the subject matter covered. It is sold with the understanding that neither the author nor the publisher is engaged in rendering legal, accounting, securities trading, or other professional services. If legal advice or other expert assistance is required, the services of a competent professional person should be sought.
  —*From a Declaration of Principles Jointly Adopted by a Committee of the American Bar Association and a Committee of Publishers and Associations*

McGraw Hill books are available at special quantity discounts to use as premiums and sales promotions or for use in corporate training programs. To contact a representative, please visit the Contact Us pages at www.mhprofessional.com.

McGraw Hill is committed to making our products accessible to all learners. To learn more about the available support and accommodations we offer, please contact us at accessibility@mheducation.com. We also participate in the Access Text Network (www.accesstext.org), and ATN members may submit requests through ATN.

To Agustina, Pilar, Tomás, and Alfonso.
I hope they live in a world in which they can enjoy
their inalienable right to pursue happiness.

To all those who suffer at the hands
of autocrats and dictators.

To the memory of my grandparents Boris and Berta,
who escaped from Nazism and Communism.

CONTENTS

PREFACE

A Fear That Stuck with Me

The idea for this book crept over me while walking in Midtown Manhattan on a chilly fall day in October 2019. I had just finished meeting with one of my clients, a very smart, pleasant, and informed investor. His insights on how politics and capital markets around the world intersect are unparalleled. My conversations with him typically energize me, but this time I walked away unsettled. I had a sinking fear that investors just like him could end up financing the demise of democracy in places like Argentina, the country of my birth.

At first blush, that fear may seem exaggerated to you. But my job as an economist is to aggregate and analyze information, and then connect all the dots and identify potential outcomes. My many years and experiences in this business increasingly told me that the relationship between investing and the health of democracies is much more direct than most people know. On that day, this relationship felt perilous and very personal.

During the fall of 2019, the political landscape in Argentina was even more circus-like than usual. Populist leader Cristina Kirchner was about to be elected vice president after serving two terms as president from 2007 to 2015, which followed her husband Nestor's presidency from 2003 to 2007. What's more, she handpicked her running mate! Alberto Fernández may have been atop the ticket as the presidential candidate, but it was quite clear that he wouldn't be the one calling the shots. Based on Kirchner's previous political reigns, that dynamic did not bode well for liberal democracy in Argentina.

Populist leaders like Cristina Kirchner undermine their country's judiciary system, free press, and minority groups, and those who dare critique their policies and practices in the wake of their own interests. It becomes extremely hard to remove them from power, even when the citizenry exercises their most fundamental right—to vote for the candidates of their choosing into public office.

As democracy experts Steven Levitsky and Daniel Ziblatt argue, mutual toleration, or the acceptance that political rivals have "an equal right to exist, compete for power, and govern,"[1] is essential to the functioning of democracy. But populist leaders like Cristina Kirchner do not accept their opponents as legitimate. In December 2015, Kirchner made a show of skipping President Mauricio Macri's inauguration and then called his election "illegitimate." In her book *Sincerely*, published in April 2019, before declaring her candidacy, she defined Macri as "chaos." She added that because he is chaos, Argentina must be "put back in order," effectively planting the seeds of how she would approach her future political life.

By the fall of 2019, my gut feeling was that it would become even more difficult to remove Kirchner should she gain power again. During the four years she was out of office, government corruption cases against her advanced in the courts. The most pressing case is about alleged money laundering. Businessman Lázaro Báez secured public works contracts for more than $3 billion during Kirchner's presidencies.[2] At issue is that Báez rented more than 1,100 rooms per month in a hotel owned by the Kirchner family—but never used them. Kirchner's children were indicted, a move that seemed to anger her. For the first time in years, she experienced what it was like to be powerless in a country like Argentina, where the powerful can run roughshod over anyone who stands in their way. I didn't think she would take too kindly to feel as helpless as so many others do.

On a personal level, I had my own brush with Kirchner's political reign and experienced firsthand what it's like to be powerless under such a regime. In October 2008, a high-ranking official of Argentina's Central Bank pressured my employer after I made an exchange rate forecast that he didn't agree with—a forecast, I might add, that proved quite accurate. After a few incredibly stressful months, my wife and I moved to the United States with our four children, as I could not continue with my job in Argentina. This example is how life can be in countries with weak democracies: something as small as an unwelcome economic forecast can force you to leave your own country.

However disruptive my experience was, it was nothing like prosecutor Alberto Nisman's. In January 2015, Nisman was investigating Cristina Kirchner and several others for conspiring to remove Interpol's red alerts against a group of Iranians suspected of being involved in the 1994 bombing of Argentina's AMIA Jewish Center. According to Nisman, the deal was impunity for the suspects in exchange for a renewed trade deal with Iran. But the day before he was set to testify before Congress, Nisman was found dead in his apartment from a single gunshot wound. His suspicious death remains unsolved.

What bothered me the most that October afternoon in Manhattan was that my clients, dedicated to investing in emerging market countries, could unwittingly provide financing to another Kirchner government. In the coming years, I feared that their money could facilitate her attempts to trespass on the limits of liberal democracy.

Emerging Market Countries Suffered a Democratic Recession

Events in Argentina were not isolated. They were part of an ongoing *democratic recession* that has affected developed, emerging, and underdeveloped countries to differing degrees for years now. Starting in the mid-1970s, the world went through what Harvard's Samuel P. Huntington called the "third wave" of global democratization. Democracy expanded to Spain, Portugal, Latin America, and then to Eastern Europe, among other regions, after the fall of the Iron Curtain. That expansion hit a wall around 2006, and democracy standards have deteriorated since then.

I will focus on the interaction between markets and democracy in emerging market countries for two reasons. First, they are a key part of the democratic recession. In the words of democracy expert Larry Diamond: "The quality or stability of democracy has been declining in a number of strategically important emerging-market countries, which I call 'swing states.'"[3] Second, these countries are typically highly dependent on foreign capital, which means developed market banks and investors, as well as international financial institutions (IFIs) such as the World Bank, play a very important role in their development.

Within the financial community, countries considered emerging markets, EM for short, include most of Latin America; Eastern European countries such as Poland, Hungary, Türkiye, and Russia; China, India, Indonesia, and Thailand in Asia; and several others, including South Africa. Emerging markets aren't as economically developed as the United States, Western Europe, or Japan, but they're not extremely poor either.

What makes emerging markets so attractive to the financial community is their growth potential. The investment thesis, that is, the argument for investing in them, is relatively straightforward: emerging market equities should benefit because EM economies have, in theory, more room to grow compared to developed markets. Along the same lines, EM bonds, both sovereigns, meaning government-issued, and corporate, should offer a higher yield relative to developed market bonds, to compensate for their higher risk, including the higher probability of default. Bonds are called fixed-income securities because they promise a predetermined stream of income. The price of a bond and its yield have an inverse relationship. The lower the price, the higher the expected yield or return of the bond, because in addition to the coupons (interest payments), debt holders gain from the increase in price as bonds converge to their par value at maturity, assuming there is no default.

Investing in EM can also provide diversification benefits, the best practice of spreading investments around so that an investor's exposure isn't overly concentrated in any one asset class or subject to one source of risk. As part of a drive for diversification and the search for higher returns, most global pension funds have been increasing their exposure to EM in recent decades, either directly or through funds dedicated to EM investment.

Bolstering EM's investment thesis in recent history is the low interest rate environment globally. EM can generate significant returns when interest rates in the more advanced economies are near zero or negative. When interest rates are high in developed markets, investors can be wary of betting on emerging markets. But when interest rates are low, as they have been from the 2008 Global

Financial Crisis until very recently, money is cheap, so investors can take on more risk.

But the risks are higher when investing in emerging markets compared to developed markets. Exchange rate risk is one, as returns in local currency must be converted to the investor's domestic currency, and thus subject to fluctuating currency rates. Also, emerging market corporate governance standards can be less comprehensive. As you might expect, political instability is a major risk too. The more unstable a government and its leadership, the more economic risks that investors must consider, such as inflation, market regulations, monetary and fiscal policies, and, ultimately, the risk of nonpayment.

A big problem is that, on its own, money doesn't discriminate between democratic and anti-democratic leaders. Even though Brazil's former president Jair Bolsonaro consistently undermined democratic ideals, markets liked him because his finance minister, Paulo Guedes, was a pro-business reformist. The market's relationship with President Recep Erdoğan in Türkiye was similar. His administration stepped on democracy at every turn, but what did the market see for many years? Attractive yields on Turkish government bonds.

The rise of anti-democratic leaders like these amid increased monetary flows into emerging markets is not a coincidence, and this story isn't new. While working as an economist with some of the most prominent EM investors on Wall Street, I saw how markets applauded Venezuela's Hugo Chávez, even when it was evident that he was destroying democracy in his country.

Goals of the Book

I feared the same deterioration of democratic standards could happen to my Argentina. Not long after that eye-opening meeting in New York, on December 10, 2019, Alberto Fernández and Cristina Kirchner were sworn in as president and vice president. Since then, the administration's actions and words have confirmed my worst fears: Alberto Fernández was indeed a puppet of Cristina Kirchner, and their government attacked the judiciary, the free press, private property, and ultimately, democracy.

This prompted me to publish, in February 2020, the seminal idea for this book in an article for *Financial Times' beyondbrics* blog under the title "Democracy is under threat, we must add a D to ESG."[4] Then the Covid-19 pandemic hit, and the world came to a standstill. The assaults on democracy worsened in the world. Several governments took advantage of the Covid-19 restrictions to further undermine civil liberties and tighten their grip on the powerless. At the same time, investors poured billions and billions of dollars into EM. In my mind, it was time to pick up the pace and write this book.

My goal with this book is to bring awareness to the fact that foreign money has helped leaders like Putin, Erdoğan, Chávez, and Orbán to build their power, at the expense of democracy and human rights in their countries. Russia's invasion of Ukraine and China's increasing clout among nondeveloped countries highlights that this feature can also have implications beyond these autocratic countries.

What I want to show is that the relationship between financial markets and the recent attack on democracy is a problem, that there are some structures and incentives in the market that help to produce this undesired result, and that something can and should be done about it. The objective is not to demonize anyone, as both sophisticated institutional money managers and retail investors end up financing autocrats. This story is for the most part not one of wrongdoing or foul play, but of lack of recognition.

We can also take action on this problem. Activism exerted through financial markets is thriving with new investment vehicles such as Green Bonds. Standards like environmental, social, and governance (ESG) criteria are now embraced by the world's biggest asset managers. Undoubtedly, asset managers want to demonstrate a commitment to ethical investing, but when financial institutions make such decisions, you can bet that they're a response to client demands as well.

In my view, similar activism should confront the global threat that financial markets pose to democracy. A major challenge to overcome is a lack of objective measures of democracy that could be applied in the same way as scientific evidence of climate change, but this challenge is not impossible to surmount. After all, this is the age of Big Data, where we have analytics for everything. Still, there won't be a solution to an issue that public opinion doesn't see as a problem.

The book is intended for readers interested in ethical investments and ESG, in emerging markets investment and politics, and for those that are concerned about the fate of democracy in the world. Combining stories and analysis in a language that is accessible for readers, I show how markets have helped to finance the deterioration of democracy in countries such as Russia, Hungary, Venezuela, and many others. I also propose some solutions for this problem, including actions that individual investors, financial advisors, and institutional investors can take to avoid financing autocrats.

Liberal Versus Illiberal Democracies

The book is about the relationship between markets and democracy, which requires a baseline definition of democracy before starting. I follow the definition that Larry Diamond uses in his book, *The Spirit of Democracy*.[5]

At its most basic level, if there are regular, free, and fair elections in which the electorate can choose and replace its leaders, one could say a country has an *electoral democracy*. But, in Diamond's words: "Competitive and uncertain elections, even frequent alternation of parties in power, can coexist with serious abuses of human rights, significant constraints on freedom in many areas of life, discrimination against minorities, a weak rule of law, a compromised or ineffectual judiciary, rampant corruption, gerrymandered electoral districts, unresponsive government, state domination of the mass media, and widespread crime and violence."[6]

Based on Diamond's assessment, the ideal democracy that I use as a benchmark in this book is what is called a *liberal democracy*. A clarification is in order for American readers. I use the word *liberal* in the classical or European sense, that is, referring to economic, political, and religious liberties, and not in the American sense, which is related to left-of-center policies such as affirmative action and the expansion of the welfare state.[7] A liberal democracy, in addition to regular free and fair elections, ensures the following attributes:[8] (1) freedom of belief, speech, assembly, and opinion; (2) freedom of religion and culture and equality in the political participation; (3) the right to vote and to run for office; (4) genuine electoral competition;

(5) legal equality of all citizens under the rule of law; (6) an independent judiciary; (7) due process of law; (8) institutional checks on the power of elected officials; (9) pluralism of the sources of information; and (10) control over the military and the security apparatus by the civilian government.

These attributes are achieved to different degrees in different countries. When they are greatly diminished, democracy turns from liberal to illiberal, or only electoral, and it can cease to exist at all. Fortunately, as I discuss in Chapters 1 and 9, there are several reliable measures of how liberal democracies are around the world.

A second point of clarification is that I use the words *populist* and *autocrat* interchangeably throughout the book. Some authors classify them as strongmen,[9] dictators, "spin dictators,"[10] or "stealth dictators."[11] Purists may have an issue with me using these broad terms. But at the end of the day, any of these types of leaders try to undermine liberal democracy. They divide society between "us" and "them," claiming only they represent the people, and fostering a cult of (their) personality. Polarization is the new normal when populists or autocrats rule. They erode all checks and balances, including the legislative and the judiciary, the independent press, and nongovernmental organizations (NGOs). They blur the lines between state and party or between state and leader, implement mass clientelism, and subject the private sector to their political whims. Corruption is rampant, as it is the way to buy their aiders and abettors. They also cut the middlemen between leader and clients. These are some of the characteristics, among many others, that populists, autocrats, strongmen and strongwomen, and dictators implement to different degrees when in office.

Plan of the Book

The book has two parts. In Part One, I interweave stories with investment data to show the financial community's pivotal role in helping anti-democratic leaders around the globe consolidate power, or at least being indifferent to the deterioration of democracy. It's a lengthy track record of markets and investment banks embracing dictator wannabes, infamous types like Venezuela's Hugo Chávez, Russia's

Vladimir Putin, Türkiye's Recep Tayyip Erdoğan, and others who make it all too clear that democracy is not their goal. Oftentimes, the high yields that the bonds of these countries offer and the attractive underlying assets of state-controlled companies such as Gazprom or Aramco cause investors to look the other way—that is, if they even know that they own the assets. I also highlight how the Covid-19 pandemic increased the assaults on democracy as governments used health and safety restrictions to further curb personal freedoms. All the while, investment flows to these countries accelerated.

In any book, the hardest job is to decide what to exclude. I chose to tell the stories of Venezuela, Türkiye, Hungary, Russia, China, Bolivia, Ecuador, Brazil, and Argentina. I also included shorter versions of events in Belarus and Poland. I left out very interesting cases, such as the Philippines, India, Israel, Mexico, El Salvador, Nicaragua, and many more. I also mention only in passing the role of international financial institutions (IFIs), international banks, and companies that work on the fringes of the commercial system but oftentimes have a close relationship with dictators, the commodity traders.

In each chapter, I also had to select specific stories and high-light the characters that best convey them for the purposes of this book. The stories selected aim to get readers up to speed on what was going on with democracy and markets in these countries in the most efficient way possible. By doing so, I left aside many interesting events and several controversial autocrat cronies to prevent the book from becoming too long. The countries and stories included serve the points that I wanted to make in highlighting the relationship between democracy and the markets; for those interested in more details, I have cited many impressive books and articles in the bibliography.

In Part Two, I explore solutions to address the democracy problem, drawing parallels to the market's development of Green Bonds and its acceptance of ESG standards. I start by reviewing the evidence on whether investing in more democratic countries is more profitable, in addition to being the right thing to do. I also look for the underlying determinant of returns at the country level, namely economic growth, and its relationship with democracy. I then go over the impressive growth of ESG investing and discuss its drivers and controversies. I argue that ESG criteria does not account for democracy standards, but it should. Finally, I propose alternatives by which investors could avoid investing in undemocratic countries, including ways to add democracy's "D" to ESG. I do not claim to have all the answers to the problem of how to account for democracy in investment decisions. My goal is to open the debate, as I think the discussion is critical to ensuring the health of democracies around the world.

What is at stake is not trivial, as Russia's invasion of Ukraine in 2022 made quite clear, and timing is of the essence. In ever greater numbers, the personal rights and freedoms of people around the world are in danger, particularly minorities and people who speak out against injustice. What these modern-day anti-democracy movements lead to isn't easy to predict. But the world learned the hard way in the first half of the twentieth century that these movements can be very damaging. In many ways, they already are. You can ask people in every corner of the globe about the hardships that they endure due to this democratic recession.

Let's make sure that we aren't unknowingly complicit through our investment portfolio. Countries are independent, and it is hard to stop them undermining their democratic standards. At the very least, we do not want them to do it with our money.

CHAPTER 1

THE UNEASY RELATIONSHIP BETWEEN WALL STREET AND DEMOCRACY

Investors care for the environment, and they are taking action in their portfolios; they should do the same with democracy.

Uncovering the Relationship Between Wall Street and Democracy

Are you in favor of autocrats such as Russia's Vladimir Putin or Venezuela's Nicolás Maduro? It's probably a question you never thought anyone would ask you. For most people, the answer is obvious: of course, you're against politicians who erode democratic standards.[1]

Yet, if you look carefully at your pension fund, your Roth IRA, or any other investment account you own, you'll probably see that you've been financing them. In fact, over the last decade, you most likely helped finance the leaders who created what is now a clear democratic recession in Türkiye, Poland, Hungary, Russia, Nicaragua, Venezuela, Bolivia, Niger, the Philippines, and India, among many others.

In 2020, the Covid-19 pandemic accelerated the ongoing assault on democracy. Freedom House, a US-based democracy advocacy group established in 1941, published a report titled *Democracy Under Lockdown* in October 2020.[2] The report concluded that "since the coronavirus outbreak began, the condition of democracy and human rights has grown worse in 80 countries" and that it is "exacerbating 14 years of consecutive decline in freedom." The Economist Intelligence Unit (EIU), a research and analysis division of the *Economist*, argued that "across the world in 2020, citizens experienced the biggest rollback of individual freedoms ever undertaken by governments during peacetime."[3]

Meanwhile, investors continued to pour massive amounts of capital into emerging markets' bonds and stocks. In January 2020, right before lockdowns went into effect, EM governments issued $33.1 billion of debt and EM corporates issued $77.5 billion, the second highest on record. After a brief Covid-induced interruption, EM government bond issuance restarted and increased in the fourth quarter of 2020. According to data from the Institute of International Finance (IIF), investors poured a record $76.5 billion into emerging market–focused funds in November 2020.[4] "The market is red-hot for higher yielding assets, and lower-rated sovereigns are particularly interesting for investors,"[5] said Stefan Weiler, head of Europe, Middle East and Africa (EMEA) debt capital markets at J.P. Morgan in a *Financial Times* article at the time. A credit rating reflects the capacity of the issuer to repay the debt. Bonds with lower ratings have higher expected yields or returns, to compensate for the higher perceived risk.

For perspective on EM's growth trajectory, in 1988, emerging economies represented just 1 percent of the global investable equity when Morgan Stanley launched the widely followed Morgan Stanley Capital International (MSCI) index.[6] At the end of 2020, EM comprised 13 percent of that index. It's a similar story in the sovereign bond market; by the third quarter of 2019, global investors could access $1.2 trillion of foreign currency EM government bonds, mostly USD and euro-denominated, up from only $394 billion in 2003.[7] The sovereign debt market denominated in local currency—that is, bonds issued in the issuer's currency, like the Brazilian real—has grown at an even faster rate. From 2003 to 2019, issuance grew at a 15 percent compound annual rate to the equivalent of more than $10 trillion, although global investors can only access a small part of this lot, as most of it is held by local investors.[8]

The problem is that many of these high-yield, lower-rated government bonds are from countries where democracy is either inexistent or in peril such as China, Russia, India, Türkiye, and Poland. The global financial community hasn't acknowledged its role in undermining these ideals. For many years, investment banks from the United States, United Kingdom, and across Europe have issued and underwritten bonds from questionable governments like those led by Venezuela's Chávez, Hungary's Viktor Orbán, and Türkiye's Recep Erdoğan. These bonds were in turn purchased by retail investors, institutional investors, and pension funds in the developed world.

These autocratic leaders are also indirectly financed when foreign investors purchase bonds or stocks issued by quasi-sovereign issuers, sometimes called state-owned enterprises (SOEs). These companies are fully or partially government-owned. Examples include energy companies such as Gazprom in Russia and PDVSA in Venezuela. The Saudi Arabian oil company Aramco offers a cautionary tale of the relationship between these quasi-sovereigns and democratic ideals.

On October 2, 2018, prominent journalist Jamal Khashoggi walked into the Saudi consulate in Istanbul to get documents that he was told he needed for his upcoming wedding. Khashoggi was once close to the Saudi royal family, but he had fallen out of favor with them due to his pointed criticism of their policies and practices and his frequent calls for reform. In something of a self-imposed exile, he moved to the United States in 2017, where he was a columnist for the *Washington Post*, whose slogan since 2017 has been "Democracy Dies in Darkness." While at the consulate, Khashoggi was assassinated, allegedly by people close to Crown Prince Mohammed bin Salman.[9]

However, Khashoggi's death and the royal family's purported role in it didn't matter much to the markets when quasi-sovereign Aramco made its market debut in December 2019. At the time, Aramco's initial public offering (IPO), the first sale of the company's shares to the public, was the world's largest on record, valuing the company at $1.7 trillion, and raising $25.6 billion.[10] The IPO had been in the works since 2018, around the time of Khashoggi's death and the international outrage that followed.

The financing of autocrats is not limited to purchases of sovereign or quasi-sovereign bonds and stocks. When foreign investors purchase bonds or stocks of private companies in nondemocratic countries, they may also be indirectly financing autocrats. The extreme case is China, where it is often argued that even privately owned companies are not independent from the directives of the Chinese Communist Party (CCP). In less extreme cases of autocracy, sometimes private companies in nondemocratic countries must engage in unprofitable ventures at the behest of the country's leader, and bribing officials is sometimes the only way to stay in business.

The bonds and stocks of nondemocratic countries often end up in the portfolios of developed countries' pension funds. These, directly or indirectly via firms that specialize in investing in EM, allocate part of their portfolios to funds that track indices like J.P. Morgan's hard currency Emerging Markets Bond Index (EMBI), a popular government-issued bond index, or to Morgan Stanley's MSCI Emerging Markets Index, a stock index.

It's not just big financial institutions that have significant stakes in EM. Individual investors have more access to EM debt and equity markets than ever before via mutual funds or through exchange-traded funds (ETFs). ETFs are investment vehicles that attempt to replicate the performance of an index such as the S&P 500 (an index of the 500 largest companies in stock exchanges of the United States); they typically have low costs (expenses and taxes) and trade like stocks. Mutual funds have higher expenses and can be passive (following an index) or active. Active mutual funds are managed by portfolio managers that have a defined trading strategy (for example, invest in Latin American bonds or European stocks), but are not constrained to replicating an index.

Exchanged-traded funds are now one of the most important vehicles for money to reach EM issuers. The iShares J.P. Morgan USD Emerging Markets Bond ETF alone was a $17.86 billion fund in February 2023.[11] All told, including both stock and bonds, the total value of EM-dedicated ETFs was more than $331 billion in January 2023.[12] For the average investor, financing EM countries' leaders, including dictator-hopefuls, is just a couple of clicks of a mouse or taps on a smartphone away.

Sometimes the link between Wall Street and democracy's demise takes a more indirect route through international financial institutions (IFIs). In his book *The Tyranny of Experts*, economist William Easterly, who specializes in economic development, concluded that these institutions' approach to economic development is based on "a technocratic illusion: the belief that poverty is purely a technical problem."[13] According to Easterly, technocrats running these institutions believe that poverty arises from a lack of expertise, not a lack of rights. In their view, roads, fertilizers, and antibiotics are the antidote for poverty, not personal freedoms, property rights, or, more broadly, liberal democracy. In this vein, the World Bank is "legally not allowed by its own charter to use the word democracy," according to Easterly.[14] Not surprisingly, a big share of its loan portfolio is directed toward nondemocratic countries.

Loans from development banks like the World Bank are funded by a combination of equity financed by member countries and by bonds. Rated AAA, the highest possible grade credit rating agencies assign to bonds, IFI's debt is usually quite attractive to investors. One reason is that development bank loans are paid out before other types of government debt in times of distress; they have what's called *seniority*. As of September 2020, the World Bank had issued a hefty $243 billion worth of bonds.[15] With so many bonds from international financial institutions in the market, there's a reasonable chance some of them are part of your portfolio. There's also a reasonable chance that bonds like these and others are financing actions that hinder liberal democracy among developing countries.

Let's Emulate How Markets Tackle Environmental Risks

Here's another question: Are you in favor of global warming, male-only company boards, or corporate malfeasance? I would like to think that was a very quick no for you. But the difference between this question and the one I asked previously is that, right now, you have the power to do something about it in your financial portfolio.

Green Bonds, which target projects that make a positive environmental impact, are part of the financial market's response to climate change. These bonds derive from the market's acceptance of substantial scientific evidence on climate change and pressure from environmental activists. Companies, governments, and international financial organizations are regular issuers of Green Bonds, a market that exceeded $1 trillion in 2021, and issuance continues to soar. New Green Bonds offered to the market totaled only $11 billion in 2013; five years later, in 2018, new issuance totaled $167.3 billion, and in 2020 that number was $269.5 billion.[16] The Covid-19 pandemic seems to have been a game changer for how investors and companies perceive the relationship between the environment and our daily lives. The total green, social, and sustainability (GSS) bond market grew to $2.9 trillion by June 2022, according to a September 2022 report by the Bank of International Settlements (BIS).[17] Importantly, issuers are encouraged to comply with a set of standards known as the Green Bond Principles, which look to promote and ensure integrity in the green market.[18]

This type of activism exerted through financial markets to achieve certain standards extends beyond climate change. Environmental, social, and governance standards used to screen and assess investments are no longer niche. Fund managers around the world are incorporating them as staple considerations in their investment framework. Like Green Bonds, the rise of ESG is fund managers' response to client preferences, many of whom want to ensure that they don't finance investments that damage the environment or companies that don't value equal rights. In 2022, ESG investments accounted for one in three dollars under professional management in the United States and one in two in Europe.[19]

BOX 1.1 ESG Investing

Environmental, social, and governance criteria are a set of extra-financial standards used to evaluate or to screen a company, a bond, or an investment project:

- The E in ESG refers to conservation of the environment, and the criteria includes energy management and the impact on climate change, carbon emissions, waste management, biodiversity loss, and air and water pollution, among others.

- The S refers to the consideration of people, and the criteria include diversity (e.g., gender, race), human rights, labor standards, community engagement, and responsible supply chains, among others.

- The G refers to the way companies are run, and the criteria include corporate governance, executive compensation, risk management practices, and the treatment of conflicts of interests and bribery, among others. In the context of sovereign bonds, the G includes criteria such as political stability and government effectiveness.

There are many ways to implement ESG investing, and it has been subject to an increasing backlash. Two facts are nevertheless uncontestable: (1) the size of assets under management that follow some type of ESG criteria has soared in recent years, and (2) ESG does not take liberal democracy considerations into account. I'll get back to ESG in Chapter 9.

Financial markets following science, listening to activists, and reacting appropriately is encouraging. With a solid precedent set, there's reason to hope that the same thought processes can be used to address the growing problem of Wall Street financing governments that are undermining democracy. The challenge is that there's no clear objective line of what is a liberal democracy and what it is not. Complicating matters is that democracy is dying in new ways, not just via the brute force of military coups, as Steven Levitsky and Daniel Ziblatt argue in their influential book *How Democracies Die*: "Because there is no single moment—no coup, declaration of martial law, or suspension of the constitution—in which the regime obviously 'crosses the line' into dictatorship, nothing may set off society's alarm bells."[20]

According to Levitsky and Ziblatt: "There is another way to break a democracy. It is less dramatic but equally destructive. Democracies may die at the hands not of generals but of elected leaders—presidents or prime ministers who subvert the very process that brought them to power. . . . More often, . . . democracies erode slowly, in barely visible

7

steps." They add that "Many government efforts to subvert democracy are 'legal,' in the sense that they are approved by the legislature or accepted by the courts."

While scientists can quantify climate change, measuring democracy's vital signs is a different story. There are, however, several trustworthy organizations that track democracy's health around the world. Their conclusions are the same: democracy is in trouble. I will focus on three of them, although there are more available.*

Published annually since 1973, Freedom House's *Freedom in the World* report now covers 195 countries and 15 territories.[21] Their index includes 26 measures of a well-functioning liberal democracy, including the electoral process, political pluralism and participation, functioning of the government, freedom of expression and/or belief, associational and organizational rights, the rule of law, and personal autonomy and individual rights. Freedom House aggregates the data into two rankings, one for political rights and another one for civil liberties, and then categorizes the countries as *Free, Partly Free,* and *Not Free.*

Data from Freedom House shows a disquieting trend: "Between 1988 and 2005, the percentage of countries ranked Not Free in the *Freedom in the World* report dropped by almost 14 points (from 37 to 23 percent), while the share of Free countries grew (from 36 to 46 percent). This surge of progress has now begun to roll back. Between 2005 and 2018, the share of Not Free countries rose to 26 percent, while the share of Free countries declined to 44 percent."[22] This trend continued after 2018. Freedom House's report, "Freedom in the World 2023: Marking 50 Years in the Struggle for Democracy," noted the seventeenth consecutive decline in global freedom. It was, however, the most upbeat "Freedom in the World" report in years, arguing that "the struggle for democracy may be approaching a turning point," since the decline in democracy was the smallest in 17 years.[23]

---

* These include the Institute for Democracy and Electoral Assistance (IDEA) Global State of Democracy Indices and some indices that encompass other aspects of liberty as well. One is Cato and Fraser Institute's Human Freedom Index, which includes personal, civil, and economic freedoms. Another one is Bertelsmann Stiftung's BTI Transformation Index, which measures the transformation process toward democracy and a market economy.

Another reliable measure of democracy is the Democracy Index, which the Economist Intelligence Unit (EIU) established in 2006, covering 165 countries and two territories. The Democracy Index gauges five categories: electoral process and pluralism, functioning of government, political participation, political culture, and civil liberties. Based on scores in these categories, the EIU's Democracy Index classifies countries into four types of regimes: Full Democracy, Flawed Democracy, Hybrid Regime, and Authoritarian Regime. In its 2019 annual report, the EIU concluded that "global democracy is in retreat."[24] In 2020, the EIU's average Democracy Index was the lowest on record.[25] Two years later, things had not improved. In its 2022 report, the EIU talked about "stagnation" of democracy, highlighting that it was a dismal result because in 2022 "the world started to move on from the pandemic-related suppression of individual liberties that persisted through 2020 and 2021."[26] The EIU concluded that 2022 was a "disappointing" year for democracy, given expectations of a rebound.

Finally, in 2014, the Varieties of Democracy Institute (V-Dem) created the Liberal Democracy Index (LDI). V-Dem classifies the countries in two forms of *democracy* (Liberal and Electoral) and two forms of *autocracy* (Electoral and Closed). In its Democracy 2020 Report, titled "Autocratization Surges—Resistance Grows,"[27] V-Dem notes that the data in the report "show a global decline in liberal democratic institutions." The decline continued in 2021 and 2022. According to V-Dem, "the level of democracy enjoyed by the average global citizen in 2022 is down to 1986 levels,"[28] noting that in 2022 the world had more Closed Autocracies than Liberal Democracies for the first time in two decades.

The democratic recession is all too evident for democracy watchers, but as we will see in the following chapters, it went mostly unnoticed by investors until Russian tanks crossed the border of Ukraine. The sound of war woke up the financial world to the perils of autocracy.

KEY TAKEAWAYS OF CHAPTER 1

This chapter:

- Introduces some of the main stakeholders, investment vehicles, and incentive mechanisms of investing in emerging market stocks and bonds. Among these are rating agencies, ETFs, mutual funds, government (sovereign) bonds, J.P. Morgan's EMBI, and Morgan Stanley's MSCI index.

- Explains some of the basic elements of fixed income (bond) investment applied to emerging markets.

- Argues that liberal democracy is backsliding globally, sometimes in subtle ways, and that autocracy is on the rise.

- Compares the market's reaction to climate change and environmental risks to its reaction to democracy's slide. The former gave rise to Green Bonds and ESG investment criteria, with investors pouring trillions of US dollars into new investment vehicles that consider the impact on the environment, among other factors. The latter has spurred little reaction until now.

- Introduces the three main democracy indices: Freedom House, V-Dem, and the Economist Intelligence Unit (EIU). Publicly available, these indices provide good insight on the current state of democracy and human rights across the world.

CHAPTER 2

FINANCING THE REVOLUTION IN VENEZUELA

Wall Street's love relationship with "El Comandante"

A Goldman Sachs Purchase That Should Have Raised Red Flags

On May 28, 2017, the *Wall Street Journal* sent shock waves through global markets when it broke the story that the asset management division of Goldman Sachs, GSAM, had purchased bonds from Venezuela. According to reporters Kejal Vyas and Anatoly Kurmanaev, GSAM paid 31 cents on the dollar, or $865 million, to purchase $2.8 billion worth of bonds issued by state-owned oil company Petróleos de Venezuela SA, known as PDVSA.[1]

Adding intrigue to the story, GSAM didn't buy the bonds through the usual Wall Street channels, namely big investment banks such as J.P. Morgan or Bank of America, but rather through a little-known intermediary called Dinosaur Securities, according to Venezuelan economist Francisco Rodriguez. Even though Rodriguez argues that the purchase was made to raise the exposure to Venezuela's debt "in anticipation of a potential change of government,"[2] the transaction's optics were as sketchy as the purchase was risky. Still, the people who made the decision to buy the bonds were not concerned enough to prevent them from making the purchase.

Only Wall Street stalwarts BlackRock (the biggest asset manager in the world with more than $8.6 trillion by December 31, 2022),[3] Vanguard, Fidelity, State Street Global Advisors, and J.P. Morgan Asset Management are bigger than GSAM and its roughly $2 trillion in assets under management (AUM) as of December 31, 2022.[4] GSAM employs more than 2,000 top-notch professionals who work in 31 offices around the globe. Its ranks are full of Ivy League and Oxford-Cambridge alumni.

Given its size and scope, it is impossible for GSAM to avoid investing in troubled countries and companies. For example, most pension funds allocate part or all of their portfolios to asset managers like GSAM—after all, they are experts in managing money. To measure their performance, these asset managers compare their returns to those of benchmark portfolios, an asset manager's scorecard.

In the emerging markets bond universe, many investment banks produce these benchmark portfolios, also called indices. J.P. Morgan produces the most closely followed emerging market benchmark indices.[5] Its three most popular indices are for government debt denominated in foreign currency, known as the EMBI for short; government debt issued in local currency, known as the GBI-EM; and corporate foreign currency debt, or the CEMBI. There are many variations of these indices.

Venezuela composed about 5 percent of the EMBI for years. But because the yield on Venezuelan debt has been about five times higher than that of other countries in the index, some years it accounted for about 20 percent of its expected return.[6] This made it impossible for asset managers like GSAM to ignore Venezuela: if it did not invest in Venezuela's bonds, other asset managers would have outperformed GSAM, given how profitable Venezuela's bonds were in some periods, and pension funds and other investors would have taken their funds out of GSAM and placed them with other asset managers.

The timing of Goldman Sachs' purchase, however, was not optimal. Just a few days before, renowned Venezuelan economist Ricardo Hausmann of Harvard University had published an op-ed in *Project Syndicate* titled "The Hunger Bonds," whose argument sounds much like the theme of this book. In this piece, Hausmann stated that "Investing often creates moral dilemmas over goals: Should we aim to do well or to do good? Is it appropriate to invest in tobacco companies? Or in companies that sell guns to drug gangs?" He then argued that investors pour money into Venezuela bonds because they have very high yields, but that doing so means "wishing for really bad things to happen to Venezuela's people."[7] The problem, Hausmann wrote, was that to pay the debt services of the bonds, the government cut imports to the point where it was literally starving the population. In addition, a few months before, Julio Borges, the National Assembly president and a member of the opposition, had warned about Deutsche Bank's possible involvement in selling some of Venezuela's gold from its international reserves. He wrote that doing so would be tantamount to acting "in favor of a government that is recognized as dictatorial by the international community."[8]

The timing of Hausmann's op-ed was not capricious. Venezuela lost any semblance of democracy in 2016 and early 2017. Events escalated after the election of December 2015, when the opposition scored an important electoral victory by getting two-thirds of the 167-seat National Assembly.

The elections took place after the economy shrank by a hefty 3.9 percent in 2014 and 6.2 percent in 2015. In hindsight, these contractions paled in comparison to what was to come, but at that point the 2014–2015 recession was one of the most devastating in Venezuela's history. The bad economy surely helped the opposition coalition known as the Democratic Unity Roundtable (MUD) to overcome the unfair electoral playing field it faced to score its biggest victory since Hugo Chávez had been elected president in 1998.

According to the Freedom House's *Freedom in the World 2017* report, "the 2015 elections were marred by a delayed initial announcement, a campaign environment clearly tilted in favor of the ruling PSUV (Partido Socialista Unido de Venezuela), disqualifications of prominent opposition candidates, government abuse of public resources to boost voter support, uneven access to state-dominated media, a lack of international observers, some violence, and reported intimidation and monitoring by superiors of state employees with the aim of ensuring that they voted for the government, followed by threats and firings after the results were announced."[9]

The PSUV became a victim not only of its economic mismanagement, but also of its own electoral rules.[10] Since coming into power, a key element of PSUV's success was its manipulation of electoral rules and its control of the Consejo Nacional Electoral (CNE), the national electoral council. As we will see in other chapters, manipulating electoral rules is common practice in most, if not all, countries governed by populists willing to undermine democracy. One method is to change the electoral rules to gerrymander and to amplify victories, no matter how sketchy the math. For example, changes implemented by the government in 2009 came into play in 2010 when the PSUV received 48.1 percent of the votes versus the opposition's 47.2 percent, but somehow, PSUV captured 59 percent of the National Assembly.

In 2015, the tables turned on the government. The opposition won 56 percent of the votes, but two-thirds of the seats in the National Assembly. Constitutional provisions allow a party or coalition that controls two-thirds of the National Assembly to introduce important changes. They could remove members of the Supreme Court (TSJ, by its Spanish acronym), and remove members of the CNE. They could also call for a Constitutional Convention, which would have had the potential to supplant all existing elected branches of government (executive, legislative, and judiciary). Many thought it was the end of the *Chavismo*.*

But 10 days after the CNE formally accepted that the opposition had reached the pivotal number of 112 seats in the National Assembly, the government's campaign chief, Jorge Rodríguez, accused a high-ranking state official from Amazonas, a region controlled by the opposition, of vote buying. Then, one of the losing candidates from Amazonas requested that the Electoral Court nullify the state's results, in which the opposition captured three out of four seats up for grabs.

This was only the beginning of a clash of powers that deprived the National Assembly of its attributions. In late 2015, before losing its majority, the government appointed 13 new justices to the 32-member TSJ. The outgoing National Assembly also granted President Nicolás Maduro, Chávez's successor, powers to rule by executive order, which he used to reform nine laws, "annulling any powers of oversight by the National Assembly from the statutes."[11] The TSJ then repeatedly struck down the bills passed by the new

---

* *Chavismo* is an ideological current based on socialism, nationalism, and anti-imperialism, inspired by the figure of Venezuelan leader Hugo Chávez (1999–2013).

National Assembly and curtailed its authority,[12] rendering it totally irrelevant for practical division-of-power purposes.

The clash deepened throughout 2016 and early 2017. In 2016, Maduro-controlled courts blocked the collection of signatures needed for a referendum to recall Maduro. Under the country's 1999 Constitution, if 20 percent of registered voters sign a petition, a referendum is held to decide whether the president or any other public official can serve for the remainder of their term. For this to happen, a majority of voters must support the decision on the ballot, among other requisites. In 2004, the opposition gathered the necessary signatures to call for such a vote, but President Chávez prevailed, as only 40.64 percent of voters supported his removal. This time, the CNE blocked the initiative from the start with dubious allegations of signature fraud.[13] With the signature collection invalidated, in October 2016 the CNE cancelled the referendum.

Populist Leaders' Common Traits

The inability to stage the recall referendum enraged the opposition, and people took to the streets in massive and often violent protests.[14] The events that preceded and followed these protests underscore five common traits of democracies under attack by populist regimes.

First, populist regimes, whether from the left or from the right, turn more authoritarian when they become less competitive electorally.[15] These regimes maintain the facade of free and fair democracies while tilting elections their way, but not so much that it leads international observers to call fraud.

Distinct from fascists, populist leaders do not plan to abolish democracy.[16] But when elections, even severely manipulated ones, put their power at even the slightest risk, they move to do away with their results. This is what happened in Venezuela in 2016. "Venezuela did not function as a representative democracy in 2016,"[17] according to Freedom House, when it lowered Venezuela's democracy status from Partly Free to Not Free. Venezuela's score in the Economist Intelligence Unit's Democracy Index also declined in 2016, although it remained a Hybrid Regime until 2017, when it received an Authoritarian Regime score.

However, that did not stop Wall Street from investing in Venezuela's bonds. By the time GSAM purchased the PDVSA bonds in May 2017, mutual fund filings showed that asset managers such as Fidelity, PIMCO, BlackRock, T. Rowe Price, and Ashmore, among many others, held Venezuela's sovereign bonds.[18] This was unsurprising: by that point, Venezuela was an important member of several bond indices tracked by institutional investors, including J.P. Morgan's EMBI.

The second, but related, trait is that populist regimes become more repressive over time. This is in the very nature of populism; populists rely on their personal appeal and not on the institutions of democracy, and they build power by creating enemies. Russian writer Leo Tolstoy's infamous phrase, "all happy families are alike, but every unhappy family is unhappy in its own way,"[19] could apply to populist regimes. They are populists in their own way, but they all aim to break down institutional systems by polarizing societies into two antagonistic camps. They divide society into the "true people" and their "enemies," claiming to be the only representatives of the interests and the voice of the true people. They do not have political adversaries, they have enemies.

What distinguishes populists is how they construct their "true people." It may be along religious lines, cultural-ethnic lines, or along political/socioeconomic lines. Chávez operated in this last bucket; to him, the true people were the forgotten majorities, left aside by the neoliberal policies supported by the United States and the IMF, and aided and abetted by, in his words, "those self-serving elites who work against the homeland."[20] Populist leaders try to establish a direct link between them and the true people, unmediated by the elite-controlled media, with total loyalty required. Chávez once said: "I demand absolute loyalty to me. I am not an individual. I am the people."[21] Said another way, Chávez thought of himself as a modern incarnation of Louis XIV's "L'état c'est moi" ("The state, that is me," or "I am the state"). Without the safety nets provided by democratic institutions or respected political adversaries to negotiate with, populist leaders can suffer catastrophic failures. The stakes of losing power are too high for them. Leaving power most likely means going to jail, so the more power they acquire, the more corrupt they become to maintain it. As Kurt Weyland, one of the leading scholars on populism, says, "populist leaders live dangerously." He suggests, "To diminish this grave risk, personalistic plebiscitarian leaders resort to political means that propel them in the authoritarian direction." In their eyes, and the eyes of their followers, "their titanic struggle justifies the use of all means, even if it transgresses the official institutional rules."[22] This is why, to the dismay of independent observers, the followers of populist leaders do not care if they are corrupt, which they often are.

The third common trait of populist governments is the attack of the free independent press. By May 2017, there was little independent press left in Venezuela. In 2013, Maduro's first year in power, he cracked down on the independent press, in particular, denying newspapers access to US dollars. The move was something of a death blow because they needed dollars to import paper, which Venezuela no longer produces. The lack of funding along with his administration's censorship tactics sent at least 12 independent regional newspapers to bankruptcy in the first 12 months of Maduro's term.[23]

Maduro also forced independent media to be sold to pro-government businessmen, including *El Universal*, one of the oldest independent newspapers in Latin America, and Globovision and Cadena Capriles, two big media companies.* These businessmen are called *Boliburgueses*, which is a play on the words *Bolivarian*— Chávez's nod to the leadership of independence hero Simon Bolivar, whom he wanted to emulate—and *bourgeoisie*.

Nicolás Maduro, a former bus driver and union leader, rose through the ranks of Hugo Chávez's government, serving as minister of foreign affairs from 2006 to 2013 and vice president starting in 2012. He was elected president in a special election held on April 14, 2013, following Chávez's death on March 5, 2013.

Although many observers described Maduro in 2012 as the "most capable administrator and politician of Chávez's inner circle,"[24] right from the beginning of his presidency he was widely seen as a poor version of Chávez. Former US Secretary of State Madeleine Albright said that he "possesses every flaw and none of the virtues of the leader he replaced."[25]

From the outset, Maduro went hard on opposition members and repressed any protest. He denied funds to opposition governors. In

---

* Cadena Capriles is unrelated to opposition politician and 2013 presidential candidate Henrique Capriles.

2013, opposition legislators were physically assaulted by government legislators on the floor of the National Assembly.[26] Beginning in 2014, the number of political prisoners started to rise. They included former presidential candidate Leopoldo López, who was in jail from February 18, 2014, to April 30, 2019, for supposedly instigating violence during 2014's protests. Daniel Ceballos, the former mayor of San Cristobal, and Yon Goicoechea, the Venezuelan Student Movement leader, among many others, have spent time in jail.[27]

Still, the crackdown on the press and the incarceration of opposition leaders did not seem to concern Wall Street analysts or investors watching Venezuela in 2014. Instead, they were worried about oil prices. "Oil Price Fall Triggers Fears of Venezuela Default" was the title of an October 16, 2014, piece in the *Financial Times*.[28] Brent oil prices tumbled from an average of $108.6 per barrel in 2013 to $52.3 on average in 2015, sending Venezuela's economy into a tailspin. Oil accounts for more than 95 percent of the country's exports, and at certain points more than 61 percent of total government revenues.[29]

Venezuela watchers discussed whether the drop in oil prices would spur a default on its government debt. On one side, academics such as Ricardo Hausmann and Harvard University professors Carmen Reinhart and Kenneth Rogoff argued that given that the government had already defaulted on its domestic obligations, default of its external debt was highly probable.[30] On the other side, Wall Street analysts such as Francisco Rodriguez from Bank of America believed that the country could serve its debt even with oil prices at $60 a barrel if the government made some adjustments.*

In November 2013, Venezuela's government couldn't issue bonds because of the high yields, but PDVSA could. Venezuela's bond yields were high because oil prices were low, not because of the government's crackdown on democratic institutions. On November 15, 2013, PDVSA placed $4.5 billion of bonds, and then on May 16, 2014, it issued $5 billion more. These bond issues also included their share of corruption.[31]

Typically, governments use one of two methods to issue debt: they use direct auctions organized by the treasuries, like the US government does, or they enlist banks to help place them in the market

---

* Disclosure: At this point, Francisco Rodriguez reported to me at Bank of America.

for a fee. Most emerging market countries use banks when they issue debt denominated in US dollars or euros. However, Venezuela did things differently, using an opaque mechanism that placed debt with government entities, which then sold the bonds to well-connected local brokers for a hefty profit.

The bonds issued by the government of Venezuela or by PDVSA eventually landed on Wall Street. They were designed to end that way. Government bonds can be issued in different currencies, such as Venezuelan bolivars or US dollars, and through different methods. They can also be subject to alternative legal jurisdictions. Most of the bonds issued by Venezuela and PDVSA are compliant with a Securities Exchange Commission (SEC) regulations called "Reg S" and/or "144A," meaning they can be sold to non-US investors and to US "qualified" institutional buyers, respectively, with a faster listing process. If they were not paid in time or any other legal dispute arose, the bonds were also subject to the United States District Court for the Southern District of New York.

These features are important for bonds to be included in benchmark portfolio indices, and thus to eventually end up in Wall Street asset managers' portfolios. Javier Corrales and Michael Penfold, two of the most prestigious political analysts in Venezuela, concluded that "International banks and local financial institutions often colluded with the regime to place foreign debt in the local market, pricing it below market levels and then reselling it above placement price on Wall Street."[32]

These bond sale procedures revealed the fourth common trait of populist governments: Corruption reaches every level of government. Competence is replaced by loyalty, loyalty must be rewarded, and corruption is the best way to keep the regime's cadres well-oiled (no pun intended).

In her book *The Twilight of Democracy*, American journalist and historian Anne Applebaum succinctly portrays anti-democratic regimes as anti-meritocratic:

> This form of soft dictatorship does not require mass violence to stay in power. Instead, it relies upon a cadre of elites to run the bureaucracy, the state media, the courts and, in some places, state companies. These modern-day *clercs* understand

their role, which is to defend the leaders, however dishonest their statements, however great their corruption, and however disastrous their impact on ordinary people and institutions. In exchange, they know they will be rewarded and advanced. Close associates of the party leader can become very wealthy, receiving lucrative contracts or seats on state company boards without having to compete for them. Others can count on government salaries as well as protection from accusations of corruption or incompetence. However badly they perform, they will not lose their jobs.[33]

In Venezuela, there are many cadres, and there are many avenues for their members to get rich, including party members, the *Boliburgueses*, and military officials. Throughout most of Chávez and Maduro's presidencies, one of the main source of profits came from government controls on the foreign currency market. Because of these controls, at any point in time since Hugo Chávez was elected president in 1998 there have been at least two exchange rates at which US dollars could be exchanged for Venezuelan bolivars (VEB).* To simplify, there has been one exchange rate for export and import transactions and for debt payments; let's call it the official exchange rate. And there have been rates for all other transactions; let's call them the black exchange rates, because they go through the black market.

For example, to exchange VEBs for US dollars, an individual or company would go through the black market, which was much more expensive because more VEBs are needed to purchase the same number of US dollars. From 2003 to 2012, on average, the black market exchange rate was twice the amount of VEB per US dollar than at the official exchange rate.[34] This spread created substantial business opportunities. Political commenter Francisco Toro from the blog *Caracas Chronicles* dubbed the politically connected elites

---

* Due to the high inflation Venezuela suffered in recent years, there have been several currency redenominations. In 2008 the Bolivar (VEB), which had been in circulation since 1879, was changed for the Bolivar Fuerte (VEF) at the rate of 1 VEF = 1,000 VEB. In 2018, the Bolivar Fuerte was replaced by the Bolivar Soberano (VES), at the rate of 1 VES = 100,000 VEF. In 2021, the government introduced the Bolivar Digital (VED), at the rate of 1 VED = 1,000,000 VES. https://es.wikipedia.org/wiki/Bol%C3%ADvar_(moneda)#Bol%C3%ADvar_fuerte_(VEF;_2008-2018). For simplicity, we will call the Venezuelan currency VEB throughout the chapter.

who profited from the purchase and sale of foreign currency the "Arbitrageur Kleptocracy."[35]

In the case of the government bond issuances, a Wall Street broker explained the mechanism to me like this: Despite being denominated in US dollars, bonds could be purchased from the government using VEB. If a bond was worth $90 in New York, and the exchange rates were 4.3 VEB per US dollar at the official exchange rate and 8.6 at the black-market rate, locals paid 540 VEB for the bond (540/90 = 6; that is, at an intermediate implicit exchange rate of 6 VEB per US dollar). Then the government registered a gain at the official exchange rate because 540 VEB equaled $125 at the official rate. Most importantly, the bond owner sold it in New York for $90, which at the parallel exchange rate was equal to 774 VEB—an instant gain of 43 percent to the seller compared to the 540 VEB paid to the government.

"Between 1999 and 2012, the government would issue a total of $43 billion in foreign currency bonds," according to Francisco Rodriguez's estimate. "Of these, 20 issuances for $34 billion would be offered directly in the local currency market, where locals could acquire them using local currency at an implicit rate that would generally be higher than the official exchange rate yet lower than the black-market rate."[36] This monumental corruption-tainted financing scheme took place while Chávez was demolishing democratic checks and balances in Venezuela. It was only the tip of the corruption iceberg, which according to some conservative estimates has cost Venezuela $70 billion.[37]

The fifth trait of a populist government surfaced during the critical months of 2016 and 2017, and it concerns the participation of well-intentioned people and institutions. These people and institutions include those who have ideological leanings close to that of the government—in Venezuela's case, on the left of the political spectrum. In their support of the policies supposedly designed to help the poor and underdogs, like those in Venezuela, they were willing to overlook the many wrongs of Chávez's regime.

Artists like Roger Waters and Spike Lee and economists like Joseph Stiglitz, among many others, fell into this camp. Stiglitz met Chávez in Caracas in 2007 and said that "Venezuela's economic growth in the last years has been very impressive."[38] Coming from a Nobel Prize winner, it was not an irrelevant endorsement. The problem in situations like this is that, although they may be well-intentioned, they obscure the truth and give the regime credibility, particularly in the eyes of the international community.

None other than Pope Francis fell victim to this fifth trait. On October 26, 2016, the opposition drew half a million protesters onto the streets of Caracas. Then, on October 30, President Maduro visited the Vatican and asked Pope Francis for help in mediating the conflict between the government and the opposition. The talks that ensued only served to advance Maduro's interests because they helped to divide the opposition, most of whom did not agree with attending them, and to delay the recall referendum. Nothing of use came out of the negotiations, and by December 6, the opposition stopped participating.[39] Maduro used the Vatican as a pawn, as he had used Wall Street before. Foreign investors are, in my view, another set of well-intentioned people that autocrats often use to achieve their anti-democratic goals.

The Aftermath: Financial Sanctions and Collapse

The battle between the government and the opposition and, relatedly, between the opposition-controlled National Assembly and the other PSUV-controlled powers deepened in 2017. That March, the TSJ stripped the National Assembly of its powers and assumed legislative functions.[40] The decision caused an international outcry before it was reversed. It did not matter, as President Maduro replaced the National Assembly with a National Constituent Assembly, whose members were elected in an election boycotted by the opposition, which did not feel it had sufficient guarantees to participate fairly. At that point, the National Assembly effectively had no role in what was left of Venezuela's institutions.

On August 25, 2017, President Donald Trump imposed financial and economic sanctions on Venezuela. Executive Order 13.808 barred the Venezuelan government, its state-owned companies, and its joint public-private ventures from international credit markets.[41] The measure has effectively impeded the country from issuing or restructuring its debt since then. US Treasury Secretary Steven Mnuchin stated the goals of the executive order: "Maduro may no longer take advantage of the American financial system to facilitate the wholesale looting of the Venezuelan economy at the expense of the Venezuelan people."[42] These lines could have been taken from this book.

These events proved quite costly for GSAM. The sanctions imposed in 2017 stopped any trading of Venezuela's debt in the United States and from non-US financial institutions that feared US sanctions. Essentially, what you had, you had to keep. As a result of this, of Venezuela's default in December 2017, and of the impact of economic sanctions on the country's economy, the price of Venezuela and PDVSA bonds collapsed. By mid-2021, most PDVSA bonds traded near 5 cents to the US dollar, and the government bonds traded near 10 cents to the US dollar, a rout for their owners, even the ones like GSAM who bought them for cheap.

The Venezuelan people have had it far worse. The country's economic and humanitarian collapse has little parallel in modern history. Between 2012 and 2020, per capita inflation-adjusted income fell by a huge 64.2 percent, and between 2017 and 2020, prices rose at an astounding annual average rate of 10,006 percent. An estimated 6.1 million people, one-sixth of the population, have left the country. Almost 90 percent of the population argued in a survey they did not have money to buy enough food for their families, and murder rates are among the highest in the world.[43] Issues like these are common traits of autocratic regimes: their management of the economy tends to be dismal. I will return to this discussion in Chapter 7, as Latin America's brand of populism is the extreme example of economic mismanagement, and in Chapter 8, where I review some formal evidence on the (negative) impact of populists on the economy.

An Institutional Blitzkrieg the Market Did Not Want to See

The most shocking part about the events in Venezuela is not how they ended, but rather how the market missed the fact that it was all written to finish that way from the very beginning. Hugo Chávez wanted to make Venezuela a new Cuba. He once said that the relationship between Cuba and Venezuela was more than an alliance, it was "a merger of two revolutions."[44] He set this goal well before becoming president, when he was Lieutenant Colonel Hugo Chávez. He came to fame when, on the morning of February 4, 1992, the government allowed him to appear on TV to convince his brothers in arms to depose of their weapons and end the coup d'état attempt that he had led. He started by saying, "Unfortunately, *for now*, the objectives that we had set have not been achieved in the capital" (emphasis added). His words would shape the evolution of Venezuelan society for years to come.[45]

Chávez then spent two years in prison for the attempted coup. (A little piece of advice here: Sending populist leaders to jail only increases their popularity. Like Chávez, Juan Domingo Perón in Argentina and Recep Erdoğan in Türkiye became more popular after stints in jail.) Shortly after his release in March 1994, he traveled to Cuba to meet President Fidel Castro. In a speech at the University of Havana, Chávez outlined his plan. He stated: "In our dreams, we have been in Cuba an infinite number of times, the Bolivarian soldiers of the Venezuelan army, which for many years have decided to give our lives to a revolutionary project, to a transformative project." He continued: "Cuba is a bastion of Latin American dignity and as such it must be seen and *as such it must be followed* and as such it must be nurtured"* (emphasis added), among many other declarations of allegiance to Castro's regime.[46]

Chávez then announced what he intended to do once in power: "The other pole that we are going to feed, push, and reinforce is the request in the street, with the people, for the call for elections for a National Constituent Assembly, to redefine the fundamental bases of the Republic that fell apart; the legal bases, the political bases, the economic bases, the moral bases, even, of Venezuela are on the ground, and that is not going to be fixed with small patches." He was elected on December 6, 1998, and assumed the presidency on February 2, 1999.

Once in power, he followed his Havana words to the letter. In a blitzkrieg that lasted for little over a year, Chávez systematically destroyed the foundations of what, until then, was considered the most solid democracy in Latin America.[47]

Freedom's House 1998–1999 *Freedom in the World* report graded Venezuela among the freest countries in Latin America, with a higher

---

* Google Translate and our own edits.

ranking than Argentina, Brazil, Colombia, and Mexico, and at par with Chile. But by 1998, the stage was set for change; Venezuela had experienced two decades of economic decline, during which its gross domestic product (GDP) per capita, a measure of the wealth an economy creates in any given year, dropped by almost 39 percent.[48] That deterioration, among other factors, eroded the power of the bipartisan system that the Christian democratic party COPEI (Comité de Organización Política Electoral Independiente) and social democratic party Acción Democrática (AD) had shared for decades. This setup allowed an outsider like Chávez to capture the presidency. This is another pattern repeated across countries that elect populist presidents: a period of economic stagnation or decline and of rising inequality precedes their rise to power, which prompts displaced voters to look for alternatives to traditional parties and politicians.

Chávez won the election with 56.2 percent of the votes, but the National Assembly had been elected only one month before the presidential elections, so his party controlled only one-third of the seats. The existing institutions constrained his ability to start the revolution he promised, prompting him to do away with them and shift course. At his inauguration on February 2, 1999, he called for a referendum to summon a constitutional assembly. Importantly, the existing constitution did not include this reform mechanism, but the Tribunal of Justice did not object, a costly mistake for Venezuela and for the TSJ's members. The elections for the National Constitutional Assembly (ANC) were in July and, with a changed electoral system, Chávez's forces won 122 of 131 seats.[49]

Immediately, the ANC claimed authority over other state institutions and dissolved the National Assembly and the TSJ. The ANC continued to work as a sovereign legislature until January 2000. To add insult to injury, the newly elected National Assembly approved an "Enabling Law" that allowed Chávez to govern by decree for 12 months. *El Comandante*, as he called himself, used these powers liberally to change the economic and political landscape of Venezuela for years to come.

At the same time, Chávez began merging Venezuela's revolution with Cuba's. He increasingly relied on Cuban intelligence, particularly after the failed coup of 2002, and as he promised in the 1994 Havana speech, he sold oil to Cuba at a steep discount. The merger strengthened when Nicolás Maduro, who had been trained in Havana when he was young and had even stronger ties to the Cuban regime than Chávez, was elected president in 2013.

These sweeping changes were not lost to democracy watchers. Freedom House reclassified Venezuela from Free to Partly Free in 1999. The 1999–2000 Freedom in the World report said this about Chávez: "He restricted the power of the democratically elected congress, created what amounts to a parallel government of military cronies, and further eroded the country's system of checks and balances by effectively ending judicial independence."[50] The V-Dem Liberal Democracy Index registered its steepest decline ever, sending it from being well above the Latin American average to being well below in just two years.

However, Wall Street ignored these infringements on democracy and initially showered Chávez with praise—and money. Wall Street's love for Chávez started before he was elected president. Many investment banks, including J.P. Morgan, Bank of America, Citigroup, and Goldman Sachs, organize investor meetings in Washington, DC, at the same time the International Monetary Fund (IMF) and the World Bank have their biannual meetings. The banks take full advantage of finance ministers, central bank governors and other public officials gathering in one place to present their views to financial investors. As a seasoned investor told me, at the 1998 Spring Meetings, J.P. Morgan organized a videoconference with Chávez, who was banned from entering the United States. To a full and enthusiastic crowd, *El Comandante* told the Wall Streeters everything they wanted to hear.

In the early days of Chávez's regime, his macroeconomic management followed the playbook of most wannabe autocrats: At the outset, they try to court markets while making moves to undermine the democratic institutions that limit their power. Chávez confirmed his predecessor's finance minister, Maritza Izaguirre, and then with oil prices still low, he implemented a sharp fiscal adjustment to balance the government books. Wall Street loves fiscal adjustments, because they increase the chances of the government's debt being repaid on time.

In June 1999, Chávez rang the bell of capitalism's altar, the New York Stock Exchange, and then visited the *Washington Post*, where he distanced himself from "irresponsible populism."[51] According to one analyst, in Wall Street "Chávez was welcomed like a pop star and enjoyed the occasion."[52] Thereafter, Venezuela issued bonds in 2001 and then again in 2003, at a time when emerging market sovereign issuances were not that common, helping him to firm his grip on power. It was a rather stark turn from the Havana speech, when he said: "We are honored as rebel soldiers not to be allowed in the North American territory."

Over time, Chávez increased the intensity of the hardball tactics that he used to tamp down any type of opposition, whether from politicians or civil society, including nongovernmental organizations (NGOs) and the independent press. His opponents responded in kind, although not successfully. There was a failed coup d'état in 2002, a failed worker strike at PDVSA that lasted from 2002 to 2003, and a failed recall referendum in 2004. To increase his grip on the country and his party, Chávez eliminated presidential term limits in 2009. He wanted to become, in the words of Madeleine Albright, a "president for life."

In the meantime, Chávez hit the commodities lottery. Oil prices, which were as low as $8.1 per barrel in his 1998 election year, soared to $103 in 2012.[53] And when commodity prices rise, Latin American asset prices tend to do well, which is natural given that these countries are mostly commodity producers.[54] Investors, knowing this empirical fact, pour money into Latin American bonds and stocks during these periods.

Higher export prices and broader access to foreign financing allowed Chávez to expand social spending to a level never seen before in Venezuela, making him a hero of the poor at home and around Latin America. A big chunk of this spending was channeled through PDVSA, whose corporate governance was altered to become an instrument of the government policies.[55] So when investors bought PDVSA bonds, they were most likely not financing oil activities. Rather, they were financing the more than 30 social programs, the *Misiones*, by which Chávez brought many goods and services to the poor—in exchange for their votes, of course.

Obviously, Wall Street also enjoyed the commodity boom. From 2003 to 2013, Venezuela issued about $30 billion and PDVSA about $34 billion in foreign currency bonds, most of which ended up in

Wall Street accounts. Their coupon rates, that is the yearly payment that bondholders are promised to receive, exceeded 10 percent of the face value of the bond in many cases. This financing allowed Chávez and then Maduro to consolidate their power.

We now know how the story ended, but we probably should have known before it was too late. Ignorance is bliss, as the saying goes, but in this case, it meant financing the path to autocracy for Chávez and Maduro.

KEY TAKEAWAYS OF CHAPTER 2

This chapter:

- Goes into greater detail on two of the main mechanisms that cause investors to (often unwittingly) finance dictators and dictator wannabes: bond and stock indices.

- Describes some of the main avenues by which autocrat wannabes undermine democracy: changing electoral rules, packing courts, dividing societies, attacking and capturing independent media, changing the country's constitution to increase their power and lift term limits, and fomenting corruption to oil their cronies.

- Claims that economic decline and rising inequality, often coming after the IMF imposes programs on democratic governments, feeds populism.

- Argues that to keep markets happy, populists often name market friendly finance ministers, who usually fall into the autocracy trap.

- Shows that while markets were oblivious to the obliteration of democracy in Venezuela, democracy watchers were flagging the decline in real time.

- Introduces the role of sanctions and the impact they have on investors. Chapter 10 includes a more thorough discussion of sanctions and their impact.

CHAPTER 3

THE CITY OF LONDON IS ERDOĞAN'S FINANCIER

The EU and the market turn a blind eye on Türkiye's "half democracy."

Green Bonds, Dark Future

On May 20, 2021, Bloomberg broke the news that the Turkish government was working on a plan that would allow it to sell ESG bonds by year-end.[1] The piece, which cited an unnamed source from the country's Treasury, said that the framework would allow the government to sell social and "Dark Green" bonds in different currencies. Dark Green Bonds are the ones whose underlying projects contribute the most to implementing climate solutions.[2]

The bonds may be dark green, but the outlook for democracy in Türkiye remains black. While the Treasury had its hands full on the ESG framework, other branches of the Turkish government were busy repressing opposition members and censoring media outlets. What happened over the following 11 days provides insight into the state of democracy in Türkiye.

On May 27, 2021, before a local court, government prosecutors accused Istanbul's mayor, Ekrem İmamoğlu, of insulting members of the Supreme Electoral Council.[3] İmamoğlu is a rising star in the opposition, and generally regarded as more popular than the President Recep Erdoğan. One reason for İmamoğlu's popularity, besides his belief in democratic norms like due process, is that he "turned the strongman's politics of aggression and arrogance on its head."[4] His platform of radical love was based on two simple rules: "ignore Erdoğan and love those who love Erdoğan."[5]

İmamoğlu knew that fair proceedings in his own legal matters, and less so radical love, were unlikely. The number of constitutional court judges increased from 11 to 17 as part of the 2010 Constitutional Reform, effectively handing control to Erdoğan. The reform also gave Erdoğan control of the High Council of Judges and Prosecutors, the committee that oversees judges and prosecutors.

Other government branches were even busier at the end of May. By May 31, 2021, news trickled out that Turkish agents had captured Selahaddin Gülen in Kenya and brought him back to Türkiye to face prosecution.[6] Selahaddin Gülen is the nephew of Muslim cleric Fethullah Gülen, who has been in self-exile in the United States since 1999. Erdoğan has a long memory, and his judiciary has an extended reach. It does not spare opposition members living abroad, especially those involved in the failed coup that Erdoğan blamed on the followers of Fethullah Gülen, the Gülenists, in 2016.

At the same time, corruption allegations against Erdoğan's government were rampant. On May 28, mafia boss Sedat Peker released seven videos on YouTube that garnered approximately 55 million views. In the videos, Peker dropped "bombshell charges that certain government officials or their family members are involved in drug running, rape and murder," according to a *Financial Times* article.[7] Peker released the videos from a hotel in Dubai. He shouldn't have felt secure had he known of Selahaddin Gülen's fate. Nonetheless, living abroad and looking over your shoulder still seems like a better option than being a member of the opposition or the media, or anyone with something to say against the government, and residing in Türkiye.

Reporting from Türkiye is increasingly difficult, even for foreign news companies such as Bloomberg. Two of its reporters faced a two-and-half-year trial that could have put them in prison for two to five years over allegations that they tried to "undermine" the economy, after publishing a story about the impact on the economy of the weakening of the Turkish lira in August 2018.[8] (They were acquitted on April 29, 2022, along with dozens of other defendants.)[9] Reporters Without Borders (RSF), a nongovernmental organization (NGO) focused on freedom of expression and information, ranked Türkiye 153 out of 180 countries in its 2021 World Press Freedom Index. RSF has also included Erdoğan on its "Predators" list since 2009.[10] In a report released on June 15, 2021, just as two journalists' trial started, RSF argued that "reporters who cover public interest stories in Turkey increasingly risk imprisonment."[11] It's no wonder why acclaimed Turkish novelist and essayist Kaya Genc calls Türkiye "the world's largest prison for journalists."[12]

By the end of May 2021, international investors had their own concerns about Türkiye, but not due to the government's attack on the media or against opposition members. On May 25, Erdoğan fired one of the central bank's deputy governors, Oğuzhan Özbaş, the third member of the central bank's monetary policy committee to be fired since March. That list also included the central bank's governor, Naci Agbal, who dared to raise policy rates to stem inflation. The central bank was supposed to be independent from the government, but met the same fate as any other nominally autonomous institution in Türkiye, such as the judiciary and the press. Erdoğan's assault on the monetary authority's independence caused the Turkish lira to slump from about 6.96 per US dollar in mid-February to 8.49 at the end of May.

Turkish bond prices suffered, but neither their drop nor Erdoğan's behavior precluded investors from financing his regime. By May 20, 2021, the Turkish government had already borrowed $3.5 billion from the Eurobond market,[13] and there would be more foreign financing available later in the year. A Eurobond is a bond that is issued in the currency of one country but sold in another country.[14] A US dollar denominated bond sold outside of the United States is an example of a Eurobond. A $2.25 billion dollar-denominated government bond offer in September "attracted vigorous demand from investors across the UK, US, and Europe" according to the *Financial Times*.[15] The article added that "the allure of high yields has also been too strong for some investors to ignore."

The story of Türkiye under Erdoğan underscores the need to incorporate democracy considerations into investment decisions.

To men like Erdoğan, financial markets can help serve his agenda, which was always, in the words of Soner Cagaptay, "to build power in order to crown himself the country's omnipotent leader."[16] One key characteristic of Recep Erdoğan's consolidation of power has been the use of different groups and institutions to get rid, in turn, of the control of other groups and institutions. Investors are likely to be used by Erdoğan in his singular pursuit of consolidating power, the history of which can be broken down into three distinct periods.

First Act: Moderation, and Then Economic Success

Erdoğan's ascent and consolidation of power bears many similarities to Hugo Chávez's and that of other populist leaders. Their standard playbook includes purging the bureaucracy, attacking opposition members and independent media, overtaking the judiciary, and twisting electoral rules. However, Erdoğan's rise has at least two key differences from Chávez's.

The first distinction is Erdoğan's use of religion as an instrument for populist politics. He built an agenda based on Islamism,[17] or "the belief that Islam should guide social and political as well as personal life."[18] The second difference is that, for many years, Erdoğan had the support of the international business community and markets. They financed Türkiye's investments and external deficit with gusto, and to a greater degree than any other country included in this book except for China.

Let's start with the first difference. To understand Türkiye's democratic decline under Erdoğan, though, we must grasp its democratic history. Importantly, Türkiye has never actually been a full democracy. Founded in 1923 and led by Mustafa Kemal, who was later named Atatürk, or "Father of the Turks," the Turkish Republic was a modernization effort built on the ashes of the Ottoman Empire's defeat in World War I. It was not an attempt at democracy, but rather a despotic, top-down effort to modernize the economy and society, and to build the state.[19] Kemal's ultimate objective was to prevent Türkiye from falling behind Western democracies more than it already had.

The new republic adopted Switzerland's civil laws, Germany's commercial regulations, France's administrative practices, and Italy's criminal code.[20] Atatürk also adopted the French's *laïcité*, promoting freedom from religion in education and politics.* The idea was to relegate religion to the private sphere; this secularist system controlled religion and "marginalized citizens who defined their identity first and foremost through their faith."[21] Even after Atatürk's death in 1938, when Türkiye became a parliamentary democracy, it still operated under the secular cage he built.[22] It was a democracy that lived under the tutelage of the military, which staged coups in 1960, 1971, 1980, and 1997.

In a country with a population that is 99 percent Muslim, *laïcité* was hard to maintain. After the 1980 military coup, successive governments strengthened the role of religion in daily life.[23] But it was not enough for the more conservative, religious, and poorer segments of the population, particularly in Türkiye's heartland. In the words of former deputy prime minister Bülent Arınç, a partner of Erdoğan in the creation of the Justice and Development Party, known by its Turkish acronym AKP, "We used to see the Turkish state as a leviathan that oppressed the religious and the poor."[24] In the context of the Cold War, the government cracked down on leftist parties after the 1980 coup, arresting half a million people and banning almost every civil society organization, including trade unions. Unable to organize around ideology, many poorer Turks came together around religion.[25]

Recep Erdoğan was the person with the right background, the right skills, and the right sense of timing to fill this demand for social change. Born in a poor neighborhood of Istanbul, from a family that had migrated from the conservative heartland of Türkiye, his parents enrolled him in an Imam Hatip school, a religious vocational school, when he was 11. Early on, he developed a talent for soccer and for politics. His political views were shaped by Necmettin Erbakan, who published his "National Vision" manifesto in 1969, when Erdoğan was 15. Erdoğan immediately joined Erbakan's National Salvation Party, the first Islamist party to enter the Turkish parliament.[26] Unlike other Islamist leaders, Erdoğan (initially) showed a strong

---

* As opposed to the American model of freedom *of* religion. See a discussion of the two models in Soner Cagaptay, *The New Sultan: Erdoğan and the Crisis of Modern Turkey* (London & New York: I.B Tauris & Co. Ltd, 2020), 95–96.

pragmatism and efficiency in handling public affairs, which distinguished him as mayor of Istanbul, a position to which he was elected in 1994.

Over time, Erdoğan amassed sufficient power to dismantle *laïcité* by using Ataturk's same tools, state institutions and top-down social engineering.[27] However, his path to power was not a straight line. In December 1997, when he was mayor of Istanbul, he was sent to prison for delivering a speech in which he cited a well-known nationalist poem, "The mosques are our barracks, the domes our helmets, the minarets our bayonets, and the faithful our soldiers."[28] He would later discover that the City of London and Wall Street are their financiers. Much like Chávez, his imprisonment helped him politically by casting him as a martyr.

Erdoğan learned his lesson: If he wanted to navigate in a regime still under the tutelage of laicists, he had to tread carefully. Formed in August 2001, the AKP embraced moderation, democracy, a pro-Western foreign policy, and importantly, a pro-market economy. Erdoğan declared his party to be a "conservative democratic" force,[29] and he "listed democratization and pluralism as its ideological cornerstones."[30] He downplayed the Islamist rhetoric and invoked universal principles of human rights and democracy.[31] But as he consolidated his power, Erdoğan started to make a bigger use of religion in politics. This shift included the debate on the use of headscarves in 2008, which was cast by Erdoğan in terms of an attack on the Muslim majority rather than on individual liberties, as well as the debates on the sale of alcohol and on abortion, among many others. The changes also included the fostering of religion through the educational system.[32]

Erdoğan was able to impose these changes as he gained popularity and power, for which, in turn, he received a boost from foreign investors. This takes us to the second difference between Erdoğan and Chávez. Like most other populist leaders in this book, AKP's rise to power with Erdoğan followed a major economic crisis, which created opportunities for anti-system candidates. In Türkiye's case, it suffered several crises; GDP contracted 5.5 percent in 1995 and 3.3 percent in 1999. But the biggest blow was the 2001 crisis, when the economy contracted 5.8 percent, the most since World War II. The government implemented brutal austerity measures under an

IMF program, including freezing salaries and dismantling what was left of Türkiye's welfare state.[33] The crisis caused the center of the political spectrum to implode, and Erdoğan and the AKP were more than happy to fill the void. They won the 2002 election with an economically liberal and pro-European Union (EU) accession agenda, although Erdoğan could not assume power until 2003 because he was still banned from political participation due to his imprisonment.

Erdoğan took advantage of the austerity measures implemented by previous administrations and delivered impressive growth while dramatically reducing inflation. During Erdoğan's first term from 2003 to 2007, average annual GDP growth was 7.3 percent. Inflation dropped from 53 percent in 2001 to 6.2 percent in 2007.

This stunning economic success was bankrolled by foreign investors who liked Erdoğan's pro-market and pro-EU accession agenda. The current account is a record of the transactions in goods and services between a country's residents and the residents of the rest of the world. Its main component is the trade balance, the difference between the exports and imports of goods. When a country registers a current account deficit, it means that the rest of the world is financing the residents of that country to consume more than what they produce; that is, to import more than what they export. In technical jargon, a current account deficit must be financed by a financial account surplus and/or a loss of international reserves. It is analogous to your personal accounts. If, in any given month, your consumption is higher than your salary, it must be the case that someone else is financing you, a family member, your bank, or—God forbid—your credit card, or else you must be drawing down your savings.

Türkiye's current account balance swung significantly from a surplus of 1.8 percent of GDP in 2001 to an average annual deficit of 4.2 percent of GDP from 2003 to 2007.[34] In fact, Türkiye's current account deficit averaged 4.2 percent of GDP per year from 2003 to 2020, the highest among major emerging market countries. For practical purposes, foreign companies and markets loved Türkiye.

A big share of the financing came through foreign direct investment (FDI)—that is, through companies investing in greenfield projects, acquiring local companies, or expanding their installed capacity in the country. Türkiye thus became, under Erdoğan's tenure, the workshop of Europe.[35] Higher investment led to higher exports, which rose almost 80 percent during Erdoğan's first term. Investment in infrastructure also boomed, allowing the population to get access to services they never had before.

Portfolio flows, or financing implemented through foreigners' purchases of local companies' shares or their debt, and government debt, were also an important part of the mix. In 2005 and 2006, foreigners acquired more than $9 billion per year of Turkish debt instruments. After a respite during the Great Recession of 2008, foreign purchases soared to more than $16 billion in 2010, and then peaked at $32 billion in 2011. This made Türkiye one of the emerging markets that received the most financing from foreigners.

Portfolio flows are naturally more volatile than FDI flows. During Erdoğan's time in power, external factors such as the US Federal Reserve's interest rate policies have caused them to fluctuate, as have his own policy blunders, such as his penchant for firing central bank officials. However, these flows have seldom fluctuated due to concerns about Türkiye's democratic standards.

Türkiye's government bonds became an important part of most debt indices tracked by institutional investors on Wall Street and in London. By 2018, Türkiye composed up to 6 percent of the J.P. Morgan EMBI Global Index and 3.7 percent of the J.P. Morgan EMBI Global Diversified Index,[36] both commonly used external debt indices denominated in US dollars. In 2005, foreigners owned less than 10 percent of Türkiye's government debt denominated in the local currency. By 2013, their ownership share peaked at close to 25 percent, although it has dropped since then.[37]

With growing acceptance from London's financiers, during his first term, Erdoğan pushed to secure Türkiye's accession to the EU, a move that most of the population supported. Human rights issues, including capital punishment, among many others, were assumed to be the main impediments to Türkiye's entry as a member state.[38] As a result, Erdoğan pushed to expand civil rights and liberties, and from 2002 to 2007, Türkiye did improve its standing in Freedom House's Freedom in the World index. Erdoğan also moved to keep religion and politics separate. Even a controversial legislative proposal, the recriminalization of adultery, was cast not in religious terms but around the "traditional and national values of the Turkish society."[39]

The EU accession attempt also highlighted how Erdoğan consolidates power by using groups and institutions against other groups and institutions. He wanted to curb the military's power, which also happened to be a requirement for Türkiye to qualify for accession talks with the EU. In 2003, he put the military's formal influence in government affairs on the negotiation table with the EU. Specifically, Erdoğan demoted the Turkish National Security Council, which until that point could independently draft Türkiye's national security and foreign policy doctrines. Reduced to an advisory council without the ability to decide policy, Erdoğan essentially stripped his own military of a voice under the guise of EU accession.[40]

Second Act: Credit Rating Rises, Democracy Rating Falls

Credit ratings are opinions about credit risk, more precisely about the capacity and the willingness of a debt issuer to meet its financial obligations in full and on time.[41] The three main credit rating agencies are Standard and Poor's (S&P), Moody's, and Fitch. To assign a credit rating, these agencies use an array of economic and political information and forecasts to assess the capacity of payment of the issuer.

For the sovereign debt markets, the sovereign's credit ratings are critical, though there is some dispute among academics and practitioners about the impact of credit rating changes on sovereign debt prices. While some argue that credit rating changes impact debt prices and that they are not anticipated by the market, others argue that the market anticipates their effects.[42]

What is not in dispute is the impact of an upgrade from speculative grade (SG) to investment grade (IG), or a downgrade in the other direction. An investment grade rating is seen as a guarantee against default, at least in the short term. Since 1975 there has not been a single default by a sovereign issuer that had been rated IG by S&P one year prior to default.[43] Most importantly, once a country receives an IG rating, more funds can invest in that country's bonds, as many funds cannot invest in SG debt. An IG rating is so important that market players refer to issuers that lose IG status as "fallen angels."

On May 16, 2013, the rating agency Moody's Investors Service raised Türkiye's government bonds one notch to Baa3 from Ba1.[44] The increase was significant because it meant Türkiye became IG for the first time since 1994. The move followed a similar upgrade from Fitch Ratings, which raised Türkiye's credit rating to BBB- from BB+, bringing it to an IG rating for the first time in almost two decades.[45] The third of the three big rating agencies, S&P, had raised Türkiye's bonds to BB+ from BB on March 27, 2013, but kept it one notch below investment grade.*

Public officials and investors celebrated the IG rating, as did market prices. Istanbul's main stock exchange rose 1.3 percent following the announcement, while government bond yields dropped. A seasoned emerging markets economist said at the time, "This should bring a whole new investor base to Turkey."[46]

I have already highlighted the importance of benchmark portfolios such as J.P. Morgan's EMBI for institutional investors. Some of these benchmark portfolios or indices, such as J.P. Morgan's EMBI and the GBI-EM, do not have a minimum credit rating requirement. They include IG and SG credits. Other indices, however, are limited to bonds rated IG, such as the FTSE World Government Bond Index (WGBI) and the Bloomberg Barclays Global Aggregate Index. For this index, countries must have IG status based on the middle rating of Fitch, Moody's, and S&P, among other requirements. For the WGBI, ratings should be at least A– by S&P, and A3 by Moody's (a more demanding rating), among other requirements. As of April 2020, only three emerging markets were included in the WGBI: Malaysia, Mexico, and Poland.[47]

This means that when an IG rating finally comes, it flings the doors opens for a wider set of foreign investors. When Mexico was included in the WGBI in 2010, foreign purchases of local Mexican bonds increased by $11 billion, and helped to expand the proportion of bonds owned by foreigners by 7 percentage points, to 31

---

* Credit ratings are, for S&P and Fitch (from highest to lowest): AAA, AA+, AA, AA–, A+, A, A+, BBB+, BBB, BBB–, BB+, BB, BB–, B+, B, B–, CCC+, CCC, CCC–, CC, C, DDD, DD, and D. From AAA to BBB– credits are considered "investment grade." Credit ratings for Moody's are (from highest to lowest): Aaa, Aa1 Aa2, Aa3, A1, A2, A3, Baa1, Baa2, Baa3, Ba1, Ba2, Ba3, B1, B2, B3, Caa1, Caa2, Caa3, Ca, C, RD, SD, and D. From Aaa to Baa3 credits are considered "investment grade."

percent.[48] When South Africa was included in the WGBI in June 2012, benchmark-driven asset managers bought an estimated $5 billion to $9 billion in South African local currency bonds, or 10 percent of the total market capitalization.[49]

By mid-May 2013, Türkiye was primed to enjoy the reputational benefit of an investment grade rating. It faced, potentially, the benefit of higher debt prices (which would mean lower yields), due to the purchases of foreign benchmark-driven investors. Soon, however, things changed.

On May 28, just a few days after Moody's upgrade, environmentalist groups organized a sit-in to protest the government's plan to cut down trees in Gezi Park, one of the last green spaces in the heart of Istanbul, to build a new shopping mall. The protests spread fast thanks to social media. The brutality that the police unleashed on the protesters sparked even bigger protests, not just in Istanbul, but in as many as 70 other cities for several weeks. The event was considered "the biggest spontaneous revolt in Turkish history."[50] Erdoğan's reaction to the protests suggested that "by 2013, the AKP was morphing from a broadly center-right movement led by Islamists and supported by liberals, to a narrowly Islamist party led by a single dominant ruler."[51]

Liberals who were once allies with Erdoğan started to distance themselves from him. Erdoğan took advantage of the situation and purged the more liberal members of AKP, including president Abdullah Gül, and declared himself a presidential candidate in 2014. A 2007 constitutional referendum allowed for a popular vote to elect the president, compared to the previous system, whereby Parliament elected the president.[52] Erdoğan's next step was to change to a pure presidential system some years later.

These events were seen as a turning point for Erdoğan and ultimately for democracy in Türkiye. However, Türkiye's democratic recession had started well before. It takes two to tango, as the saying goes, and by 2007 it seemed clear that neither Türkiye nor the EU wanted to continue the accession dance. The EU helped Erdoğan to strip the military of its influence by requiring a reduction in its power, but it also dragged its feet, and the process stalled. Accession to the EU may have been the last best shot at democracy in Türkiye under Erdoğan (although the story of Hungary—see Chapter 4—casts doubt on the effect of EU accession on democracy). In case Türkiye's liberals needed any more convincing, the Ergenekon trials that began in 2008 and the 2010 Constitutional Reform provided sufficient evidence.

The Ergenekon affair started in January 2007 with the murder of Hrant Dink, a Turkish Armenian journalist who had called the Ottoman Empire's 1915 killing of Armenians a genocide. Given that he was killed by a youngster from the conservative heartland of Türkiye, many people were convinced the "Deep State" was behind the murder. The idea that there is a nationalistic, state-connected underworld, an anti-Islamist "Deep State" that controls Türkiye's politics, has a long history.[53]

Ergenekon is an enigmatic "terror group" group linked to the Deep State, named for an ancient Turkish myth.[54] Erdoğan took the opportunity to attack this "Deep State." Prosecutors, supported by leading members of the AKP, accused hundreds of military officers and civilians, including journalists, academics, lawyers, and politicians, of being members of Ergenekon. These investigations, along with the investigations related to an alleged coup, known as the "Sledgehammer case," included severe violations of due process; some defendants, for example, were jailed for years.

In this crackdown, Erdoğan counted on the help of the Gülenists, who follow self-exiled cleric Fethullah Gülen. The AKP and the Gülenist movement were rooted in different Islamic traditions, but their common aversion to the influence of the military in Türkiye's politics bonded them into an alliance.[55] The Gülenist movement had important interests in the media, including the popular newspaper *Zaman*, which promoted the Ergenekon trials,[56] and interests in education. The Gülenists also ran an important network in the bureaucracy and the judiciary. By the time of the Ergenekon trials, Gülen had effectively created "a state within the Turkish state, gaining a strong foothold in the police force, the judiciary, and the bureaucracy," according to Dani Rodrik, a Turkish-born Harvard economics professor.[57]

The Gülenists used the Ergenekon trials as an opportunity to oust Erdoğan's opponents and replace them with Gülenists, in an attempt to shape Turkish society along its own conservative-religious lines. In my view, they were just being used by Erdoğan, who in turn would eventually dispose of them as well.

In September 2010, the Ergenekon trials were coming to an end, but Erdoğan's thirst for power was not. That month, Türkiye held a referendum on whether to approve 26 proposed constitutional reforms. Allegedly, the reforms were to align Türkiye's constitution with the constitutions of EU member states, thereby facilitating Türkiye's accession.* By then, the EU accession was a long shot at best. The referendum was approved with 58 percent of the vote, and it allowed Erdoğan to pack the Supreme Court and the committee that oversees judges and prosecutors. Even then, it came as no surprise that in 2012 "Erdoğan complained about the separation of powers, which he described as 'an obstacle' to be overcome."[58] He skillfully removed this obstacle.

Once Erdoğan controlled the judiciary, he went after the opposition media. As in most other countries where democracy is sliding, the AKP passed a new media law in 2018. The result was impressive, as several large independent or anti-government newspapers ended up in the hands of Erdoğan's cronies.[59]

Türkiye's democracy may have been sliding during Erdoğan's second act, but its credit ratings weren't. That is not to say that credit rating agencies are oblivious to the state of institutions in the countries they rate. Fitch's sovereign rating model (SRM) includes four main pillars: structural features; macroeconomic performance, policies, and prospects; public finances; and external finances.[60] The structural features pillar, which has a weight of more than 50 percent in the final rating, includes many quantitative and qualitative factors that overlap with those tracked by democracy indices. Among the quantitative factors are six World Bank Governance Indicators, including "Rule of Law" and "Voice and Accountability." The qualitative factors include assessments of political stability.

S&P has a similar setup. Its Sovereign Rating Methodology considers five factors when making a sovereign credit rating call: (1) institutional and governance effectiveness and security risks; (2) economic structure and growth prospects; (3) external liquidity and international investment position; (4) fiscal performance and flexibility and debt burden; and (5) monetary flexibility.[61] The first

---

* This is a frequent plot used by autocrats: they modify legislation with one stated purpose that is the exact opposite of what they want to achieve.

factor includes "the transparency and accountability of institutions," among other institutional factors. I return to this topic in Part Two of the book.

Yet despite all those checks, from 2007 to 2013, S&P improved Türkiye's sovereign rating by two notches, from BB– to BB+. Fitch bumped up its rating on Türkiye by three notches to BBB–. Moody's went up by three as well, from Ba3 to Baa3. Meanwhile, Türkiye's standing in the democracy indices tumbled. Its Freedom House ranking fell from 3 in 2007 to 3.5 in 2013, which indicates less freedom, following a drop in its civil liberties ranking. Freedom House considered it Partly Free until 2017. Türkiye's fall in the V-Dem's index was more dramatic. The country's deliberative democracy index score fell from 0.48 in 2007 to 0.21 in 2013, the steepest decline among the 21 major emerging market countries for that period. In 2013, V-Dem changed Türkiye's status from an Electoral Democracy to an Electoral Autocracy. Türkiye's score also dropped significantly in EIU's Democracy Index, from 5.7 in 2006 to 5.63 in 2013, and then to 4.35 in 2021, but it remained classified as a Hybrid Regime since 2006.

Third Act: Turn on the Gülenists

Since that eventful 2013, democracy in Türkiye has continued its downward path, and so has its relationship with foreign investors. But one decline did not beget the other.

Having curbed the military's influence, tamped down liberal opposition, stacked the judiciary in his favor, and gained control of the press, by 2013 it was time for Erdoğan to turn on the Gülenists. Their relationship started to sour after Erdoğan's second reelection as prime minister in 2011. Suddenly, Erdoğan began to cut Gülen-related businesses out of government contracts.[62] He denied loyal Gülenists promotions and jobs in his administration. He cut them from AKP lists for the parliamentary elections.[63] In 2013, Erdoğan even started to close elite Gülen-sponsored schools.

The Gülenists retaliated in various ways. Mostly, they launched corruption investigations and probably were behind the leaked tapes that cast Erdoğan in a bad light, including an alleged conversation that he had with his son about managing millions of US dollars. But the confrontation escalated significantly in July 2016 when Gülenist members of the armed forces allegedly staged a coup d'état that, had it been better organized, likely would have taken Erdoğan's life. Thereafter, Erdoğan used the failed coup as an excuse to purge the military and the bureaucracy of thousands of Gülenists, and to prosecute anyone with links to his former ally, Fethullah Gülen.

According to former US Secretary of State Madeleine Albright, the purge hit the judiciary particularly hard, as one of every five judges were forced to resign. She said that "the scope of the government's response went far beyond legitimate law enforcement."[64] Ironically, or not, writers from newspapers *Taraf* and *Zaman*, who sided with Erdoğan during the Ergenekon trials, were arrested for allegedly plotting against Erdoğan in 2016.[65] *Taraf* was closed by decree in 2016, along with another 112 media outlets.[66]

In 2017, without the constraints of the Gülenists, Erdoğan further consolidated his power when voters supported a constitutional reform that shifted the government from a parliamentary system to a presidential regime. However, his political victory was by a razor-thin margin of 1.41 percent.

In July 2018, Erdoğan was elected president with a term that lasted until 2023. Prior to his victory, in 2017, Freedom House changed Türkiye's rating from Partly Free to Not Free as its Political Rights rating declined from 4 to 5, and its Civil Liberties rating declined from 5 to 6. Freedom House said the changes were "due to a deeply flawed constitutional referendum that centralized power in the presidency, the mass replacement of elected mayors with government appointees, arbitrary prosecutions of rights activists and other perceived enemies of the state, and continued purges of state employees."[67]

Freedom House didn't lack cause. There are countless examples of the deterioration of democracy, as well as the assaults on equality and basic human rights under Erdoğan: Türkiye has banned gay and transgender pride marches since 2015; Wikipedia has been blocked since 2017.[68] In June 2016, Erdoğan called women who work "half persons."[69] Under him, in my view Türkiye only has a "half democracy," which in practice means that the individual rights of minorities and opposition members are not respected.

Investors have had, shall we say, different concerns. Without any-one or any institution to keep him in check, Erdoğan also meddled in economic affairs, favoring a pro-growth agenda regardless of its cost on inflation. His mismanagement of monetary policy and the ele-vated current account deficit has drawn investors' ire.

International reserves were a scant $49.2 billion, or 6.9 percent of GDP, by the end of 2020. Inflation hit 14.6 percent in 2020. The cur-rent account deficit averaged 3.1 percent of GDP from 2014 to 2021. Investors started to pull away from Türkiye's government bonds.[70] By mid-2021, the share of Turkish local currency government debt was less than 5 percent of the total local currency debt, and close to its minimum since 2005.[71]

In many respects, Türkiye's economy looked like an acci-dent waiting to happen. Its democracy did too. In December 2022, Istanbul mayor and opposition star Ekrem İmamoğlu, whose story we started this chapter with, was sentenced to two years, seven months, and 15 days in prison, and banned from politics.[72] Despite this, mar-kets continued financing Erdoğan. On April 6, 2023, little more than one month before the May 14 presidential election, Türkiye's govern-ment finally issued its first Green Bond. It raised $2.5 billion with a bond that pays a coupon of 9.125 percent annually and matures in 2030.[73] Including this issue, the government raised $7.5 billion from international capital markets in the first four months of 2023.

There were widespread expectations that Erdoğan could be unseated in 2023. His popularity dropped as inflation reached a peak of 86 percent during 2022 and remained over 42 percent at the time of the election, and the lira plummeted. On top of this, most of the opposition was able to coalesce around the candidacy of 74-year-old Kemal Kiliçdaroğlu. Erdoğan, however, defied polls and received 49.5 percent of the votes on May 14, just short of the 50 percent needed to win in the first round. His party also secured a majority in the parliamentary election. On May 28, 2023, Erdoğan won the run-off election and was reelected for a new five-year presidential term.

In the weeks before the elections, Erdoğan bolstered public spending to increase his electoral chances. He cut "the ribbon on one megaproject after another,"[74] on April 20 he announced "free natural gas" for households for one year,[75] and he raised public sector wages, among other populist measures.

It is rather strange that the market fails to see the connection between these government actions, their impact on democracy, and the issuance of Green Bonds with which they may have financed them, directly or indirectly. Green Bonds are issued to finance worthy projects like wind farms, but money is fungible. With someone like Erdoğan in power, ESG bonds are likely to end up financing his autocratic adventures. In ESG parlance, investors risk being "greenwashed," a word used when someone is deceived into believing that a company or a government is eco-friendly, green, or sustainable.

KEY TAKEAWAYS OF CHAPTER 3

This chapter:

- Emphasizes how ESG and Green Bonds can sometimes be used as "greenwashing" at the national level. Money is fungible, and when autocrats issue Green Bonds, the money could end up financing repression.

- Goes into further detail about the roles of rating agencies and the market and their interplay in investment indices. Rating agencies do not take democracy into consideration. As a result, sometimes autocratic countries have high credit ratings, which are in turn a precondition to be admitted into investment indices that attract huge sums of money, such as the WGBI.

- Compares Türkiye's autocratic history with Venezuela's. Although the details of their stories differ, autocratic attacks on democracy always involve the same elements: divide society, change the country's constitution, change term limits, attack the media, capture the bureaucracy, and dismantle the judiciary, among others. While markets were oblivious to the obliteration of democracy in Türkiye and Venezuela, democracy watchers flagged the decline of their democracies in real time.

- Demonstrates how markets continued to provide ample financing to Erdoğan, even when any semblance of a liberal economy was lost.

CHAPTER 4

LIBERAL FUNDING YIELDS AN ILLIBERAL DEMOCRACY IN HUNGARY

Conservative populists in Eastern Europe: Orbán, the leader

The European Union Finances Antidemocratic Forces That Threaten the Bloc from Within

Few people outside Hungary know who Lőrinc Mészáros is. Yet, with an estimated net worth of $1.4 billion, this former gas and water pipefitter was the richest person in Hungary in 2022.[1] How did he become so wealthy? In his words: "God, luck and Viktor Orbán."[2] He conveniently forgot to mention the European Union.

In 2010, the same year Orbán was elected prime minister for the second time, Mészáros became mayor of Felcsút, Orbán's hometown. Orbán and Mészáros attended the same school as children, only three years apart, but it wasn't until later in life that they reconnected through their shared passion for football. The connection proved fruitful for Mészáros: it helped the 20 businesses that he owned directly or had ties with to land EUR 1 billion worth of contracts by 2016.[3] One contract was for the construction of a football stadium next to Orbán's farm in Felcsút.[4] The town only has 1,800 inhabitants, but the state-of-the-art stadium, which is known as "the most beautiful stadium in the country," seats 3,800 people.[5]

Mészáros is probably the most conspicuous of Hungary's "new rich," but he is certainly not the only one. Orbán's beneficiaries generally share two traits. The first is obvious: they made their fortunes thanks to the corruption of the government's procurement system.

The Corruption Research Center of Budapest (CRCB) investigated this issue. They analyzed the role of crony companies, which they called "MGTS+," an acronym for Mészáros, Garancsi, Tiborcz, Simicska, also including a total of 35 companies of businessmen linked to Orbán, in 248,404 public procurement contracts between 2005 and 2020. The CRCB's conclusion wasn't a surprise: "the share of public procurement won by crony companies within the total public procurement value has increased significantly since 2011."[6] In other words: the odds of crony companies winning contracts are extraordinarily high, much higher than ordinary Hungarian companies. The CRCB also found that corruption risk at the beginning of 2020 was at its highest level since 2005. Forty-one percent of the auctions had only one competitor. In addition, contract terms had become increasingly opaque.

What was really mind-boggling is that approximately 60 percent of the government procurement contracts that made Orbán's friends rich were financed by the European Union.[7] In fact, Hungary is one of the biggest beneficiaries of EU funds. Between 2014 and 2020, Hungary received EUR 39.5 billion, well in excess of the EUR 8.2 billion it contributed to the EU over the same period.[8] The net flow of funds from the EU to Hungary between 2014 and 2020 was equivalent to 2 to 3 percent of Hungary's GDP per year.

European Anti-Fraud Office (OLAF) investigations found numerous anomalies in EU-funded public tenders.[9] Hungary has led the list of member states where irregularities have been found in EU funds, and OLAF recommended the EU Commission recover 3.93 percent of the payments made to Hungary, compared to 0.36 percent average for all EU countries.[10] Following these investigations, the CRCB determined that EU-funded projects became more competitive than Hungary-funded projects, but only marginally so. In 2020, Hungary topped OLAF's anti-fraud investigation list for the second year in a row.[11]

The second trait the "new rich" share is that many of them built influential media empires that helped consolidate Orbán's power by spreading his message, in exchange, it seems, for generous financial support from the government. The origin of Lajos Simicska's fortune is an example of the benefits of being close to Orbán. Simicska was also a friend of Orbán from their school days. When they were kids, Orbán considered him "the cleverest of us all."[12] Simicska was very poor. But, like Mészáros, he caught a lucky break in knowing Orbán. By 2016 he had become the ninth richest person in Hungary. This was accomplished by making an alliance of sorts: according to Rényi Pál Dániel, a Hungarian journalist, "until 2014, Simicska and Orbán managed Hungary together."[13]

Beginning in 2010, "Simicska and his partners won about 40 percent of all tenders in which the EU transfers to Hungary were awarded."[14] Add them all up, and these tenders were worth several billion euros, which he used to build a media empire that included two daily newspapers, among them *Magyar Nemzet*, the most influential conservative newspaper in Hungary. His media portfolio also included two radio stations, TV stations, and a weekly newsmagazine.[15]

After the 2014 election, Orbán and Simicska started drifting apart. Differences in values and interests were behind their dispute, which was bitter.[16] Simicska had become too mighty for Orbán.[17] Public officials linked to Simicska were replaced, and his construction company, Kozgep, stopped winning government contracts. In February 2015, Simicska publicly attacked Orbán, saying he wanted to establish a new dictatorship. Orbán launched a vicious counter-offensive against Simicska's media outlets. After the falling out, the government's share of advertisement in *Magyar Nemzet* fell by more than 80 percent in two years.[18] Eventually, *Magyar Nemzet* and Simicska's other media outlets were closed, or sold to Orbán's new friends.[19] By 2020, with his construction and media empires in decline, Simicska was only the forty-ninth richest person in the country.

Another lucky media mogul who got rich off Orbán included Andrew Vajna, a Hungarian American film producer. Before he died in 2019, Vajna was widely considered the second most important media personality in Hungary. He was also the country's sixteenth richest person.[20] A producer of Hollywood action films like *Rambo* and *Total Recall*, Vajna seemed to have a well-developed plan to build his wealth. Scoring five casino concessions without going through a single auction helped, of course. His most aggressive move was his 2015 purchase of TV2, Hungary's second-largest TV channel.[21] To get the deal done, he outmaneuvered none other than Simicska, with help from a loan from state-owned Export-Import Bank,[22] a bank that is supposed to finance export companies.

Another beneficiary was Árpád Habony, who is often referred to Orbán's unofficial public relations "spin doctor." Habony is Orbán's most influential media adviser. For comparison's sake, Habony is to Orbán what Steve Bannon was to American president Donald Trump, except Habony kept a low profile, working in the shadows.[23] His role did not stop at that; Habony became a media entrepreneur himself. He owns Modern Media Group, bought in part with interest-free loans from people close to Orbán. His outlets have received more than a few large advertisement contracts from government bodies over the years.[24]

This way of making money is not surprising for those who have been following Orbán's party, Fidesz (short for Alliance of Young Democrats), since its beginnings. It was, from the start, a band of brothers. According to Tamás Sárközy, an independent legal expert, "nowhere in the world . . . is there a democratic country in which a small group of ten to twenty former students, who have known each other for 30 years, occupies to such a degree so many key positions of power. . . . The core of power in the Hungarian state is formed by a band of friends."[25] Andras Lánczi, an Orbán confidante, political philosopher, and president of a think tank that receives generous government support, summarizes the corruption in Hungary: "What is called corruption is practically the main policy of Fidesz. By this I mean that the government has set such goals as the establishment of the Hungarian entrepreneurial class."[26]

An Up-Front Attack on Liberal Democracy Institutions

Orbán did not leave his control over the media to chance. Like Hugo Chávez and other wannabe autocrats, he implemented his anti-democratization push right at the beginning of his second mandate in 2010. Previously, he was prime minister from 1998 to 2002.

On December 20, 2010, Hungary's Parliament passed the New Press and Media Act. Orbán had to backtrack on several particularly controversial aspects of the law after strong international pressure. But the law's core was left untouched, including the creation of the National Media and Infocommunications Authority (NMHH), through which all national media outlets must register.[27] The law is broad in scope, giving government officials control over what the population sees and hears and from whom. Following its implementation, over 1,000 workers in the media sector were dismissed without notice and replaced with Fidesz-friendly supporters, and popular television and radio programs were canceled and replaced with Fidesz-friendly content.[28] For example, in February 2021, a tribunal in Budapest supported the media authority's decision to not renegotiate the license for Klubrádió, Hungary's main independent radio station.[29]

In *Orbán: Hungary's Strongman*, journalist Paul Lendvai estimated that with these actions, Fidesz ensured that "80% of viewers and listeners receive only information provided directly or indirectly by the government."[30] The state's favorable tax treatments and generous advertising budgets for Orbán's media friends likely helped as well. Following the law's passage, Hungary's position in the World Press Freedom Index, compiled by Reporters Without Borders (RWB), slid from twenty-third in 2010 to ninety-second out of 180 countries in 2021. Hungary fell behind countries such as Haiti and Sierra Leona.[31]

The results of the 2010 election essentially gave Orbán carte blanche. He did not waste much time changing the constitution and taking over other levers of power. Hungary's majoritarian electoral system delivered Fidesz an overwhelming victory in 2010. With 57.2 percent of the vote, Orbán's party won 67 percent of Parliament's 263 seats. Hungary's political center collapsed: 80 percent of the new members of parliament (MPs) were from the right or the extreme right. Not happy with this, Fidesz, using its two-thirds majority in Parliament, passed an electoral reform in 2012 as part of a constitutional reform, increasing the majoritarian nature of the system and reshaping the constituency boundaries.[32] In the 2014 election, the new electoral law benefitted Orbán's party; it received 44.54 percent of the votes, but it was able to retain a two-thirds majority.[33]

Orbán took full advantage of the lack of political checks and balances. In *The Hungarian Post-Communist Mafia State*, former minister of education and former member of Parliament Bálint Magyar argues that Orbán proceeded to establish a "mafia state." He argued that "the mafia state is a privatized form of parasite state, an economic venture belonging to the adopted political family managed through the bloodlessly coercive and illegitimate instruments of public authority."[34]

Among other illiberal reforms, Orbán pushed amendments into parliamentary procedure, including the adoption of urgent legislation without debate. According to global democracy experts such as Steven Levitsky, Daniel Ziblatt, and Larry Diamond, democracy not only needs "mutual toleration" between rivals, but it also needs "forbearance" or self-restraint from those exercising power.[35] Forbearance doesn't appear to exist in Orbán's regime.

In the first 19 months after the 2010 election, Fidesz passed 26 reforms embedded in 12 constitutional amendments. One of them reduced the majority needed to prepare the new constitution.[36] Fidesz didn't waste time putting the clause into practice: on January 1, 2012, Hungary's constitution was renamed the new Fundamental Law of Hungary. It took less than two months to be drafted and nine days to pass through Parliament.

At the same time, Orbán took over the judiciary, using similar strategies as autocrats in other countries. Among other moves, Orbán changed the procedures for the selection of constitutional court justices. To take advantage of Fidesz's majority in Parliament, he increased the number of justices from 11 to 15, increased their term limits from 9 years to 12, and reduced their mandatory retirement age from 70 to 62, which forced nearly 300 judges into retirement.[37] Later, Parliament reduced the constitutional court's reach by putting the state's finances off limits, which was particularly convenient for Orbán and his cronies. He also effectively abolished the Supreme Court and renamed it the Curia of Hungary. This new format made replacing the court's independent president, András Baka, easier.[38] For additional insurance that the judiciary would remain loyal to him, Orbán appointed Tünde Handó, a longtime family friend, as head of the newly created National Judiciary Office. This position allowed him to appoint judges who were also loyal to Orbán.[39]

The bureaucracy wasn't spared either. Orbán replaced person-nel in key departments, including the State Audit Office and the Hungarian Central Statistical Office, and gave their jobs to Fidesz supporters. At the Office of the Prosecutor General, the country's top prosecutor, Péter Polt, was allowed to serve beyond his term limit, and then his term was extended for nine years. Orbán also made it so that Parliament can no longer question the prosecutor general, effec-tively placing the country's highest attorney above the law.[40]

Political commentator David Frum summarized the descent of Hungary's democracy in a 2017 article in the *Atlantic*: "The transition has been nonviolent, often not even very dramatic. Opponents of the regime are not murdered or imprisoned, although many are harassed with building inspections and tax audits. If they work for the govern-ment, or for a company susceptible to government pressure, they risk their jobs by speaking out. . . . Day in and day out, the regime works more through inducements than through intimidation. The courts are packed and forgiving of the regime's allies. Friends of the gov-ernment win state contracts at high prices and borrow on easy terms from the central bank. Those on the inside grow rich through favorit-ism; those on the outside suffer from the general deterioration of the economy. As one shrewd observer told me on a recent visit, 'The ben-efit of controlling a modern state is less the power to persecute the innocent, more the power to protect the guilty.'"[41]

Let's Stop My Financiers!

The most astonishing aspect of Orbán's regime is that he has man-aged to turn the EU, or Brussels, as many, including Orbán, call it, into Hungary's main villain while at the same time getting them to finance his power grab.* That the European Union project has been a top-down enterprise,[42] an elite project pushed on reluctant

---

* Leaving Hungarian-born billionaire investor and philanthropist George Soros as his second enemy. In his youth, Orbán worked for Soros's Open Society Foundation, which also financed his studies in Oxford. But following Orbán's chameleon-like change from a pro-European liberal to an anti-European "illiberal" leader, Soros moved from friend to enemy. As Orbán speaks for the "true Hungarians," Soros is considered the enemy of all "true Hungarians."

populations by intellectuals and high officials[43] that has meddled with an increasing number of domains, makes it an easy scapegoat. But Orbán, in my opinion, went too far.

Orbán even staged a national campaign against the EU. In April 2017, the government launched a survey called the "National Consultation," where it solicited feedback from eligible Hungarian voters about what to do about the EU. The questionnaire, titled "Let's stop Brussels!"[44] included six questions on "what Hungary should do" about EU policies. Among them were questions about economic policies like utility prices, job creation, and taxes. Other questions focused on hot-button issues like immigration. The questions were biased, clumsily so, and there was no independent body to check the real number of returned questionnaires.

But that wasn't the point of the campaign against the EU. Orbán is deliberate in the strategies he uses to build and maintain unchecked power. Like many wannabe autocrats, he develops narratives that call on Hungary's "true" citizens to unite against common enemies that "threaten" their way of life and his reign. That is an easy task in a country like Hungary and a region like Eastern Europe.

Historically, conservative populists who led illiberal revolutions in Eastern Europe staked their movements on bloodlines. For example, Orbán, according to former US Secretary of State Madeleine Albright, appeals increasingly to "ethnic pride based on shared history, values, religion and tongue."[45] It is an easy argument to make to predominantly homogeneous, aging societies who have long memories of past traumas.[46] Only 6 percent of Hungarians are foreign born, compared to 15 percent in neighboring Austria. Fear of immigration is high in these countries, and Orbán preyed upon this fear. In 2015, he set up more than 100 miles of razor wire as waves of refugees from war-torn Syria reached Europe. As part of his justification for the move, he said that "we shouldn't forget that the people who are coming here grew up in a different religion and represent a completely different culture."[47]

Eastern European countries also suffer from what political scientist Ivan Krastev calls "geopolitical insecurity," as they have always been dominated by foreign powers. Hungary lost two-thirds of its territory and one-half of its population in the 1920 Treaty of Trianon, which Orbán often references in speeches.[48] Yet, in the 1990s, countries like Hungary rushed to join the EU because they saw membership as a way to sever ties with Moscow and find economic prosperity with the West. It didn't take Hungarians long to realize that membership came with many strings attached. Given their traumatic history, those strings made them skeptical.[49]According to Krastev, they have learned to be "suspicious of any cosmopolitan ideology that crosses their borders."[50]

In the case of the EU, that ideology is "founded on the values of respect for human dignity, freedom, democracy, equality, the rule of law and respect for human rights, including the rights of persons belonging to minorities" (Art. 2 of the Union Treaty); that is, on the basic values of a liberal democracy.[51] Orbán has been pushing for another brand of democracy, an "illiberal" one. In his words: "A democracy is not necessarily liberal. Just because something is not liberal, it still can be a democracy," to which he added that "we have to abandon liberal methods and principles of organizing a society."[52]

Orbán's Attack on Democracy Was Only Missed by the Markets

Democracy watchers have kept tabs on Orbán's dismantling of Hungary's liberal democratic institutions. Hungary's standing in democracy rankings has plummeted under Orbán. V-Dem downgraded Hungary from Liberal Democracy to Electoral Democracy in 2010, and then to Electoral Autocracy in 2018. Freedom House downgraded Hungary from Free to Partly Free in 2018. The Economist Intelligence Unit has labeled Hungary a Flawed Democracy since 2006, but its democracy index has declined almost every year since 2006. In 2002, Hungary had a score of 7.53, not far from the 8 that would classify it as a Full Democracy. By the end of 2022, Hungary had a score of 6.64, not far from the 4–5.99 range that would classify it as a Hybrid Regime.

Democracy watchers also noticed how Orbán's grip in Hungary has tightened during the Covid-19 pandemic. On March 30, 2020, Parliament passed an "enabling" law that authorized Orbán to rule by decree, without parliamentary oversight. The broad powers conferred to him contrast with the more limited powers other parliaments, such as France's National Assembly, conferred to the executive branch during the pandemic. In December 2020, Hungary's Parliament adopted the Ninth Amendment to the Fundamental Law, giving even more powers to the executive starting in 2023.[53]

Despite mountains of evidence that highlight Orbán's improprieties, the EU took years to implement meaningful economic sanctions against his regime and, in fact, it generously financed Hungary's descent into an illiberal economy.[54]

The EU has implemented a few measures to curb Orbán over the years, but until 2022 the sanctions lacked the teeth to stop Hungary's democratic decline. In 2017, for example, the European Commission began infringement proceedings against Hungary over a law that attempted to close Central European University (CEU), which was founded in 1991 with the backing of George Soros.* Other EU proceedings against Hungary include its rules on asylum-seekers, NGOs, and LGBTQIA rights, whose rights have been severely curtailed.[55]

Why did it take so long for the EU to address this dynamic? My research assistant, Miranda Cortizo, argues in her paper, "The European Union's Response to Internal Democratic Backsliding: Evidence from Hungary and Poland," that several factors contributed to the EU's response time. A design problem in EU's bylaws, political maneuvers by Hungary and Poland, and strategic interests that these two countries satisfied for the EU all played a role.[56]

This, fortunately, started to change in 2022 when the European Union activated a new mechanism to protect the EU's budget against illiberal regimes: the Rule of Law Conditionality Regulation. This mechanism is based on the suspension of certain payments due to breaches of the rule of law principle.[57] In theory, it is not an instrument to protect the rule of law because it is separate from Article 7 of the EU treaty, but in practice it is a strong incentive for countries to abide by EU values.

The European Commission took this step against Hungary in April 2022, and then in September 2022 the European Council froze EUR 7.5 billion from Hungary's regional funds for 2021–2027.[58] These funds represent 20 percent of the EU funds allocated for Hungary and 3 percent of the country's annual GDP.[59] In addition, EUR 5.8 billion pandemic recovery funds were blocked.[60]

---

*The CEU remained open as of 2023.

The EU established remedial measures that Hungary needs to meet to unlock these funds, particularly regarding judicial independence. In response, Orbán created the Integrity Authority, an independent body assigned to ensure that the EU's financial interests are met, and he passed several anti-corruption laws. However, in November 2022 the European Commission found that "further essential steps will be needed to eliminate remaining risks for the EU budget in Hungary."[61] The Fidesz government pledged to meet EU demands on judicial independence by the end of March 2023.[62] With these moves, the EU took a turn in the right direction to combat Orbán's illiberalism.

The EU has yet to impose any restrictions on Hungary's sovereign bond issuance or on EU asset managers' capacity to hold Hungary's government bonds in their portfolios. It's not for a lack of regulatory clout. In fact, many political and economic observers argue that the EU regulates too much. The Markets in Financial Instruments Directive (MiFID) is the EU's legislative framework for regulating financial markets.[63] Its scope is so pervasive that the preparation for the framework's second version, MiFID II, cost companies an estimated $2.1 billion.[64] However, it is silent on the issue of human rights and democracy.

Hungary's democratic backslide with Orbán has been ignored by Wall Street and the City of London, which have always been ready to finance it. Driven, as in other markets, by the guidance of bond indices, bond issuances have been worth several billion dollars almost every year during Orbán's tenure. In April 2020, right after he gained unchecked decree powers, the government issued two bonds worth a combined EUR 2 billion at rates below 2 percent.[65] In 2020, the government issued more than the equivalent of $7.5 billion in bonds denominated in euros and yen. In September 2021, as Hungary faced delays in receiving funds from the EU, Orbán's government issued three more bonds, two in US dollars and one in euros, for a total of about $5.3 billion.[66]

In April 2022, Orbán won a fourth consecutive term, and again with a supermajority. Fidesz got 135 of the 199 parliamentary seats, although it received 53.7 percent of the votes in an election that raised many eyebrows among international observers.[67] Orbán dedicated his triumph to the EU, remaining true to his agenda. He said,

"The entire world can see that our brand of Christian democratic, conservative, patriotic politics has won."[68] He added, "We are sending Europe a message that this is not the past—this is the future."[69] Markets also celebrated his triumph. On June 9, 2022, the government issued $3.8 billion of foreign currency bonds. Investor demand was almost double the amount issued.[70]

KEY TAKEAWAYS OF CHAPTER 4

This chapter:

- Shows yet another avenue by which democracy can come under attack. In Venezuela, populism was defined along socioeconomic lines (the poor against the rich), and in Türkiye along religious lines ("the mosques are our barracks"). Hungary's case illustrates a line of populism, defined along cultural-ethnic lines (the talk among Polish right-wing nationalists about "true" Poles).

- Highlights how attacks on democracy have the same objectives and consequences, much like the discussions in Chapter 2 and 3. In all cases, markets missed them because they did not pay attention to what democracy watchers were saying.

- Describes how investors can end up financing autocrats indirectly through supra-national institutions, in this case the European Union. The same applies to the IMF (see Chapter 7) and the World Bank. These organizations issue bonds that are highly rated and end up in pensioners' portfolios.

CHAPTER 5

RUSSIA: FINANCING "PUTIN THE GREAT"

How the market turned a blind eye to an autocrat longing for Russian imperialism

Putin's Point of No Return

Russia's invasion of Ukraine on February 24, 2022, brought renewed uproar about former German Chancellor Gerhard Schröder's role as the chairman of the Nord Stream AG pipeline.[1] Schröder became its chairman in 2006, just weeks after signing as chancellor the country's Nord Stream deal with Russia, which was then known as the North European Gas Pipeline.[2]

The public backlash to his appointment was reasonable. Switzerland-based Nord Stream AG was established in 2005 by five companies from Russia, Germany, France, and the Netherlands to construct and operate a natural gas pipeline from Russia to Germany and other European countries through the Baltic Sea. Gazprom, Russia's state-controlled gas company, owns a 51 percent stake in the company,[3] and before the war started it supplied 55 percent of Germany's gas.[4] The bet of relying on Russia's gas proved disastrous for Germany, as Russia cut off supply in a retaliatory move following

Western sanctions related to the Ukraine invasion. The move left Germany scrambling for energy.

In 2022, Schröder, a personal and unapologetic friend of Vladimir Putin, was offered a position on Gazprom's board three weeks before the war started, according to an article in the *New York Times*.[5] His ties to Russian energy don't end with Gazprom; he has also presided over the board of Rosneft, a government-controlled Russian oil company, since 2017.

There was, however, another influential German national on Nord Stream's board who has gone largely unnoticed by the public, Matthias Warnig.[6] Compared to Schröder, Warnig is much more important to understanding the oligarchic servile system Putin created, his roots as a KGB agent, and the role that international markets and bankers played in his consolidation of power. In the late 1980s, Putin met Matthias Warnig in Dresden, East Germany, where he was stationed in his first and only overseas KGB post from 1985 to 1989, and Warnig was a Stasi agent. The Stasi's functions in East Germany were much like the KGB's in Russia, only the Stasi executed theirs to a higher degree of perfection. Warnig's job was industrial espionage.[7] There is some controversy about Putin's KGB assignments in Dresden, but most accounts suggest he held a rather low-level job.[8] No matter their roles, Warnig and Putin became close in Dresden, and Warnig eventually became an integral part of Putin's regime.[9]

After the collapse of the Berlin Wall and the beginning of the German reunification, Warnig went to work for Dresdner Bank in March 1990, and Putin returned to his hometown, Leningrad, to lead Leningrad State University's international relations efforts. In June 1991, simultaneous with Russia's first multiparty presidential election, Leningrad held its first multiparty direct mayoral election and a referendum on whether to rename it Saint Petersburg. Anatoly Sobchack, a prominent and promising pro-democracy reformer and Putin's former law professor, won the election. Putin worked with Sobchack when he was chairman of the Leningrad City Council before being elected mayor. Whether the KGB played a role in linking their careers is subject to debate.[10]

Taking advantage of his command of the German language and his international experience, Putin was put in charge of the city's international relations and international investments. According to American political scientist Karen Dawisha, "when it was time for St. Petersburg to set up branches of foreign banks, Putin chose from among the many applicants his friend and Dresden coworker Matthias Warnig."[11]

Warnig's career in Russia was stellar. By 2002 he was leading all Dresdner Bank operations in Russia from Moscow.[12] He would later become a board member, and in certain cases a small shareholder, of some of the most important firms in Russia. In 2012, he joined the board of directors of Bank Rossiya, which Leningrad Communist Party insiders founded in 1990.[13] The bank, owned mostly by Putin's close friends, "was important not as a bank but as the treasury of the Putin group."[14] In 2011, Warnig joined Rosneft's board, a company in which he is a small shareholder. He is also on the boards of influential companies in Russia, including VTB Bank, Verbundnetz Gas, pipeline transport company Transneft, and aluminum company Rusal.

Warnig, along with many other non-Russian businessmen and companies, and with support from international markets, played an important role in the 2003 takeover of Yukos Oil from Mikhail Khodorkovsky. Catherine Belton, former Moscow correspondent for the *Financial Times*, argued in her book *Putin's People: How the KGB Took Back Russia and Then Took on the West* that this operation marked the "point of no return" for Putin's entourage, the point from which they strayed away from the West and fostered instead a revival of the Russian state.[15]

Khodorkovsky studied chemistry at the Moscow Mendeleev Chemical Technology Institute,[16] driven by a desire to leave a difficult upbringing in the northeast of Moscow. His life took a turn when Mikhail Gorbachev's perestroika allowed for the creation of "cooperatives," the first private enterprises in Russia. In 1987, Khodorkovsky and some friends established a computer cooperative, Menatep.[17] The group did well, and eventually they set up one of the first private banks in Russia, later called Menatep Bank, and diversified into other businesses.

Khodorkovsky hit the jackpot in the mid-1990s when Russia's government finances were in shambles and it was running wage arrears. Behind in the polls for the 1996 presidential election,

President Boris Yeltsin needed cash to ramp up public spending and win reelection. So, to that purpose, Yeltsin's government pledged state-owned enterprises as collateral for cash advances, the so-called "loans-for-shares" program.[18] This scheme also marked the birth of many other oligarchs, including Roman Abramovich.

Khodorkovsky paid $309 million for a 78 percent stake in Yukos[19] in 1996. By 2003, that stake was worth billions of dollars, and it made Khodorkovsky the richest person in Russia. The impressive rise in the company's value was both the result of surging oil prices and of Khodorkovsky reinvesting profits in new technologies and introducing Western-style management best practices that helped Yukos's productivity soar.[20] Intense lobbying against higher taxes on oil and aggressive tax saving schemes, which many oil companies resorted to,[21] took care of the rest.

What ultimately caused Khodorkovsky's downfall was that he also wanted to improve Russia's governance by bringing it more into line with Western democracies. Based on the mold of George Soros's Open Society Institute, Khodorkovsky founded Open Russia in 2001 to disseminate the values of democracy and free market capitalism.[22] He even named former US Secretary of State Henry Kissinger to its board.

Khodorkovsky was concerned about the increasing role of the so-called *siloviki* in Putin's administration. These former KGB men, including Igor Sechin, Viktor Ivanov, and Nikolai Patrushev, wanted to reassert the role of the state and had an aversion to free markets.[23] He funded many political parties in the State Duma, the lower house of the Federal Assembly of Russia, and toyed with a political career himself. At one point, he said that he would step down from Yukos on his forty-fifth birthday. He would turn 45 in 2007, and the next presidential elections were scheduled for 2008.

But Khodorkovsky ran into the wrong men. While the *siloviki* tried to establish a quasi-capitalism where companies would not be renationalized but managed by oligarchs that "served at the pleasure of state officials,"[24] Khodorkovsky took over VNK, also known as Eastern Oil Company. The problem was that some officials in the FSB, the KGB's successor, had interests in VNK, and "seeing it seized from under their noses had been the final straw for Putin's men."[25] It also did not help that Khodorkovsky thought about merging

YukosSibneft, the combination of Yukos and Roman Abramovich's Sibneft, with America's ExxonMobil.

A meeting between Putin and the oligarchs on February 19, 2003, sealed Khodorkovsky's fate. The theme of discussion was "the fight against corruption."[26] Khodorkovsky, live on national TV, made a presentation in which he accused Rosneft of grossly overpaying for a small company, Severnaya Neft. "All those present knew I was accusing the president of Russia's inner circle of personal involvement in a crooked business deal," recounted Khodorkovsky. He added, "unbeknownst to me at the time, the beneficiary of the Severnaya deal was not merely a sidekick of the president, but the president himself."[27] According to Swedish economist and Russia expert Anders Åslund, Khodorkovsky told him that he had reliable information that the kickback totaled $200 million.[28] Putin was angry and, unusually for him, he replied with a veiled threat against Khodorkovsky.

Showing political ambitions, highlighting the administration's corruption, and selling energy assets to the Americans were too much for the *siloviki* and Putin. They set out to strip Khodorkovsky of his assets, a process in which Warnig and many others in the Western financial system played supporting roles. First, the government imprisoned Yukos's security chief, Alexei Pichugin, in June 2003, and then it imprisoned Platon Lebedev, Khodorkovsky's partner, in July. The market did not respond well. Yukos's market capitalization dropped by $2 billion in one day,[29] and in two weeks Russia's stock market value fell by $20 billion.[30]

Then it was Khodorkovsky's turn: he was arrested by the FSB in October 2003 on charges of fraud and tax evasion while his private plane stopped to refuel in Novosibirsk, Siberia. Yukos's shares lost more than half of their value from their peak the previous fall.[31] Ultimately, Khodorkovsky was sentenced to nine years in labor camp after a trial full of procedural violations, including applying laws retroactively.

The government produced a never-ending bill of allegedly unpaid back taxes for Yukos, a bill that eventually reached $24 billion. Instead of allowing the company to reorganize, the government announced that it would sell Yukos's main production unit, Yuganskneftegaz, which produced 60 percent of Yukos's total output.[32] Its valuation was awarded to the Moscow branch of Dresdner Bank, which was led by none other than Matthias Warnig. Along with other Western investment bankers, Charles Ryan, a US citizen who headed United Financial Group, a brokerage in which Deutsche Bank bought a 40 percent stake in November 2003 to form Deutsche-United Financial Group, advised the government on the Yukos takeover.[33]

Gazprom wanted to buy Yuganskneftegaz using a loan of more than $13 billion from a syndicate of banks led by Deutsche Bank and Dresdner Bank.[34] But the Western banks providing the loans pulled the deal off due to a preventive action of Yukos in US courts. Rosneft ended up buying Yukos through a shady proxy for less than half of Dresdner Bank's valuation.[35] Western oil majors and financial institutions facilitated the acquisition of Yukos's remaining assets, including by filing the bankruptcy petition for Yukos's debts, which Rosneft later acquired, and by providing a $22 billion loan to Rosneft.[36]

The markets did not seem to care that property rights and individual rights were obliterated in the Yukos affair. Putin played with them, as he seemingly believes in a version of a phrase often attributed to Lenin: "Capitalists will sell us the rope with which to hang them." According to Belton, he thinks that "anyone in the West could be bought, and that commercial imperatives would always outweigh any moral or other concerns."[37]

While the Yukos dismemberment was happening, and right after he announced that he would suspend the election of governors, Putin stated that he planned to create the world's biggest energy major. He would merge Gazprom with Rosneft, presumably in a move to appease investors. Because the government would own more than 50 percent of the combined company, the restrictions on foreign ownership would be removed.[38] This news was very well received by the international investor community; one investor summarized the situation: "They are buying off the loyalty of the foreign investor community as they create what looks like a political dictatorship. And it's working."[39]

Ultimately, the government called off the prospective merger in 2005 as it was a complex solution to the government's ultimate desire—to raise its participation in Gazprom to 51 percent—and also due to a pushback from Rosneft.[40] Foreign investors were allowed to own a noncontrolling minority stake in Gazprom,[41] as the government increased its stake in the company from 38 percent to 51 percent. To do so, the government borrowed $7 billion from international banks, just a few weeks after Khodorkovsky was declared guilty of fraud and tax evasion, among other charges. International investors reveled in the opportunity to participate in Gazprom, and Russia's RTS Index doubled in six months.[42]

Rosneft's survival was seen as a triumph for its chairman, Igor Sechin, who fought to keep the company independent. One of Putin's closest advisers since 1991,[43] Sechin was a key architect of Russia's moves to regain of control of its energy assets. Thanks to the "acquisition" of Yukos's assets, Rosneft tripled its oil production, and foreign investors were happy that they could get a piece of the action. In July 2006, Rosneft carried out an initial public offering (IPO), receiving more than $10 billion. The IPO left $120 million in fees for the 26 banks that participated in the deal.[44]

Rosneft's second expansion phase was in 2012 when it bought TNK-BP.[45] British Petroleum (BP) initially invested $8 billion in 2003 for 50 percent of this joint venture with Russia's privately owned and vertically integrated oil company TNK. Production and profits soared. Less than 10 years later, Rosneft acquired TNK-BP for $55 billion. BP received $12.5 billion in cash, 18.5 percent of Rosneft's shares, worth $14.5 billion, and a dividend of $8 billion. BP made 350 percent on its initial investment.[46]

Rosneft's buying spree did not end there. In 2016, Rosneft bought Bashneft from Sistema, a private company, in an "auction" for $5.3 billion.[47] The procedure was not much different from the dismantling of Yukos. Sistema's owner, Vladimir Yevtushenkov, was arrested on money laundering charges in 2014. Although he was later acquitted, Yevtushenkov lost almost all his wealth. As if this was not enough, in May 2017, Rosneft claimed damages against Sistema, arguing that Sistema had stripped assets from Bashneft. Sistema's stock plunged 37 percent, and the Russian stock market fell 14 percent, with investors concerned about a repeat of Khodorkovsky's story. In August, courts awarded Rosneft $2.3 billion, by which point Sistema's stock had lost half its value.[48] At the end of the spending binge, Rosneft produced about half of Russia's oil.[49]

However, neither Yevtushenkov's downfall nor, for that matter, Russia's annexation of Crimea in 2014 were a deterrent for the market that was still looking to add Russian oil and gas assets to their portfolios. In December 2016, the government sold 19.5 percent of Rosneft shares to a consortium of Glencore, then a public company whose shares floated in the market, and Qatar's sovereign wealth fund, although the real beneficiaries remain unknown according to Anders Åslund.[50] The EUR 10.5 billion from the sale went to the government's coffers.

Instruments of Domestic and International Power

Foreign investors were largely oblivious to the fact that these *siloviki*-controlled enterprises were instruments of domestic and international power for Putin's regime. All investors saw, or wanted to see, were Russia's oil and gas reserves and the booming profits that they generated.

The oil and gas wealth that flowed into Russia skyrocketed from $30 billion in 1995 to an average of $175 billion annually a decade later,[51] but only a select few benefitted. Widespread corruption left very little for the population. Instead, hundreds of billions of dollars, mostly stashed outside of Russia, went to regime insiders. In her book *Putin's Kleptocracy*, Karen Dawisha noted that despite receiving $1.6 trillion from oil and gas exports from 2000 to 2011, Russia did not build a single multilane highway during that period.[52]

Money is power, and power requires money. To build both, Putin's regime raided the oil and gas companies, filled them with cronies, and siphoned resources from them. One way the regime went about it was to pay for acquisitions at higher-than-market prices, as was allegedly the case with Rosneft subsidiary Severnaya Neft.

Roman Abramovich's sale of Sibneft to Gazprom is another suspected example of this tactic. Gazprom used the $7 billion it received from the government to increase its stake in Sibneft[53] and ultimately bought it for $13.1 billion, making it the biggest takeover deal in Russia's history. There is some dispute about whether or not the deal was made at market prices,[54] but there is agreement that Abramovich was remarkably luckier than Khodorkovsky.

Another way to plunder these companies was to force them to award contracts to cronies. Anders Åslund noted, "Gazprom has regularly overinvested in pipelines that are not commercially viable. These contracts have been awarded to companies controlled by a few close friends of Putin."[55] Arkady Rotenberg, Putin's childhood sambo friend from Leningrad, bought five construction subsidiaries from Gazprom in 2008 and founded Stroygazmontazh, the largest construction company for gas pipelines and electrical power supply lines in Russia. Like Lázaro Báez in Argentina (see Chapter 7), Rotenberg is a very lucky man: he won a major tender for the construction of Nord Stream just a few weeks after forming Stroygazmontazh.[56]

Gennady Timchenko was a close friend of Putin from their days in post-communist Saint Petersburg. In 2004, Putin even gifted Timchenko a dog, the offspring of Putin's Labrador. Timchenko made Putin, who still had a passion for sambo and judo, honorary chairman of a judo club he cosponsored.[57] His oil trading company, Gunvor, was one of the main beneficiaries of Gazprom's acquisition of Yukos and Sibneft.[58] By 2008 it was trading 30 percent of all seaborne oil exports from Russia.[59]

Actions like these showed a significant disregard for the outside minority investors, including US and European pension funds. The shares of Rosneft, Gazprom, and other companies traded at lower multiples to sales than similar Western companies, as bad management and corruption caused Russian companies to generate lower profits for each US dollar of sales.

Gazprom's board, for instance, was packed with former KGB men and Putin's friends from Saint Petersburg. In May 2014, Gazprom traded at a 43 percent discount, compared to an average of 3 percent for other European energy companies.[60] Jim Grant, the founder of financial markets journal *Grant's Interest Rate Observer*, called it "by acclamation the world's worst company managed by the worst kleptocrats ever assembled on one continent."[61]

Evidence of this disregard occurred when TNK-BP's shares dropped 40 percent in response to Rosneft's offer to buy it. Igor Sechin, Rosneft chief, responded that "minority shareholders shouldn't expect to be treated equally and that they shouldn't expect large dividends in the future, since Rosneft is 'not a charity fund.'"[62]

These companies also served to expand Russia's foreign policy clout, right under the noses of foreign investors. According to Dawisha, from the very beginning of his presidency, Putin made clear in public speeches that Russia's foreign policy would be exercised not only by the state but also by its oil and gas companies.[63] According to Åslund, "Gazprom is probably Russia's foremost geopolitical tool in the former Soviet Union and Eastern Europe."[64] It has cut gas supplies and engaged in other predatory policies dozens of times, with Lithuania, Georgia, Belarus, Ukraine, and Moldova as some of its main targets.

Of course, Russia wielded Gazprom as a foreign policy tool the most in Ukraine. The company cut Ukraine's gas supply in January 2006 and January 2009 due to disputes about pricing and transit fees. But when Viktor Yanukovych, Ukraine's pro-Kremlin president, was in power, Gazprom sold the country gas at a deep discount.[65] After Yanukovych was ousted as president and with Putin's help fled Ukraine in April 2014, Gazprom hiked the price by 80 percent.[66]

Rosneft's use in foreign policy also extended far from the homeland. In May 2015, Rosneft committed to invest $14 billion in Venezuela's oil industry, which made little commercial sense given Venezuela's government disastrous management of the ventures in which it participated, including those in the oil business.[67] It may have been to support Nicolás Maduro, who was then tightening his grip on power and destroying what remained of Venezuela's democracy (see Chapter 2). Unsurprisingly, the Rosneft venture did not prosper, and in March 2020 Rosneft sold its Venezuelan assets to a company owned by the Russian government.[68]

The market continually looked the other way as it benefitted from the oil and gas price–driven boom in Russia. After nearly hitting near $12 per barrel on average in 1998, oil prices rose to nearly $24 per barrel when Putin became president in 2000. By 2012, oil was up to $109 per barrel.[69] "In 2003, oil and gas output represented 20% of Russia's GDP, 55% of its export earnings, and 40% of its tax revenues."[70] Russia became a petrostate, with a kleptocrat at its helm.

After suffering a huge crisis at the end of the twentieth century that included a debt default and the effects of a harsh IMF-driven fiscal adjustment, Russia's economy started to surge. The economy's average yearly GDP growth rate between 2000 and 2008 was 7 percent, a stark contrast to an average contraction of about 5 percent during Boris Yeltsin's presidency (July 1991 to December 1999). The economy soared from about $270 billion in 2000 to more than $1.75

trillion in 2008. This growth, along with a significant expansion of civil services, gave Russian citizens a quality of life that they had never experienced before. Putin's approval ratings averaged 74 percent during his first 20 years in power,[71] and hovered near 80 percent during his first two terms.[72]

Like other autocrats chronicled in this book, Putin appointed a liberal—in the European sense of the word—economic cabinet and implemented structural market-friendly reforms. He kept Mikhail Kasyanov as prime minister, and he brought back Aleksandr Voloshin as the Kremlin's chief of staff, a signal of continuity with the Yeltsin era and market-friendliness. Putin appointed Herman Gref, a liberal from Saint Petersburg, as minister of economic development and trade, and the liberal Alexei Kudrin as minister of finance to continue the impressive market reforms of Yegor Gaidar and Anatoly Chubais.[73] Andrei Illarionov, a libertarian economist, was appointed as economic adviser.[74]

The cabinet successfully implemented an impressive set of reforms that spanned taxes, land, and the civil code. The cabinet also established new labor laws, a bankruptcy code, a private pension plan, and it deregulated several sectors of the economy.[75] The government went from running huge fiscal deficits in the 1990s to fiscal surpluses, bringing down government debt levels and building international reserves of $412 billion by 2008, an increase of $387 billion from 2000.[76]

The market loved all of it. Foreign capital flows into Russia soared, including portfolio flows, foreign direct investment, and loans. From outflows in 2000 and 2001, and a small inflow in 2002, foreign capital flows rose to an average of $87 billion per year from 2003 to 2008, with a high of $212 billion in 2007.[77]

Other participants played the happy market tune as well, including rating agencies. In 2004, Moody's rated Russia as Baa3, the lowest investment grade category. On October 6, 2004, it raised Russia's outlook from stable to positive, citing the economy's strength. A *Financial Times* article commented that the move was a surprise given that economic reforms had stalled, and that the move "shrugs aside worries about property rights reawakened by the government's campaign against Yukos, the oil company that is lurching towards bankruptcy because of back taxes."[78]

Dismantling Democracy from Day One

The benefits of Russia's oil and gas bounty were too great for markets to look past, but democracy watchers recognized Putin's moves to destroy democratic checks and balances early on. They were too obvious to ignore; even before his inauguration, Putin spoke about "a more rigid, vertically structured system of administration,"[79] and he stayed true to his words.

As most dictators and wannabe dictators depicted in this book, Putin took to obliterating democracy's checks and balances in Russia right from the start of his presidency. Putin was inaugurated on May 7, 2000, in a lavish ceremony reminiscent of Tsarist times.[80] Only four days later, police special forces units raided the offices of Media-Most, the largest media company in Russia. Media-Most owned, among many other entities, NTV, one of the three the most important TV channels and "the most hard-hitting of them."[81] The accusations against Media-Most and its owner, Vladimir Gusinsky, did not add up, but that did not matter. The police were there to intimidate.[82]

A month after the raid, Gusinsky was arrested. According to Putin biographer Philip Short, Mikhail Lesin, the press minister, offered him a deal: Gusinsky could sell his shares in Media-Most to Gazprom, to which the company owed US$ 200 million, and all would be forgiven, or else he would return to prison.[83] Gusinsky argued that he signed the deal under duress,[84] and he left Russia in July 2000. In April 2001, the editorial staff of NTV was forced out,[85] and a week later two liberal Media-Most publications, the weekly political newsmagazine *Itogi* and the daily newspaper *Segodnya*, were closed.[86]

Next on the list was Boris Berezovsky, who owned ORT, the TV channel with the biggest national audience,[87] and other companies in media and beyond. He knew Putin from the 1990s, and he was instrumental in getting him elected president in May 2000.[88] However, after the election, Berezovsky publicly distanced himself from Putin and threw his support behind the opposition when Putin tried to reduce the power of regional governors. Problems for Berezovsky escalated when Putin faced his first major crisis as president.

In August 2000, the Russian submarine *Kursk* sank to the bottom of the Barents Sea after torpedoes exploded inside the vessel.

The accident killed 118 crewmembers. According to Short, Putin was outraged at ORT's coverage of the disaster, which he deemed critical of the government. He decided that Berezovsky "was not just an enemy but a traitor."[89] Shortly thereafter, Berezovsky sold his shares in ORT to Abramovich's Sibneft, left Russia, and ended up living in London, where he was found dead in 2013. On January 21, 2002, Berezovsky's other TV channel, TV6, was suddenly taken off the air.[90] Other cases like these followed; independent media, except for some small outlets, was dead in Russia.

Six days after his inauguration, Putin signed legislation that reduced the power of regional governors by implementing a super-structure of seven districts, each encompassing several regions. The district heads, appointed by the president, would supervise the work of elected governors. Of the first seven appointed district heads, only two were civilians, and according to journalist Masha Gessen, one of them had the résumé of an undercover KGB agent.[91] Another law allowed regional governors to be removed without due process. They were effectively under Putin's command. Then in September 2004, Putin canceled the gubernatorial elections altogether. From then on, regional governors would be appointed by the president.[92]

Putin appeared to next set his sights on rigging elections, eliminating term limits, muting political rivals, cracking down on demonstrators, and controlling NGOs. After the December 2003 parliamentary elections, the Organization for Security and Cooperation in Europe (OSCE) stated that "The State Duma elections failed to meet any OSCE and Council of Europe commitments for democratic elections."[93] Elections were not free anymore. In his second term, Putin took aim at NGOs, promulgating a law that gives the government "numerous means to harass, weaken, and even close down NGOs considered too political."[94] In his third term, he signed a new law that required NGOs to register as "foreign agents."[95]

As Putin extended his stay in power, he went harder against opposition leaders. Alexei Navalny's imprisonment and poisoning is one of many examples. Putin also exerted his control by criminalizing protests. In 2020, he rewrote the 1993 constitution, a process that took less than a week of debate in the Duma.[96] The new constitution allowed him to seek reelection in 2024 and 2030 and gave him more powers over the judiciary.[97]

While markets were too distracted by their outsized returns, Western politicians were largely indifferent, if not complicit, in the deterioration of democracy in Russia. Some seemed gullible, some seemed driven by economic or geopolitical interests. Putin charmed President George W. Bush, who after his first meeting with the Russian president said that he "got a sense of his soul."[98] Putin had just started destroying democracy then, so perhaps Bush's misjudgment can be forgiven. Worse was President Barack Obama's "Reset," an attempt to improve relations between the United States and Russia,[99] which took place when Russia's anti-democratic actions at home and at its near abroad were well known. In August 2012, Russia joined the World Trade Organization, which gave it better and cheaper access to many markets for its goods and services sector. According to Garry Kasparov, the former chess champion and human rights activist, the United States put significant pressure on the country of Georgia so that it would not block Russia's accession to the WTO, even though a large part of its territory had been occupied by Russian forces since 2008.[100]

Democracy watchers saw the situation in Russia with clearer eyes. V-Dem considered Russia as an Electoral Autocracy beginning in 2001, but its scores deteriorated significantly during Putin's reign. Freedom House had a Partially Free ranking on Russia from 2001 to 2003 but changed it to Not Free after the 2004 presidential election in which Putin received 71.4 percent of the votes and after his decision to appoint the governors. Freedom House said that the change was due to "the virtual elimination of influential opposition parties within the country and the further concentration of executive power."[101] Russia's scores have declined almost systematically since then. The Economist Intelligence Unit classified Russia as a Hybrid Regime from the inception of its democracy index in 2006 to 2010, and as an Authoritarian Regime from 2010 on.

Sanctions Initially Left Markets Out

If investors paid attention to the deterioration of democratic standards and the consequent deterioration in property rights and human rights in Russia, they would have avoided many hardships, both financial and personal. When Russia invaded Crimea in 2014,

Russia's MICEX stock index dropped 11 percent,[102] Gazprom's stock dropped more than 12 percent, and Rosneft's dropped almost 6 percent.[103] All told, investors lost $34 billion on one of MICEX's biggest one-day falls in years. However, those losses paled in comparison to the loss investors suffered when Russia invaded Ukraine in 2022. On February 24, the RTS Index dropped 38 percent.[104] The MOEX, as the MICEX is now called, dropped 29 percent in the aftermath, after being down as much as 50 percent in early trading.[105]

Investor losses in nondemocratic countries are often not only financial. The story of William (Bill) Browder is a testament to the personal risks that investors face in Putin's Russia. Fresh out of Stanford Graduate School of Business and the grandson of Earl Browder, former head of the Communist Party USA, Bill landed a consulting assignment in post-communist Poland. It was in Poland that Browder learned that there was plenty of money to be made in Eastern Europe's privatization process, so he left consulting and entered the investment world in 1991. He worked for famed financier Robert Maxwell, before moving to Salomon Brothers.[106] There he discovered that the privatization vouchers given to 150 million Russians, for about 30 percent of Russian companies, were valued at only $10 billion.[107]

In 1996, Browder launched Hermitage Capital, a hedge fund dedicated to investing in Russia that would reach $4.5 billion in assets under management (AUM). Named after the Hermitage Museum in Saint Petersburg, Hermitage Capital became the biggest foreign investor in Russia. In 2000, Browder's firm was named the best performing emerging markets fund in the world. Since its inception and until 2000, the fund had generated returns of 1,500 percent.[108]

Hermitage was not only about money, but its purpose was to help build a capitalist future for Russia. Browder's style was shareholder activism.[109] He would buy stakes in companies that were being robbed by their majority shareholders, that is, the oligarchs and corrupt officials. Browder and his small team would investigate how the money was stolen, and then they would use this information to file lawsuits, contest the control of the company, and brief government officials. They would also expose this dirt in the international media.[110]

The strategy worked very well, until it didn't. Khodorkovsky's imprisonment in 2003 ushered in a new era in Russa, though Browder did not recognize it right away. Instead, he applauded Khodorkovsky's arrest, writing in the *Moscow Times* that "we should . . . fully support [Putin] in his task of taking back control of the country from oligarchs."[111] Shortly thereafter, Browder drew the government's ire by exposing corrupt officials. In November 2005, Browder was expelled from Russia after the government deemed him a threat to national security.

Browder liquidated the fund's holdings and took most of his team out of Russia. In May 2007, what was left of Hermitage's offices in Moscow were raided, as were the offices of the firm's lawyers.[112] In the raids, government officials took the seals and certificates of Browder's investment holding companies. With these documents in hand, some government officials forged debts of $1 billion with three empty companies and successfully applied for a $230 million tax rebate.[113]

Two lawyers representing Hermitage Capital fled to London after being interrogated by the Interior Ministry. A third, Sergei Magnitsky, decided to stay. He was imprisoned, and died in 2009 after 358 days in custody, having suffered severe abuse and mistreatment.[114] After his death, Browder set out to ensure that the thugs who robbed Hermitage and the Russian taxpayers, and those who were responsible for Magnitsky's death, could not use their ill-gotten fortunes. In Browder's words, "this idea slowly evolved into a legislative proposal called the Magnitsky Act."[115]

In December 2012, President Obama signed the bipartisan Magnitsky Act into law following Browder's tireless efforts to convince congressional lawmakers of its significance. Initially, the act allowed the US government to freeze the assets and ban the Russian officials responsible for Magnitsky's death from entering the United States. In 2016, the act was broadened to the Global Magnitsky Act, which allows the US government to sanction government officials of any country who are human rights offenders. By April 2022, the United States had sanctioned 420 human right abusers from 43 countries under the act.[116] Several other Western countries followed the United States' lead and devised similar laws.

The number of sanctions on Russian officials and Russian entities ballooned after Russia invaded Crimea in 2014, and even more came after Russia invaded Ukraine in February 2022. After Russia annexed Crimea, US policymakers had to contemplate the interests of their European allies, according to Jacob J. Lew, former US Treasury Secretary, and Richard Nephew, former State Department principal deputy coordinator for sanctions policy.[117] This consideration meant concentrating the sanctions on key decision makers while leaving Russia's energy exports to Europe intact. In particular, the sanctions targeted Putin's cronies and Bank Rossiya.

The 2014 sanctions package hit the Russian economy hard, but it was not a fatal blow. Economic growth slowed to 0.7 percent in 2014 from 4 percent in 2012 and 1.8 percent in 2013, it contracted 2 percent in 2015, and it expanded only 0.2 percent in 2016. By 2017, Russia's economy was about the same size as it was in 2014. After receiving net foreign capital inflows of $110 billion in 2012 and $133 billion in 2013, capital started to flow out of the country. Outflows averaged $26 billion per year in 2014 and 2015.[118] The central bank lost $130 billion of international reserves in 2014, and $21 billion in 2015 and 2016. Then, things returned somewhat to normal business. Foreign capital flows to Russia resumed in 2017, although not to the same extent as before 2014. The economy delivered modest growth, and the central bank was able to buy international reserves again.

For the most part, the sanctions imposed on Russia after it annexed Crimea did not restrict US investors from accessing Russia's debt and equity markets. It was only in 2021 that the US government banned US financial institutions from participating in Russian Federation debt issuance. Only after Russia invaded Ukraine did the United States prohibit its financial firms from participating in Russia's sovereign debt secondary market. This issue is discussed further in Chapter 10.

Money in, Tanks Out

Russia took advantage of this gap in the sanctions and remained an active issuer of foreign currency debt, which often found its way into the portfolios of Western investors, including their pension funds. In 2016, Russia's government was able to issue bonds again, including a Eurobond of $1.75 billion before July 2016,[119] another one for $1.25 billion in September 2016, and two bonds for a total of $3 billion in June 2017.[120]

In April 2018 the United States sanctioned Oleg Deripaska,[121] an oligarch who owns important industrial companies, including aluminum producer Rusal. Bond yields, which move opposite to bond prices, dropped 25 basis points to above 5 percent. Market participants did not seem to care because they did not think that sanctions would have "a profound impact on the Russian economy."[122] Investors gobbled up December's $1,750 million government debt issue.

The issuance continued in 2019, 2020, and 2021.[123] According to an article in the *Financial Times*, by the end of 2021 foreign investors owned at least $150 billion in Russian securities, including $86 billion of Russian equities, $20 billion dollar-denominated debt, and $41 billion of ruble-denominated sovereign bonds.[124]

In most cases in this book, the consequences of foreign investors' participation in financial markets of a country that slips into autocracy stay within that country's borders. That is not the case with Russia, at least since its intervention in Georgia in 2008. Putin's shift from a more friendly to confrontational stance with Western countries started with the "color revolutions" in Georgia in 2003 and Ukraine in 2004–2005 to protest electoral fraud.

Putin became obsessed that the "virus" of pro-democratic mobilizations in former Soviet republics could spread to Russia,[125] as they could "risk reinfecting his own people with democratic aspirations."[126] That Putin intended to invade all of Ukraine was written clearly on the wall for anyone willing to read it. In 2015, Garry Kasparov warned, "Those who say the Ukraine conflict is far away and unlikely to lead to global instability miss the clear warning Putin has given us. There is no reason to believe his announced vision of a 'Greater Russia' will end with Eastern Ukraine and many reasons to believe it will not. Dictators stop only when they are stopped, and appeasing Putin with Ukraine will only stoke his appetite for more conquests."[127] He did so, with devastating consequences for Ukrainians and the global economy at large.

Russia's interventions abroad reach well beyond its former republics. In the words of democracy expert Larry Diamond, "Putin's regime has been embarked for some years now on an opportunistic but sophisticated campaign to sabotage democracy and bend it toward his interests, not just in some marginal fragile places but at the very core of the liberal democratic order, Europe and the United States."[128]

Russia's government has supported the campaigns of illiberal parties from the far right to the far left in France, Austria, Hungary, Greece, the Czech Republic, and others.[129] Putin has counted the likes of Italy's Silvio Berlusconi and Germany's Gerhard Schröder as friends.

In an interview with the *Financial Times* in 2019, Putin argued that "the liberal idea has become obsolete" and that "traditional values are more stable and more important for millions of people."[130] In the same interview, Putin said that the world leader that he most admired is Peter the Great, a comment that reveals the truth of Putin's reign.[131] The goal of his presidency is to restore Russia's imperial grandeur, no matter the cost. In my view, the most amazing part of this story is that investors continued pouring money to finance Putin's imperial ambitions even after he so openly admitted and demonstrated what his plan was.

KEY TAKEAWAYS OF CHAPTER 5

This chapter:

- Highlights that support for autocrats can come not only through purchases of government bonds, but also by buying shares or bonds of SOEs or quasi-sovereign issuers such as Rosneft and Gazprom. Autocrats use these companies to build power domestically and abroad.

- Shows the perils that investors face when pouring money into autocratic countries. Many of the stocks and government bonds that they invested in suffered great losses even before 2022. These perils are mostly financial, but they can also be personal, as was the case of Bill Browder in Russia.

- Provides more details on sanctions, including the origins and the scope of the Magnitsky Act. Also, discusses how most government sanctions packages do not restrict investing in bonds and stocks of autocratic countries until it is too late.

- Argues that sometimes financing an autocratic country has implications beyond its borders, as we learned the hard way with Russia's invasion of Ukraine.

CHAPTER 6

CHINA: FINANCING XI JINPING'S "NEW WORLD ORDER"

International financing increased as autocracy intensified

China's Government Bonds Go Global

In May 2021, index provider FTSE Russell decided to include Chinese government local currency denominated bonds in its FTSE Russell World Government Bond Index (WGBI). Shortly thereafter, a report by Robin Marshall and Zhaoyi Yang from the London Stock Exchange Group (LSEG), of which FTSE Russell is a subsidiary, put the decision in perspective. They argued that China's inclusion in global indexes "changes the nature of the asset allocation decision for global investors benchmarked against these indexes." They said that "investors may now need reasons to justify *not* [emphasis added] investing strategically in Chinese government bonds, rather than a justification for doing so . . . when they were not included in benchmark indexes."[1]

In truth, from a purely financial point of view there had been, for many years, ample reasons for foreign investors to add Chinese government bonds to their portfolios. It's just that, until recently, China's government regulations didn't allow them to.

First, according to a July 2020 report by Marshall and Yang of FTSE Russell, the risk-adjusted returns of China's government bonds were much higher, on average, than the risk-adjusted returns of US Treasuries and Eurozone government bonds during the 2009–2020 period.[2] Risk-adjusted returns compare the returns—or the money you make when you sell a bond minus the money you paid for it—plus all accrued interest, scaled for the volatility of the returns. So, if two investments have the same returns, investors prefer the one with returns that fluctuate the least: in financial parlance, the one with lower volatility. From 2009 to 2020, the standard deviation of China's government bonds, meaning the statistical measure of their volatility, was the lowest of all major bond markets according to Marshall and Yang.

Second, China's bonds offer substantial diversification benefits to global investors, one of the main drivers of investment in emerging markets. Diversification in an investment portfolio is akin to putting the proverbial eggs in different baskets. When one source of risk hits your portfolio, perhaps a change in the interest rate set by the US Federal Reserve, having assets that are not as affected by that risk helps reduce the overall volatility of your portfolio. Markets gauge diversification benefits through a statistical measure called correlation, which measures how close two variables move together. If two markets move perfectly in tandem, the correlation coefficient is 1.0. In the case of China's government bonds, their return correlation with the US, Eurozone, and other major government bond market returns is very low. High risk-adjusted returns and low correlation with other assets? Bingo!

In addition, Chinese government bonds are one of the safest among emerging markets. They are rated A+ by Standard and Poor's and by Fitch, and the equivalent A1 by Moody's. They are investment grade, which means that their probability of default is considered very low. For comparison, in Latin America the only government with a similar rating was Chile, until March 2021, when it was downgraded to A.

Like the Chinese economy's ascent on the global stage, China's bond market growth is a relatively recent phenomenon. The massive size of China's economy has made it impossible to ignore for any company in the world. The same can be said for China's government bond market, though it has developed somewhat less spectacularly than China's economy. One of the key metrics used by ratings agencies is government debt as a percentage of GDP, and China's has been rising. However, at 76.9 percent of GDP as of December 2022, it remained below the average developed country.[3]

At the beginning of the 2000s, China's bond market capitalization, the total value of all the bonds traded in China including government and corporate bonds, was about 1 percent of the global GDP. By the end of 2017, it was 9 percent, and it has continued to grow.[4] China's government bonds outstanding were a little more than 6 trillion yuan by December 2010. By April 2020, they were 2.5 times more at more than 16 trillion yuan, equivalent to roughly $2.3 trillion.[5]

Until recently, these bonds were off-limits for foreign investors. Before 2013, if foreign investors wanted to purchase to Chinese bonds, they could only access the much smaller offshore bond market in Hong Kong. The bonds issued and traded in Hong Kong are known as dim sum bonds, named after a cuisine in southern China that features small delicacies. In 2013, the government allowed institutions approved under two programs, the Qualified Foreign Institutional Investor (QFII) and the Renminbi Qualified Foreign Institutional Investor (RQFII), to access its local bond market, but they were subject to quotas.[6] By 2016, foreigners owned only about 3 percent of Chinese government bonds.[7]

That same year, the government allowed foreigners quota-free access using the China Interbank Bond Market Direct (CIBMD), a platform where 90 percent of the onshore bonds trade. Other measures that made it easier to trade Chinese government bonds followed, such as the 2017 launch of Bond Connect. This mutual market access scheme allowed investors from Mainland China and overseas to trade in each other's markets through a China/Hong Kong connect facility.[8]

In 2016, China also took a momentous step to internationalize its currency, and thus its domestic financial market. On October 1, 2016, the renminbi (RMB), also known as the yuan (CNY), was added to the basket of the IMF's Special Drawing Rights (SDR), an international reserve asset created by the IMF in 1969. The SDR is a basket of currencies that includes the

US dollar (41.73 percent), the euro (30.93 percent), the Japanese yen (8.33 percent), the British pound (8.09 percent) and the yuan (10.9 percent).

The renminbi's internationalization has two main effects on the Chinese government bond market. First, international reserve managers at central banks around the world will increase their holdings of assets denominated in renminbi over time. Worldwide composition of international reserves does not directly match the composition of the SDR basket, as about 59 percent of them are invested in US dollars, but they do resemble each other.[9] Given that the renminbi has a weight of 10.9 percent in the SDR's basket, its percentage of the central bank's international reserves is likely to rise from its 2022 share of 2.3 percent.

This move will increase the demand for Chinese government bonds. We can draw this conclusion because the international reserves holdings of central banks are mostly held in the bonds of the respective treasuries, not in cash. For example, if a central bank has 100 percent of its reserves in US dollars, it most likely has only a small part of them in US dollar bills. The rest will be invested in US government bonds. Therefore, to gradually increase their exposure to the yuan, central banks will buy China's government bonds.

Second, a convertible currency allows investors to hedge the currency exposure of their bond holdings. When foreign investors buy local currency bonds of other countries, they run several risks at once. First, they run interest rate risks; if rates increase, the price of the bonds fall. Second, they run default risks; they may not be paid in full if the government cannot make its debt and interest payments. In emerging markets, sovereign defaults and restructuring stories are common.[10] Third, foreign investors run currency risks when the bond is denominated in the currency of the issuer country as opposed to the currency of the bond buyer's home country.

For example, if an investor based in the United States buys local currency denominated government debt from China, and after the purchase the renminbi weakens against the US dollar, the investor will get fewer US dollars for the investment. This is why many asset managers choose to hedge the currency risk in the currency derivatives market, where the exchange rates between two currencies at future dates can be fixed in advance. The more liquid and actively traded a currency is, the easier it is to hedge exposure to assets in that currency.

Finally, the step that solidified the internationalization of China's financial market was the inclusion of China's government bonds in major indexes. In March 2018, the Bloomberg Barclays Global Aggregate Index agreed to start including China from April 2019. In February 2020, J.P. Morgan's Government Bond Index—Emerging Markets (GBI-EM) included China. By March 2021, foreign ownership of China's government local currency denominated bonds had jumped to 10 percent of the total.[11]

The biggest milestone China reached was its's inclusion in the FTSE World Government Bond Index (WBGI), a process that started in October 2021 and will take place over a period of 36 months. To be included in the WBGI, remember, the government's bonds ratings should be at least A– by S&P and A3 by Moody's. The WBGI is the major prize among benchmark indices given its size; by mid-2021 an estimated $2.5–$3 trillion in assets tracked the index. In other words, funds with $2.5–$3 trillion in assets used the WGBI's financial return as the benchmark of their own success.[12] For comparison, by the end of 2019 there was an estimated $330 billion of assets under management benchmarked to the GBI-EM local currency debt market. Estimates of the demand that inclusion in the WGBI would create for Chinese government bonds ranged between $130 and $160 billion, given that China's weight is around 5 percent of the total index.

However, even after China's inclusion in the WBGI, foreign ownership of domestic government bonds will still be below 15 percent of the total, compared to more than 25 percent for the United States and the United Kingdom, and more than 40 percent for Germany. It has never been the Chinese government's plan to fully integrate its domestic capital market with the global market. Like its goods and services trade relationship with the rest of the world, China wants the best of global integration without all the costs. David Lubin, head of emerging market economics at Citi, remarks in his book *Dance of the Trillions* that, as opposed to the "Washington Consensus," which promotes free capital mobility, the "Beijing Consensus" wants internationalization, yet not a complete liberalization of capital flows.[13] In China, the state still has tight control of markets.

China's bond market may be more limited than other countries. However, it hasn't stopped hundreds of billions of US dollars of foreign financing from flowing into China, at the same time Beijing was becoming "more repressive at home and aggressive abroad."[14]

Beijing Turned More Autocratic with Xi Jinping

The challenge with China's bond market is that it is too big for global investors to ignore. Total outstanding local currency Chinese government bonds were equivalent to $1.77 trillion by mid-2021, well below the $8.93 trillion US Treasuries market and the Eurozone's $8.47 trillion, but more than the United Kingdom's $1.37 and Germany's $1.56 markets.[15] But that doesn't tell the whole story: China's government bonds compose less than 20 percent of the total Chinese bonds now accessible to foreigners. Other local bond markets include the Policy Bank Bonds issued by the Export-Import Bank of China, local government bonds, corporate bonds, financial bonds, and enterprise bonds.[16] It's a pool too big and too attractive to leave behind.

The same is true of China's economy, to an even greater degree. The Chinese economy is too big, too efficient, and too cost-effective for companies not to source part of their production there. In 2001, when China entered the World Trade Organization (WTO), which allowed it to benefit from deeper rules-based trade relations with the world, China's gross domestic product (GDP) represented 4 percent of the world's GDP. Its exports represented 3.5 percent of the world's total. By 2021, China's share of global GDP was 18 percent, and its share of global exports was 12.7 percent. In 20 years, China went from the sixth largest economy in the world to the second largest. From 2001 to 2011, its middle class expanded by 203 million people.[17] China's rise is one of those once-in-a-century events.

Many in the West hoped that when they brought China into the global trade system, economic progress would promote freedom and democracy. President Bill Clinton said in 1997 that "it will become increasingly difficult to maintain the closed political system in an ever more open economy and society."[18] Several years later, Clinton's successor, George W. Bush, said that "once a measure of economic freedom is permitted, a measure of political freedom will follow."[19]

We could dismiss these declarations as politicians' naive justifications of their actions, but they are not.

The claim that economic modernization creates favorable conditions for a stable democracy, posed by Harvard University's Seymour Martin Lipset, is one of the most influential and time-tested theories in the social sciences.[20] Lipset posed this "thesis" in "Some Social Requisites of Democracy: Economic Development and Political Legitimacy" in 1959. Since then, it has become conventional wisdom[21] and has inspired countless debates and research. Another prominent scholar, Adam Przeworski, along with some colleagues, found that "there was in fact a striking relationship between development level and the probability of sustaining democracy between 1950 and 1990."[22]

Economic development and a more open financial market did not bring about more democracy in China. In fact, the opposite has happened in recent years; the Chinese Communist Party (CCP) increased its grip on society and the economy, becoming more repressive.

A Western-style democracy was never the plan for the Chinese authorities who implemented the modernization effort, starting with Deng Xiaoping, who assumed power of the CCP in 1978. According to former US Secretary of State Henry Kissinger, a Deng confidant, the Chinese leader "remained convinced that, in China, Western political principles would produce chaos and thwart development."[23] China's leaders were baffled by Mikhail Gorbachev prioritizing political reform (*Glasnost*) in Russia over economic restructuring (*Perestroika*), and later by the implosion of the USSR. Deng's successor, Jiang Zemin, said to Kissinger that "efforts to find a Chinese Gorbachev will be of no avail."[24]

However, for about two decades, from 1992 to 2012, there were some improvements to democracy in China. A balance of power among rival factions within the CCP made collective leadership possible,[25] and the presidency of China was term limited. Julian Gewirtz, author of the book *Never Turn Back: China and the Forbidden History of the 1980s*, argues that "the 1980s were a period of extraordinary open-ended contestation and imagination. Chinese elites argued fiercely about the future."[26] These discussions included the political system. One of the priorities of Zhao Ziyang, premier

85

between September 1980 and November 1987 and general secretary of the CCP between January 1987 and June 1989, was to separate party from government and "to increase accountability, transparency, and efficiency."[27] Reforms included a degree of freedom of expression not experienced before. Part of this progress toward democracy came to an end with the Tiananmen protests, and later with the collapse of the Soviet Union. Moreover, the lack of democratic reform meant that there were no mechanisms in place to avoid the rise of a strongman that could concentrate even more power and put an end to the era of collective leadership. That strongman was Xi Jinping, who became president in November 2012.

Xi made his priorities clear from the start. In his first press conference, Xi outlined his vision of a "rejuvenation" of the Chinese nation, a narrative that evoked memories of China as the Middle Kingdom demanding tribute from the rest of the world.[28] The Chinese Communist Party's April 2013 *Communique on the Current State of the Ideological Sphere*, known as Document 9 because it was the ninth one issued that year, also made the anti-liberal approach crystal clear. It depicted a CCP fighting against seven Western values that wanted to infiltrate China's society: "constitutionalism, universal values, civil society, neoliberalism and market economics, freedom of the press, reassessing China's history, and suggesting that China's reforms should be evaluated according to Western standards.[29]

Xi's political initiatives revolved around fighting those "threats." In the words of the Council on Foreign Relations' Elizabeth Economy, Xi's strategy involved "the dramatic centralization of authority under his personal leadership; the intensified penetration of society by the State; the creation of a wall of regulations and restrictions that more tightly controls the flow of ideas, culture and capital into and out of the country; and the significant projection of Chinese power."[30]

He tightened control of the main government bodies. In his first seven years in power, Xi jailed 42 members, or 11 percent, of the CCP's Central Committee,[31] which comprises the party's top officials. By the 19th Party Congress in 2017, Xi could count as allies as many as 4 out of 7 members of the executive Politburo Standing Committee (PSC), excluding himself. Additionally, 18 of the 25-member Politburo of the CCP, the party's main decision-making body, were aligned with Xi.[32] In March 2018, a few months after the

18th Party Congress, Xi abolished the constitutional two-term limit on the presidency, allowing him to stay in power after 2022.

What followed came straight from the usual playbook of autocrats. Xi implemented controls on the media, through censorship and by increasing the CCP's presence in the media. Xi even went so far as to say that the media "must be surnamed party."[33] China ranks second in the world, after Turkey, in the number of journalists in prison.[34] News organizations are expected to pledge their loyalty to the party.[35] Under Xi, the CCP promotes the idea of "internet sovereignty," which is code for giving the state free rein to censor unwanted information and opinions. Almost all Western social media is blocked in China, with the exception of Microsoft-owned LinkedIn, which adheres to Chinese government requirements, such as blocking the accounts of dissidents.

The government also clamped down on civil society, mandating foreign nongovernmental organizations (NGOs) to register with the Ministry of Public Security (MPS) in January 2017. These and other restrictions caused the number of foreign NGOs in China to collapse from more than 7,000 to fewer than 400 in only a few years.[36] According to political scientist Minxin Pei, "most of China's so-called civil society groups are in fact, to use Orwellian double-speak, 'government-organized non-governmental organizations.'"[37] These civil society groups include a growing number of think tanks, which are often presented as independent in the West, but policy ensures that they are controlled by the CCP.[38]

The deterioration of human rights and the greater concentration of power under Xi is not lost on democracy watchers. Freedom House's 2015 Freedom in the World report stated: "Xi Jinping, who had assumed his post as part of a broader leadership rotation in November 2012, continued to consolidate his power in 2014." Referring to the anti-corruption campaign that Xi initiated, the report added: "such initiatives were accompanied by hard-line policies on political freedoms and civil liberties and a rejection of judicial oversight of party actions. Harassment of previously tolerated civil society organizations, labor leaders, academics, and state-sanctioned churches intensified. Internet controls continued to tighten, and several activists who had been detained in 2013 were sentenced to prison on politically motivated charges."[39] In the same vein, China's standing in the V-Dems Deliberative Democracy Index, which had been improving almost without interruption since Deng came to power in 1978, started to drop as soon as Xi became president.

The Deterioration of Human Rights Was Conveniently Overlooked by Market Players

Many companies, bond and equity index providers, rating agencies, banks, and investment houses conveniently overlooked the deterioration of human rights in China. The prizes, both in the bond market and in the stock market, were too attractive to ignore or to be left unattended due to human rights considerations. In their provocative book *Hidden Hand*, Clive Hamilton, an Australian academic, and Mareikhe Ohlberg, a senior fellow at the German Marshall Fund, argue that "Beijing has been working on Wall Street for a long time"[40] and that "financial institutions have been Beijing's most powerful advocates in Washington."

Among the many close ties between Wall Street and China worth chronicling, those at Goldman Sachs are particularly revealing. John L. Thornton, copresident until 2003, led Goldman's entry into China and, after leaving the bank, he became director of the Global Leadership Program at Beijing's Tsinghua University.[41] He sits on the board of several Chinese companies, and since 2009 he has been part of the International Advisory Council of China's sovereign wealth fund,* China Investment Corporation.[42] In 2006, he made a significant donation to what is now named the John L. Thornton China Center at the prestigious Brookings Institution.[43] The objective of this center is to provide analysis and policy recommendations on US-China relations and China's internal development, and is recognized as one of the leading research centers on China's political system and its foreign and economic policies.[44]

---

* Sovereign wealth funds (SWF) are state-owned investment funds that invest in stocks, bonds, privately owned companies, commodities, real estate, and other investments. They are usually built from funds generated through extraordinary revenues, such as those from oil. Some well-known SWFs are Norway's government pension fund, which generates from oil and gas revenues and has more than $1.5 trillion in assets under management (AUM). Singapore's GIC has more than $550 billion in AUM.

Henry Paulson, Goldman's CEO from 1999 until 2006, visited China 70 times before becoming US Treasury Secretary in 2006.[45] Goldman was the lead underwriter of major Chinese state-owned enterprises (SOEs) in 2003. One way to keep Wall Street leaders close to Beijing interests, according to Hamilton and Ohlberg, is to grant them special access to high-ranking public officials in China. Paulson was granted a rare opportunity for someone who is not a foreign president: a one-on-one briefing with President Hu Jintao.[46] After leaving public office, he launched the Paulson Institute, a "think and do tank dedicated to fostering a US-China relationship that serves to maintain global order in a rapidly evolving world."[47]

China drew in other Wall Street leaders as well. In 2019, Larry Fink, CEO of BlackRock, the biggest asset manager in the world, told company shareholders that he planned to turn the company into one of China's leading asset managers.[48] In August 2021, the firm launched a set of mutual funds and other investment products for Chinese investors, being the first foreign-owned company allowed to offer products in China.[49] This inroad is unsurprising for a leader such as Fink, who once said that "markets like actually totalitarian governments."[50] He added that markets do not like uncertainty, and that in totalitarian governments "you have an understanding of what's out there" and that "democracies are very messy."[51]

Bridgewater Associates, the largest hedge fund in the world, was the first foreign-owned alternative management company to establish a Chinese asset management company permitted to invest in China.[52] When Ray Dalio, the founder of Bridgewater Associates, was asked in November 2021 about a Chinese tennis player who allegedly disappeared under mysterious circumstances, Dalio said that he "can't be an expert in those types of things," and that he looks at the policies in place in each country.[53] He added, "I look at the United States, and I say, well, what's going on in the United States? And should I not invest in the United States because of our own human-rights issues, or other things?" and then continued, saying that "I am not trying to make political comparisons; I am basically just trying to follow the rules." He finally said that China's political system behaves as a "as a top-down country; what they are doing is—they behave like a strict parent."

I could continue with more stories about Wall Street leaders who have been strategically ambiguous in how they characterize China under Xi Jinping's rule. Wall Street normalized China, no matter the consequences of that normalization. They should have known better; The CCP's crackdown on dissenters is well-known to foreign observers, and what happened in Xinjiang and with Hong Kong are prime examples.

In 2017, in China's Xinjiang region, the government launched a campaign to "sinicize" (make Chinese) the Muslim Uyghur population. The campaign included the detention of over one million Uyghurs in Chinese reeducation and indoctrination camps.[54] The Uyghurs' plight brought substantial and well-deserved international attention to China's human rights practices, to a degree impossible to miss by anyone.

In Hong Kong, the crackdown on civil liberties coincided with increasing foreign participation in China's domestic bond market. A few months after China's government bonds were included in J.P. Morgan's GBI-EM index in 2020, and a few months before they were included in the WBGI in 2021, the government made a move to crack down on dissent, and ultimately freedom, in Hong Kong. On June 30, 2020, it replaced the liberal constitutional order of Hong Kong's Basic Law with the new National Security Law.

In the Sino-British Joint Declaration signed by China and the United Kingdom in 1984,[55] which set the terms of the July 1, 1997, handover of Hong Kong to China, Beijing "promised (under a formula called 'one country, two systems') to preserve the city's way of life for at least fifty years by giving it a 'high degree of autonomy' and by respecting its core values of human rights and the rule of law."[56] These commitments were embedded in the Basic Law enacted in 1990, though the law did not stop Beijing from attempting to encroach on Hong Kong's autonomy over the years. In 2003, for instance, the government of Hong Kong, pushed by the Chinese government, proposed an illiberal law for the national security provision of the Basic Law (Article 23), which it later withdrew after the move sparked massive protests.[57]

The National Security Law of 2020 took the crackdown on Hong Kong's civil liberties to a different level. The law includes four vaguely defined crimes: secession, subversion, terrorist activities, and collusion with foreign forces. At its core, the law overrides the Basic Law by restricting freedom of speech and the right to assemble, among other basic rights. Only a few months after it was enacted, "nearly the entire pan democratic opposition in Hong Kong has been arrested or has fled into exile. Opposition organizations of all stripes have been shuttered. The press and universities have largely been cowed into silence. The courts and the legal profession are under attack."[58]

Complementing the National Security Law was an amendment to the Basic Law's electoral provisions in March 2021, which increased Hong Kong's Election Committee (EC) from 1,200 to 1,500 members and expanded its power. The amendment followed the November 2019 elections, in which Beijing's preferred candidates lost by a landslide. The practical effect of the amendment is to bar the pan democratic camp from the electoral process, according to Michael C. Davies, author of *Making Hong Kong China: The Rollback of Human Rights and the Rule of Law*.[59]

Almost incomprehensively, while the Chinese government took steps to strip Hong Kong's residents of their individual rights, some of Hong Kong's money may have been invested in China's government bonds and in companies. By year-end 2020, the Hong Kong Monetary Authority (HKMA), Hong Kong's central bank, had about $573 billion in investments.[60] From this total, $227 billion were part of a portfolio invested in bond and equity markets, both in developed and emerging market economies. Detailed investment portfolio data is not available, but the HKMA's 2020 Annual Report includes the renminbi in its investment's currency composition table, and it mentions MSCI's Emerging Markets Index returns in 2020. Even though the report does not explicitly state that the HKMA invests in funds indexed to the MSCI and/or in assets denominated in renminbi, it would be awkward to mention the MSCI Emerging Markets Index returns and the renminbi in its currency composition table if it didn't. As it happens, the MSCI Emerging Markets Index includes Chinese companies. Too many of them, as I will argue in the coming pages and in Chapter 10.

Are All Companies Quasi-Sovereign in China?

The relationship between private corporations and the dictators and wannabe autocrats of the countries they are located in is often quite convoluted. Some companies are their pawns, and most are their victims. The owners and managers try to walk a fine line to try to remain independent. In China, it could be argued that they all cross that fine line, and that there is no such thing as a purely independent private sector, because every company must follow the rules set by the Chinese Communist Party. This means that when global investors finance China's companies, it can be said that they, ipso facto, finance the CCP.

The expansion of the power of the state in recent years or, better said, of the CCP, also included the economy. The state has always played a central role in managing the Chinese economy. The reforms that started under Deng in 1978 and then deepened in the 1990s gave entrepreneurs and the private sector important roles in the economy. In 1978, economic output from private firms was essentially zero. By 2012, private firms accounted for a robust 70 percent of China's output.[61] But during Xi's term, as outlined in Nicholas Lardy's aptly named book *The State Strikes Back*, the state expanded its reach in the economy again.[62] In several speeches in 2017 and 2018, Xi called for "an expanded role of the party, including the role of party committees, even in private enterprises."[63] Today, according to Hamilton and Ohlberg, almost all large and medium-sized private enterprises, including foreign-owned ones, have CCP committees operating inside them.[64]

One important way in which the party controls the economy is through state-owned enterprises. Technically, the number of SOEs declined significantly in the 2000s. By 2011, 106,000 companies, 40 percent of all SOEs, were corporatized—that is, turned into limited liability or joint stock companies. At the national level, 92 percent of the subsidiaries of 101 central state firms had been corporatized by 2016.[65] However, the line between private and public property is often blurred, as many companies have mixed (public and private) ownership.

SOEs still dominate, and in most cases monopolize, crucial sectors of China's economy, such as financial services, telecommunications, energy, automotive production, and transport.[66] As of 2019, SOEs were responsible for about a third of industrial output[67] and employed 54 million people, making China's rising middle class much more dependent on the state than in other countries.[68]

Their top executives are appointed by the CCP's Organization Department, and Xi believes that SOEs should be "important forces to implement" the party's decisions.[69]

But the arm's length of the CCP on the economy is not restricted to SOEs; its purview expands to all of the economy. In my view, all companies in China are quasi-sovereigns. According to Stanford University professor Curtis Milhaupt and University of Florida professor Wentong Zheng, "private ownership in China does not necessarily mean autonomy from the State."[70] For starters, the distinction between privately owned and state-owned enterprises is blurred in China; as of 2003, mixed-ownership enterprises accounted for 40 percent of China's GDP, including some well-known ones such as TCL and Lenovo, according to Milhaupt and Zheng.[71] One prominent example is ZTE Corporation, the second largest maker of telecommunications equipment, which has been subject to US sanctions.[72] Its shares are listed on the Shenzhen and the Hong Kong stock exchanges. Although ZTE Holdings has 30.76 percent of ZTE's shares and could be considered its controlling shareholder, when all SOE holdings in ZTE are added, they total 51 percent of the company.

According to Milhaupt and Zheng, several additional mechanisms make private companies bear a striking resemblance to SOEs. One mechanism is a dense political network linking the CCP to the leadership of the private companies, which they found after studying the party affiliations of the founders and controllers of the biggest 110 companies in China. Milhaupt and Zheng concluded that 95 out of the largest 100 private firms, and 8 out of the top 10 internet firms, have or had their founder or de facto controller as part of a political organization such as the People's Congresses.[73] Participation in these networks signal allegiance to the political system and proximity to the state actors that can facilitate the firm's success.

A second mechanism is the government's legal and extralegal control over private firms, which adds to the ambiguous property structures to blur the line between private and state ownership.[74] One extralegal mechanism to control private firms is the so-called "industrial associations," which were built from the scraps of disbanded ministries. They are designed to coordinate activities within an industry, having retained much of the power formerly exercised by the respective ministry.

Although every country has regulations that affect how private companies operate, China is unique. The degree of state intervention

93

in the economy is much higher than, for example, in an industrial country. The Heritage Foundation's 2022 Index of Economic Freedom categorizes China's economy as "Repressed"* and ranks it 158 out of the 177 countries included in the index. Also, procedural checks on government regulation are lacking. Milhaupt and Zheng argue that "real lawmaker power in China resides with the Communist Party," which has broad discretion in setting administrative rules.[75]

A third mechanism that makes private companies act like SOEs is the influence that the government exerts through subsidies and financial support. Banks are almost entirely state-owned, and before making important decisions, the boards of the four largest banks are required by their articles of association to take into account the opinions of the CCP committee.[76] In addition, the government "imposes a ceiling on deposit rates and channels credit at below-market cost to firms favored by the state."[77] Firms' political connections are a strong indicator of their access to bank loans.[78] "National champions," defined as companies that are given a dominant position and special regulatory treatment, are favored, whether they are private or state-owned. For instance, Huawei, the telecommunications giant, receives major funding from state banks.[79]

The common thread that unites these three mechanisms is industrial policy. Whether they are public or private, firms in selected sectors or industries receive favorable government regulation, including being shielded from foreign competition, and receiving subsidies and low-cost financing. The electric vehicle industry is a perfect example: Many years ago, the government started to take steps to convert the biggest car market in the world toward clean energy. These steps included substantial funds for research and development (R&D); quantitative targets; subsidies, most of which were decentralized to local governments (as most policies are in China); and discrimination against foreign companies.

Although most of these efforts had SOEs as recipients, the story of Wang Chuanfu, founder of electric vehicle (EV) and battery company BYD, demonstrates how blurred the line has become between

---

* The categories are Free, Mostly Free, Moderately Free, Mostly Unfree, and Repressed.

public and private companies. Wang, a member of the Shenzhen City PC (Standing Committee),[80] started in the rechargeable battery market, and then transitioned to EVs. According to Elizabeth Economy, "Wang benefited significantly from government support, partnering with the Shenzhen local government in the ten cities program, and receiving an estimated $435 million in subsidies from the Shenzhen government during 2010–2015."[81]

Subsidies to purchasers and tax reductions, available only to local producers, incentivized EV sales. BYD's battery production also benefited from regulations that effectively cut out foreign companies, such as Samsung and LG, from providing to Chinese EVs producers.[82] A tight relationship like this between the CCP and the private sector cuts several ways; private companies get special advantages from the central and local governments by aligning with CCP objectives,[83] and the CCP gets to wield its power over sectors.

As the CCP tightened its grip on private companies, foreign investment in private companies in China increased. The opening of China's equity market to foreign investors followed a similar path as the sovereign bond market. Initially, foreigners could only access the so-called H-shares, or those Chinese companies listed in Hong Kong. In 2014, HK Connect, a collaboration between the Hong Kong, Shanghai, and Shenzhen markets, was launched, giving foreign investors access to the $8 trillion A-share market, which includes companies listed in Shanghai and Shenzhen.[84] Then, in May 2018, 234 A shares were added to the MSCI Emerging Markets Index, which includes 1,398 companies from 24 emerging market countries. Other indices, such as the FTSE Russell, also included Chinese A-shares in recent years.

For perspective on the growing influence of China in the MSCI Emerging Markets Index, in May 2018 Chinese companies represented only 0.7 percent of the index,[85] but by April 29, 2022, Chinese companies composed 30.57 percent of this index, almost twice as much as the next country, Taiwan, and more than twice as much as India and South Korea.[86]

Hundreds of mutual funds and ETFs track the MSCI Emerging Markets Index. These funds include professionally managed mutual funds and retail investor–oriented ETFs. By November 2017, the index had $1.6 trillion in assets benchmarked to it.[87] Although I found no more updated information on the assets benchmarked to the MSCI Emerging Market Index, had they remained stable, 30 percent of the $1.6 trillion, or almost $500 billion, would have been invested in Chinese equities in April 2022. The total invested in China must be much higher now, as assets benchmarked to the index are likely to have grown since 2017.

The ETF market provides a good metric on this growth. By the end of 2021, there were $374 billion in ETF assets benchmarked to the MSCI Emerging Markets Index,[88] compared to $707 billion in ETF assets benchmarked to *all* the MSCI indices by November 2017. For reference, there are about eight times more assets benchmarked to all MSCI indices than to the MSCI EM Index.

Five Chinese companies were among the top 10 constituents of the MSCI Emerging Markets Index in April 2022: Tencent, Alibaba, Meituan, China Construction Bank, and JD.com. The leaders of Tencent, Alibaba, and JD.com are members of the CCP,[89] and China Construction Bank is an SOE, one of the so-called four big banks. Only Wang Xing, founder of Meituan, seems to have a more adversarial stance with the government. For instance, he once posted a millennium-old poem of China's first emperor Qin Shihuang decreeing the burning of books, which was interpreted as anti-establishment.[90]

For an example of how these companies, now financed by Western investors, collaborate with CCP's media machine, we can look to Alibaba's purchase of Hong Kong *South China Morning Post* in December 2015.[91] After the purchase, Alibaba brought down the paywall on the newspaper, making it more accessible around the world, and "giving a platform to a growing number of pro-CCP voices."[92] In addition, Alibaba removed the Chinese version of the website.

Sarah Cook, a research director at Freedom House, also argued that "technology giants such as Huawei and Tencent retain close ties with the PRC government and security services, routinely providing censorship and surveillance assistance to the party-state."[93,*]

---

* There are an estimated 100,000 people employed by the government and private companies to do manual censorship in China. Elizabeth Economy, *The Third Revolution: Xi Jinping and the New Chinese State* (Oxford University Press, 2018), 82.

The hand of the CCP can sometimes be too heavy on private companies, and thus on international investors. The regulatory crackdown on China's tech sector in the second half of 2021, for instance, caused a sharp sell-off. By March 2022, almost $2 trillion of market value in Chinese tech stocks had evaporated.[94]

The crackdown encompassed tech companies across multiple sectors. The attack on the education technology sector was allegedly a desire to benefit struggling middle-class families.[95] The gaming sector also took a hit. On September 9, 2021, Tencent and Netease lost $60 billion in value as fears of tighter regulation on the gaming industry grew among traders. The next day, the stocks recovered some of what they lost when a newspaper report clarified that there would be no freeze on new game approvals.[96] Other tech sector stocks moved as though riding a seesaw.

A report indicating that the government intended to break up Ant Group Co's Alipay business took tech stocks down on September 12, 2021. Equity strategists at the time came to the conclusion that investors should "sell business that politicians want to reform and buy the ones they want to build," according to a Bloomberg report.[97] Such a strategy is one you would hardly find in countries that operate under the rule of law. I will return to the impact of this crackdown on markets in Chapter 8.

How China Challenges Democracy in the World

As is the case with Russia, financing autocracy in China has global implications. The substantial increase in foreign financing to China's government and companies occurred while the country began an unprecedented expansion of its international reach. In its 2021 Democracy Index report, the Economist Intelligence Unit called China's global ascent "the China challenge," because it created a formidable competitor to the United States that offered an alternative model to Western capitalist democracy.[98]

Larry Diamond was even more dramatic. He argued that "no global development of the twenty-first century has been more damaging to the cause of freedom than the emergence of the People's Republic of China (PRC) as the world's next superpower, with the world's fastest-growing military, a worldwide propaganda apparatus, and a program of global infrastructure development."[99]

The change in China's foreign policy stance started with the 2008 Global Financial Crisis, which hit the United States and Europe hard but left China unscathed. Perhaps this relative success made Beijing think it was time to leave behind 100 years of perceived humiliation by Western powers and reassert China's dominance, the place it had had for centuries, and the one the leadership thought it deserved.

However, it was not until Xi Jinping rose to power in 2012 that China's new international attitude began to materialize across economic, military, and cultural spheres. Before Xi, Chinese officials referred to China as an emerging or regional power, and the motto driving foreign policy was Deng Xiaoping's aphorism "hide one's capacities and bide one's time." In contrast, during the 19th Congress of the Chinese Communist Party, Xi stated that China was entering a new era, in which all would "see China moving closer to center stage and making greater contributions to mankind."[100] At that point, CCP officials started to refer to China as "a big power."[101]

What does China or, better said, the CCP want? Its goal seems not to be to expand China's physical borders, but instead to spread Chinese influence and build "a new order in which other states are drawn into its orbit."[102] According to Elizabeth Economy, Xi "has stated and demonstrated desire to shape the international system, to use China's power to influence others, and to establish the global rules of the game."[103] His goal seems to be to transform the international order from a rules-based one, centered on individual liberties and the market, to a state-centered one.

We can see Xi increasing China's international clout in three areas: in organizations such as the United Nations (UN), in its media machine, and in various economic channels and initiatives. China has "focused on manipulating existing international organizations to serve CCP interests" according to Nedège Rolland, senior fellow at the National Bureau of Asian Research in Washington, DC.[104] Its work in different bodies and agencies of the UN covers multiple angles. For example, China has played an increasing role in the Human Rights Council (HRC), limiting the role of international

NGOs working on human rights across the world.[105] China has also used its weight in the International Telecommunications Union to promote policies that help authoritarian governments use technology to repress citizens and impose its concept of internet sovereignty, which allows governments to censure the web.[106] When China could not reform international organizations such as the IMF and the World Bank, it simply created new ones, such as the Asian Infrastructure Investment Bank (AIIB).*

To achieve its goals, China seeks the help of non-democratic countries, such as the Like Minded Group, a coalition of primarily authoritarian countries.[107] According to Rana Iboden, a senior fellow with the Robert Strauss Center for International Security and Law at the University of Texas at Austin, this group does not have a formal membership but expanded to 51 nations, including Belarus, Cuba, Iran, Russia, Sudan, Syria, and Venezuela, and has been very active in the United Nation's Human Rights Council (HRC). Charles Edel, a Global Fellow at the Wilson Center, and David O. Shullman, director of the China Global Hub at the Atlantic Council, argue that the way to keep corrupt elites from other (nondemocratic) countries under control is through propaganda, training, resources, economic influence, and technological expertise to cement their power.[108]

China has tried for long to influence public debates and media coverage about China in other countries, according to Sarah Cook, research director for China, Hong Kong, and Taiwan at Freedom House.[109] In particular, China uses media to present itself as a benign regime and a model for governance and development, using tactics from traditional diplomacy to "more covert and coercive moves."[110] According to Cook, China spends hundreds of millions of dollars on propaganda to spread its message, disinformation through Western social media and other channels, and on censorship tactics, including by providing positive and negative incentives for media owners.[111]

The biggest muscle China flexes, however, is its supersized economic power. Xi's most important international project is the Belt

---

* https://www.aiib.org/en/index.html. Disclosure: In 2018, I was paid by the AIIB to serve as a host for a presentation of its chairman Jin Liqun on the occasion of IADB's annual meeting in the province of Mendoza, Argentina.

and Road Initiative (BRI). Launched in 2013, the BRI is "an infrastructure plan to connect China to other parts of the world through ports, railroads, highways, and energy infrastructure."[112] It encompasses about 147 countries and more than $200 billion in investment. According to Elizabeth Economy, "Xi has also conceived the BRI as a conduit through which China can transmit its political and cultural values."[113]

The BRI has received substantial attention from Western analysts, but China's expanded role in international finance is less understood. China's financing abroad has taken two routes: foreign direct investment (FDI) and loans. While the economic determinants of China's FDI have been widely scrutinized, their political motives are less so, and China's role as international creditor has been mostly ignored until recently, given the opacity of the available data.

China is not only one of the largest recipients of FDI flows in the world,[114] but it is also a major source of FDI, investing an average of $143 billion per year from 2013 to 2020.[115] In Latin America, China's FDI expanded from about $20 billion in 2006 to almost $250 billion in 2017.[116] Initially, China's FDI in Latin America focused on natural resources like fossil fuels, metals, and agriculture, as it tried to secure critical primary goods needed to sustain its impressive domestic investment program. But over time, China shifted its investments toward manufacturing and services, such as transport and electricity generation and distribution.[117]

The geopolitical dimension of China's FDI has received little attention. Evelyn Simoni of UCLA, using Chinese FDI data in Latin America from 2005 to 2018, concluded that investment is attracted to "countries with weaker perceived liberal democracies, providing evidence to the hypothesis of FDI as an essential part of China's economic statecraft abroad."[118] China's increasing economic clout seems to have a geopolitical aim.

China's role as international creditor has also changed dramatically in recent years. Its loans and trade credits soared from almost zero in 1998 to $1.6 trillion by 2018. In 2017, it was the world's largest official creditor, surpassing the World Bank and the IMF.[119] Unfortunately, information about China's lending abroad is scant. According to World Bank economists Sebastian Horn, Carmen Reinhart, and Christoph Trebesch, who compiled an impressive database of Chinese loans, half of Chinese loans abroad are not registered in the standard international debt databases. For instance, China does not provide details on direct financing under the Belt and Road Initiative.[120] The same applies to its trade credit. This has been regularly used to finance autocrats from oil-producing countries such as Venezuela's Chávez and Maduro[121] and Ecuador's Correa, usually with punitive terms for the debtors. For the 50 countries most indebted to China, the debt increased from 1 percent of the debtor's GDP in 2005 to 15 percent in 2017. This type of debt typically has high rates, much higher than the concessional lending of the World Bank and the IMF, and short maturities.[122] High debt, high rates, and low maturities: a great way to keep debtor governments in China's hands.

China's growing FDI and loan business occurred at the same time international investors were pouring money into Chinese government bonds. Given that money is fungible, the argument could be made that institutional and retail investors in places like New York or Boston—or anywhere else, for that matter—have been bankrolling China's financing adventures abroad. These adventures have a clear aim of exporting China's authoritarian model to the rest of the world.

KEY TAKEAWAYS OF CHAPTER 6

This chapter:

- Dives deeper into the significant impact that bond and equity indices have on investors' decisions, and on how rating agencies and equity and bond index providers do not properly factor in democracy standards.

- Demonstrates that China's inclusion in many bond and equity indices meant that foreigners' financing to China's government and Chinese companies increased significantly when the country turned more autocratic under Xi Jinping.

- Argues that when investors buy shares of private companies domiciled in autocratic countries like China, they may be financing their autocratic rulers. Some argue there is no such thing as a private independent firm in China: they are all under the control of the CCP.

- Highlights how financing autocratic countries like China and Russia can have implications beyond their borders. China embarked on a broader international effort to spread its influence and its illiberal model just as investors increased their financing to the regime, directly and indirectly.

CHAPTER 7

THE LATIN AMERICAN AUTOCRATS THAT WEREN'T

Populists' incompetence, the main deterrent of autocracy in Latin America

Latin America, the Land of Populism

I wanted to finish this first part of the book writing about Latin America, the land of populism. The region is full of wannabe autocrats, from Mexico in the north to Argentina in the south. But so far, most have been unsuccessful in turning their regimes into electoral autocracies, excepting Venezuela and Nicaragua. This failure is not for a lack of trying or, for the matter at stake in this book, for lack of market support, but largely because these populists haven't been able to manage their economies. Truth to fact is that these populist leaders have received ample support from the market that has been willing to overlook their attack on democratic institutions.

Like Chávez, most Latin American populists exploit the "feelings and emotions of exclusion, and anger at political elites that pretend that neoliberalism is the only technically acceptable economic policy."[1] They generally cater to the forgotten and the betrodden with government handouts that allow them to reach, for a short time, consumption levels that they had never experienced before. By promoting short-term consumption and income redistribution at the expense of fiscal and external account health, economic instability is not a bug but a feature of Latin America's populism.[2]

Commodities compose the bulk of the region's exports, so the typical populist cycle starts when commodity prices rise. The populists spend their commodities windfalls indiscriminately, and the cycle ends with the nation's economy in disarray when commodity prices plummet. Not all Latin American populists follow this script closely, but many do, and the most fiscally prudent tend to be the ones who stay in power the longest.

Another factor that has limited the success of Latin American wannabe autocrats is civil society's resilience and the strength of their democratic institutions. When Latin America turned to the left at the beginning of the century, the question was what these governments would do, not only in terms of economic and social policy, but also with liberal democracy. Many leftist parties in the region had rejected liberal democracy in the past.

Professors Steven Levitsky and Kenneth Roberts argued that where democratic regimes and party systems were consolidated—namely in Brazil, Chile, and Uruguay—liberal democratic approaches prevailed. In turn, where democratic regimes and party systems were in crisis—namely in Bolivia, Ecuador, and Venezuela—Levitsky and Roberts argued that plebiscitarian tendencies, meaning leaders who can use mechanisms such as referenda and mass mobilization and have a non-intermediated relationship with the population, emerged.[3] This distinction, made in 2011, endured time.

For this chapter, I chose to tell stories about some Latin American populist leaders who by and large were unsuccessful in their autocratic attempts. I could have included Mexico under Andrés Manuel López Obrador, or AMLO as he is commonly known, given that Mexico's democracy is under severe threat,[4] but I chose to include Brazil instead, because Jair Bolsonaro's undemocratic attempt came from the right, not the left, as was the case in all other Latin American countries. Attacks on democracy can come from the left or right, but investors typically appreciate populists from the right more, because they expand the market and are generally perceived to be more fiscally conservative. I indulged myself with a longer subsection about Argentina; you may think it is simply because it is my country of birth, but the real reason is that I believe most international watchers underestimate the extent of Néstor and Cristina Kirchner's attacks on democracy.

Bolivia: Morales Turned into an Autocrat, but Wall Street Looked the Other Way

In November 2019, President Evo Morales abruptly fled Bolivia in exile after a series of corruption allegations and violent mass protests. Evo's supporters claimed that his departure amounted to a coup d'état; right before he left, Bolivia's chief military commander, Williams Kaliman, called for Evo to "renounce his presidential mandate in order to restore peace and maintain stability, for the good of Bolivia."[5] Whether it was a coup or a rebellion, it was a dramatic turn of events for a president who had been so popular since his rise to power in 2005, a turn that had also been missed by market watchers.

The leader of the Movement for Socialism party (Movimiento al Socialismo, or MAS), Morales won the presidency in December 2005 with more than 50 percent of the vote. He ran on an anti-US and anti–Washington Consensus platform, promoting the nationalization of Bolivia's natural resources. The Washington Consensus is a 10-point economic playbook for developing nations in economic crisis devised by the IMF, World Bank, and the US Treasury Department. It encourages privatization, deregulation, the opening of the economy, prudent fiscal policies, market-set prices, and the protection of property rights.

The MAS emerged from rural social movements, which opposed traditional parties and retained some power throughout Morales's presidency, although his leadership became more personalistic over time. As a personalistic leader, he consolidated the control of the party,[6] using "divide-and-rule tactics to boost his own predominance and enhance his top-down control."[7] He was the first indigenous president in Bolivia, and he devoted his regime to deepening indigenous rights, which made him very popular. According to the National Census in 2012, approximately 40 percent of the Bolivian population has indigenous roots.[8] Additionally, Evo's first years in office coincided with a global boom in commodity prices and a nationalization of hydrocarbon resources, which contributed to his positive image within the country.[9]

The MAS's two-thirds majority in both chambers of Congress allowed Morales to modify the Constitution in February 2009. However, the party did not win a two-thirds majority in the Constituent Assembly, the margin necessary to introduce changes. The pressure the MAS exerted to override this limit resulted in protests and the opposition walking out of the Constituent Assembly. Nevertheless, the new Constitution was approved.[10] The new regulations also gave Morales the opportunity to control the judiciary.

The market was unfazed by the illegal constitutional reform and the packing of courts. In October 2012, the Bolivian government tapped international markets with a 10-year $500 million bond issuance, led by Goldman Sachs and Bank of America Merrill Lynch. It was the country's first US dollar denominated government bond issuance in almost a century.

That $500 million bond issuance may seem small, but Bolivia's GDP was roughly $23.7 billion in 2012, which means that the issuance was equivalent to the US Treasury placing bonds for nearly $442 billion in just one transaction in 2022. Bolivia placed a second government bond of $500 million in 2013. Because the bonds are denominated in US dollars and are listed in the United States, they were included in J.P. Morgan's EMBI Global index, which "forced" investors in mutual funds and ETFs tracking the index to buy them. In April 2018, Bolivia represented 0.4 percent of the index.

When analyzing the first bond, as usual, Wall Street analysts focused on Morales's prudent fiscal policies and not on his attacks on checks and balances.[11] I don't blame them one bit. Having worked for Wall Street banks as an economist for 10 years, I think it's likely that their legal and compliance departments would not let them posit anything too risqué about politics and democracy.

The new Constitution stated that a president could be reelected, but only once. Morales exerted this right and won the December 2009 presidential election with a comfortable 64 percent of the vote. But the slide toward autocracy intensified throughout his second term, and then Morales broke his word. In 2014, although he had been in power for two terms, the Constitution's new limit, he ran for a third term, claiming that his first term "did not count" because it was under a different constitutional regime. In negotiations with the opposition in 2008, which led to the call for a constitutional reform, he pledged to run only one term under the new Constitution.[12] His claim was backed and legally approved by Bolivia's Plurinational Constitutional Tribunal, whose judges Evo appointed. Still, Morales remained very popular among Bolivians, and he benefited from a disorganized opposition. As a result, Morales won the 2014 presidential election with a commanding 61 percent of the vote.

The decline of Bolivia's checks and balances became clear, and democracy watchers noted it. The EIU demoted Bolivia from Flawed Democracy to Hybrid Regime in its 2010 report. Among other reasons, the EIU argued that "the central government has assumed a growing range of powers since 2008."[13] V-Dem's Liberal Democracy Index dropped almost steadily from the time Evo assumed power until he left office, but classified Bolivia as an Electoral Democracy until 2018. Similarly, though Bolivia's score declined, Freedom House continued to classify it as Partly Free.

The final inflection point in Morales's story occurred in 2016 when, for the first time, he did not have enough popular support to back his autocratic adventures. In February 2016, his government conducted a referendum to amend the Constitution that would allow unlimited reelections, but it failed to pass. The "no" vote narrowly won 51.3 percent to 48.7 percent.[14] The downturn in Evo's popularity can be partially explained by a shift in economic conditions. Commodities declined, and hydrocarbon revenues followed suit. Fortunately, Bolivia's relatively conservative macroeconomic policies allowed it to stash substantial international reserves during the commodity boom, and they spared the country from crises such as the one that hit Venezuela, at least until 2023. However, consumption growth decelerated in 2016.

As is usual in Latin America, there was a pint of drama with the referendum. Eight days before the vote, Evo confirmed that he had fathered an out-of-wedlock child with Gabriela Zapata, who worked for China CAMC Engineering. Zapata's firm received $560 million in a Bolivian government contract.[15] The publication of the story probably helped Evo lose the election.

However, the story did not stop Evo from going to the Plurinational Constitutional Tribunal, which ruled on the term-limits issue on November 2017. The partial court overruled the referendum result and effectively eliminated the reelection limitation, allowing Morales to run for president in 2019.[16] Freedom House gave Bolivia a downward trend arrow in its 2018 annual report due to the 2017 Constitutional Court ruling.[17] In addition, Transparency International's Corruption Perception Index declined from 34 in 2015 (98th out of 167 countries covered) to 29 in 2018 (132nd out of 172 countries). The index ranges from 0 (very corrupt) to 100 (not corrupt).[18] Both indicators suggested that Bolivia's democracy was in decline.

These events did not deter the market, of course. In March 2017, the government placed its biggest bond ever, $1 billion, at a rate of 4.5 percent. The book built to purchase these bonds registered demand for up to $3 billion from investors from all over the world.[19]

In October 2019, Evo effectively ignored the will of the people and ran for president again. By this time, the opposition had organized behind Carlos Mesa, president from 2003 to 2005, and vice president from 2002 to 2003.[20] Heading into the election, several polls indicated that Mesa had a real chance of defeating Morales in a runoff.* However, Morales beat Mesa in the first round, though he did so under rather suspicious circumstances.

Said another way, the election was probably rigged. This election was no different than many elections in Latin America, where incumbents often put state resources to work for them and have a disproportionate share of public media resources at their disposal. But the actual counting of votes made this election particularly unique. On election day, the Transmission of Preliminary Electoral Results (TREP) was interrupted at 7:40 p.m., when 83.8 percent of the votes had been counted. At the time, Morales was up by only 6 percentage points, an insufficient margin to win in the first round. But the next day, the TREP announced that Morales won with a 10.57-point difference, enough to carry the election in the first round.

The Organization of American States (OAS), which went to Bolivia to observe the election, later concluded that "the first-round victory of Evo Morales was statistically improbable . . . and calls into question the credibility of the process."[21] While some claimed that there were no irregularities in the count, rumors of a rigged election quickly spread among the population, and triggered violent protests in multiple Bolivian cities.[22] The unrest left 804 injured and 33 dead.[23]

---

* Bolivia's electoral system requires a candidate to get 50 percent of the vote, or 40 percent and a 10 percent lead over the runner-up to get elected in the first round.

At first, the government tried to downplay the protests, but then Kaliman and the armed forces got involved, and the situation escalated for Morales. He immediately flew to Mexico, where he claimed that he was the victim of an international conspiracy and a coup d'état. Whether it was a coup or not, Morales clearly took Bolivia from a democracy to a competitive authoritarian regime.[24]

In fact, Bolivia's worse democratic score in V-Dem's Liberal Democracy Index in the twenty-first century was in 2020 (measuring democracy in 2019). Its Deliberative Democracy Index score dropped from 0.42 in 2018 to 0.25 in 2020. Bolivia's Freedom House score also plunged from 67/100 for 2018 to 63/100 for 2019, although it remained classified as a Partly Free country.[25] It was an eventful and tragic year for Bolivia.

Evo Morales's thirst for power was not finished. In 2023, he was trying to return to power. The infighting between Morales's faction of the MAS and those loyal to President Luis Arce, his former finance minister, paralyzed the country and plunged it into a currency and debt crisis. The country had run out of international reserves, and investors panicked, fearing the government's capacity to repay them was in danger. Bolivia's government bond prices collapsed to 57 cents on the dollar on March 28, down from 70 cents at the beginning of that month.[26] On September 24, 2023, Evo announced via X (formerly known as Twitter) that he intended to run for president in the 2025 election. Bond prices dropped by another 10 cents on the dollar immediately. Once again, investing in autocratic countries proved to be the wrong financial decision in the medium to long term.

Ecuador: The Blinding Power of High Yields

Hardly a better example exists of how promises of high sovereign bond yields can make investors forget anything else than Ecuador's government bond sale of 2014. That June, the government of this oil-exporting, $100 billion economy raised $2 billion in 10-year US-dollar-denominated bonds that promised to pay investors an annual interest rate of 7.95 percent. The rate was about three times what a comparable US Treasury bond paid then.[27]

A Bloomberg report said that the sale took place after Ecuador rebuilt "its credibility with investors."[28] By 2014, President Rafael Correa had been in power for seven years, and he had already undermined Ecuador's democracy. As we now know, that is not a deterrent for markets. What makes the successful 2014 bond sale incredible is that Correa's government had defaulted on US-dollar-denominated bonds as recently as 2008—despite his government having the means to pay for them.

Government bond defaults are quite common in emerging markets. In their 2009 masterpiece, *This Time Is Different: Eight Centuries of Financial Folly*, Carmen Reinhart and Kenneth Rogoff documented 250 sovereign defaults.[29] As of 2014, Ecuador was among the top defaulters in the world, with 11 different defaults.[30] Sovereign defaults differ from corporate defaults. When a corporation can't pay its debts, legal mechanisms can settle the disputes with creditors in each country—for example, the Chapter 11 legislation that exists in the United States. Among other powers, these mechanisms give the judges the capacity to seize the assets of the debtor to repay its dues.

No such international mechanism or institution exists to manage countries' defaults. Most international sovereign debt disputes are settled in courts in the United States and the United Kingdom, but the judges have no power to seize domestic assets of the borrower. The creditors' only enforcement mechanism to make borrowers stay current is to exclude the country from credit markets upon default.[31] For this reason, countries usually default only when they are under dire economic stress.

Ecuador's 2008 default was different, in that Ecuador could pay its debt. The country's foreign debt was at a low of nearly 20 percent of GDP, compared to 70 percent in 2000, and its central bank international reserves were at a high of $6.5 billion. Interest payments on the 2012 and 2030 government bonds totaled only $331 million in 2008.[32]

Quite simply, Correa caused the default because he didn't want to pay the debt. Before becoming president, Correa argued that part of Ecuador's foreign debt was "illegitimate," not an unusual claim to hear from Latin American leftists. Six months after becoming president, he signed a decree to create the CAIC, an auditing commission for public credit. The CAIC's mission was to determine the "legitimacy, legality, transparency, quality, efficacy and efficiency" of the public debt contracted between 1976 and 2006. In November 2008, the CAIC delivered its report. Correa, who received a preliminary draft of the report by October 23, ordered his administration to miss a $31 million coupon payment on the government bond maturing in 2012. A formal default was declared on December 12, 2008.[33]

It was inconceivable then that Ecuador would be able return to the market any time soon, with many expecting it to take decades. But Ecuador did return, and quickly, as high coupon yields made investors forget this absurd and unlikely default in less than six years and made them look past Correa's autocratic behavior.

Like other wannabe autocrats, Correa's demolition of checks and balances was immediate. He took office in January 2007 and called for a constitutional convention on his first day. To get things done, he adopted a take-no-prisoners approach. "Congressional opponents of the referendum found themselves stripped of their seats by the electoral tribunal on the grounds of 'election obstruction' and replaced by pliable substitute legislators."[34] In total, 57 legislators of the at the time 100-seat National Congress were expelled.[35] "With the newly configured pro-government majority in Congress, the Constitutional Tribunal became the next target. When the Constitutional Tribunal judges ruled against the unprecedented removal of the dissident legislators by the Electoral Tribunal, the pro-government congressional majority responded by sacking them."[36]

Correa's party got 80 out of 130 seats in the Constitutional Convention, which proceeded to suspend the Congress. Unsurprisingly, the new Constitution allowed the president to be reelected once, and it significantly strengthened the powers of the president vis-à-vis the Congress, now called the National Assembly. The enhanced presidential powers included the ability to appoint members of the Judiciary Council, the attorney general, the National Electoral Council (CNE) and other important government bodies.[37] Correa was elected president twice under the new Constitution, in 2009 and 2013, surpassing the 50 percent vote threshold in the first round of both elections.

Correa often said that the media was his "greatest enemy," so he systematically undermined free speech and access to information. In the process, he effectively dismantled independent media.[38] Correa's legislative masterpiece was the Communications Law of 2013, which gave the government broad powers to limit free speech by demanding that all information shared by media be "verified" and "precise." The law prohibited media from "either directly or indirectly promoting any given candidate, proposal, options, electoral preferences or political thesis, through articles, specials or any other form of message."[39] Ecuadorian journalists said the law intended to censor them, even though, in a case of Orwellian doublethink, it explicitly prohibited censorship.[40]

Correa sued journalists, editors, and media directors, targeting the ones who exposed the corrupt network that financed his government and himself. He jailed many, often suffocated their media outlets financially,[41] and he closed over 20 radio stations.[42] In 2012, Correa ordered by decree that the state should stop paying private media outlets for official advertising. He said, "We do not have a reason, with money from Ecuadorians, to benefit the business of six families from this country," referring to the media owners.[43] Even more, Correa used the state's *cadenas nacionales*, or joint broadcasts, to promote his government free of charge and on primetime television.[44]

The Supercom, the government agency in charge of implementing ambiguous content restrictions on the independent media, wielded its power widely. In one case, the Supercom issued a $90,000 fine on newspaper *El Universo* for a cartoon that exposed a government corruption scandal, under the guise that it risked causing "social agitation," among other charges.[45] By mid-2014, more than 125 cases against the media were registered at the Supercom.[46]

International media and democracy watchers were well aware of the attack on democracy in Ecuador. The *New York Times* denounced Correa's campaign against free speech,[47] and the *Washington Post* said that Correa ought to be known for "the most comprehensive and ruthless assault on free media under way in the Western Hemisphere."[48] But markets were unfazed, and in 2014 they happily purchased the new government bond issues.

At the outset of his second term, Correa had a pliant media, control of the judiciary, super-presidential powers, high approval ratings, and his party, Alianza Pais (AP), held 100 seats in the unicameral legislature. With 73 percent of the total seats, he could amend the Constitution.[49] Correa's ability to stay in power beyond the existing constitutional limits seemed like a given. And he tried; in 2015, his party passed 16 constitutional amendments, including the elimination of term limits.[50]

However, as with other Latin American populist leaders, the combination of an active civil society and their own incompetence prevented Correa from staying in power. In Correa's case, a major reason behind his failure was a lack of self-control. An oil bonanza caused government revenues to rise from $4.5 billion in 2002 to $8.5 billion in 2007, when Correa was first elected. Revenues then soared to a peak of $20.4 billion in 2013. In typical Latin American populist style, he went on a spending spree, which made him very popular. The government ran fiscal deficits every single year of his presidency, reaching $5.5 billion in 2013 and $6.4 billion in 2014, driving Correa to issue bonds in 2014. When oil prices started to decline in 2013 and almost halved in 2015, public finances were left in shambles. The government adjusted its spending, but not enough, which contributed to a slowing of the economy. GDP was almost flat in 2015 and contracted 1.2 percent in 2016. Unsurprisingly, Correa's popularity dropped from about 60 percent in 2014 to nearly 42 percent by the end of 2016.

In civil society, indigenous organizations, public sector workers, environmentalists, and independent citizens staged protests against Correa's reelection.[51] The protests, and the calculations that showed he might not win in the first round, made him handpick former Vice President Lenin Moreno as his successor. The expectation was that Correa would return for another run at the presidency in 2021, but Moreno had other plans. In April 2020, exiled Rafael Correa was convicted of overseeing bribery schemes during his presidency. That August, the National Court of Justice sentenced him to eight years in prison.

Correa's influence, however, is not dead. His party was instrumental in starting an impeachment process against Moreno's successor, pro-market Guillermo Lasso, in 2023. Before his impeachment was finalized, Lasso used a constitutional clause allowing for the dissolution of the National Assembly and called for general elections. Correa's candidate, Luisa Gonzalez, got the most votes (33.6 percent) in the August 20, 2023, first round election, although she lost the run-off election against Daniel Noboa on October 1, 2023.

Brazil: Bolsonaro, the "Trump of the Tropics"*

The first time that I attended a presentation by former Brazilian Finance Minister Paulo Guedes, my instinctive reaction after he finished talking was to write him a check so that he could manage my personal finances. The 72-year-old University of Chicago–trained former hedge fund manager is a larger-than-life figure whose conviction in presenting his ideas has immense appeal to investors. His script has all the usual components that get market watchers excited, highlighted by his belief in reducing the size of the government, public debt, and taxes. He also champions deregulation and increased international trade. After you hear Guedes speak, you don't doubt that investing in Brazil is a good idea.

Guedes also presented something of a paradox in that he was Jair Bolsonaro's finance minister. Bolsonaro, a born-again Christian former army captain, is a completely different type of populist than other Latin American populists. He won office in 2018 on three basic promises: combating corruption, promoting economic growth, and being the law-and-order president. For Bolsonaro, the bad people are not the neoliberals or the International Monetary Fund, but rather the left-wing Workers Party (PT), former government officials, and their efforts to impose gender ideology and a state-centered economy.

Bolsonaro's biographer Michael Lepper described his populist coalition as "beef, Bible and bullets."[52] His supporters include those who want to do away with environmental restrictions to expand agriculture and cattle ranching, the 30 percent of the population who identify as Evangelical Christians, and those who have suffered from Brazil's rise in violent crime and drug trafficking in recent decades. Bolsonaro did share something with other populists: by the time of his election, an economic crisis and widespread corruption had rendered the political class disgraced, so "the conditions were ripe for the rise of a populist, anti-system politician." At that point, only 13 percent of Brazilians had faith in their country's democracy.[53]

Bolsonaro has much in common with former US President Donald Trump, with whom he has become "great friends."[54] First,

---

* This is how Jair Bolsonaro fancied himself, Serhan, *Atlantic*, October 28, 2021. I base parts of this section on what my colleague Patricio Navia has written about Jair Bolsonaro to our clients.

like Trump, Bolsonaro was an unlikely president. Bolsonaro began his political career in 1990 in the lower chamber of Congress, but his career as a lawmaker was as unremarkable as his career in the military. He switched parties eight times in seven legislative terms, and his track record as legislator was dismal, having only one of the 150 bills he presented throughout three decades passed by Congress.[55]

Second, Bolsonaro considered the presidency a family business.[56] Bolsonaro's three sons, Carlos, Flavio, and Eduardo, are all involved in politics and had an "unprecedented influence" during his presidency, according to Aline Souza, an analyst from consultancy firm Prospective,[57] Eduardo, nicknamed "the pit bull," was the most influential. He attended a rally supporting leftist President Dilma Rousseff's impeachment with a firearm in his waist, and he pretended to fire a machine gun after justifying his vote in favor of her impeachment in Congress. (Eduardo's attitude paled in comparison to his father's, who dedicated his vote in favor of impeachment to Colonel Carlos Alberto Brilhante Ustra, a famous torturer during Brazil's dictatorship.)[58] Eduardo has an active foreign policy agenda, with links to right-wing leaders in many countries, including Donald Trump and his son-in-law Jared Kushner.[59]

Both Trump and Bolsonaro gathered huge social media followings and were avid users of the social platform X. Bolsonaro even adopted many of Trump's slogans, denouncing "fake news" and "globalism."[60] Both also promoted culture wars and post-truth. "Post-truthism is not chiefly about getting lies accepted as truths but about muddying the waters to the point that it becomes difficult to discern the difference between truth and falsehood."[61]

These shared traits help explain some similarities in their approach to the Covid-19 pandemic, including their contempt for science. They "appeared personally convinced of some of the most far-fetched conspiracy theories they peddled," according to Moisés Naím, Distinguished Fellow at the Carnegie Endowment for International Peace.[62] For Bolsonaro, Covid-19 is just a "little flu."[63] His inaction had a disastrous impact: Brazil accounted for more than one in ten Covid-related deaths globally.[64] This anti-science belief also helps explain Bolsonaro's approach to the deforestation of the Amazon; neither Bolsonaro nor Minister of the Environment Ricardo Salles believe in climate change. They countered the international criticism they received over the issue by assuming the role of culture warriors, fighting "globalism" and the "cultural Marxism" of international NGOs.[65]

Perhaps the biggest similarity Bolsonaro and Trump share is their attack on the sanctity of the democratic process. In Trump's case, his anti-democratic agenda "culminated in his effort to overturn the 2020 presidential election result,"[66] and in his supporter's storming of the Capitol in January 2021. Bolsonaro flirted with the military, attacked the independence of the judiciary, and cast doubts over the electoral process, among other tactics.

Bolsonaro's appointment of Alexandre Ramagem as director of the Federal Police illustrated this well. Previously, Ramagem led the Agência Brasileira de Inteligência (ABIN), Brazil's version of the Central Intelligence Agency. Judge Alexandre de Moraes vetoed the nomination, arguing it was unconstitutional because Ramagem had strong links to Bolsonaro's family.[67] The ruling angered Bolsonaro, who considered it an intrusion on his right to govern. He responded by stating: "I am the Constitution."[68]

In April and May 2020, his supporters held demonstrations against the Congress and the Supreme Court and called for a military intervention.[69] Bolsonaro followed Trump's playbook, publicly doubting the sanctity of the electoral process. In Bolsonaro's case, he targeted the electronic vote, suggesting it spurs fraud, and proposed a return to paper ballots. In 2021, one year before the election, he said fraud was the only way he could be defeated. In July 2022, he summoned foreign ambassadors to his residence, and told them the electronic voting machines can be compromised.[70] The claim contradicted both the Supreme Federal Court of Brazil and the Superior Electoral Court, which had assured that the electronic vote system, implemented in 1996, is transparent and secure.[71]

In Brazil, tinkering with the electoral process is a more menacing idea than in the United States. In a country that has not completely asserted civilian control over the military, more than 6,000 military personnel worked in Bolsonaro's administration, many in prominent positions. Many of them glorified the military dictatorship of the 1960s and 1970s.[72]

Investors dismissed Bolsonaro's autocratic tendencies and his dismal environmental track record and welcomed his market-friendly agenda. Guedes was named "Finance Minister of the Year" in 2019 by *LatinFinance*, a magazine that provides intelligence on Latin America's financial markets and economies.[73]* Investors who left Brazil in droves during President Dilma Rousseff's impeachment crisis and during her successor Michel Temer's tenure returned when Bolsonaro came to power. Portfolio flows, foreigners' purchases or sales of local bonds and stocks, were negative from early 2016 to 2019, but turned positive with Bolsonaro in power. Total capital flows to Brazil soared, including portfolio flows, foreign direct investment, and foreign loans.

Foreign investors weren't completely on board with Brazil under Guedes and Bolsonaro, but the reason had nothing to do with Bolsonaro's undemocratic tendencies. Guedes's economic strategy involved slashing the budget deficit, which allowed the central bank to cut interest rates. This combination of tight fiscal policy and lax monetary policy caused government bonds to carry a lower yield. As a result, the percentage of foreign investors participating in the domestic currency government debt market dropped from 11.2 percent of the total in December 2018 to 10.4 percent in December 2019. During Bolsonaro's term, it fluctuated between 9 percent and 11 percent.[74]

As with other Latin American wannabe autocrats, Bolsonaro was quite inefficient. By the end of his term, he had few accomplishments on the three agendas that he promoted as candidate. Corruption scandals marred his government, economic growth was scant, and the post-Covid inflation bout sent millions into poverty. Crime increased rapidly as the pandemic receded. Only his cultural agenda was alive. It is no wonder then that he lost the election in a runoff against former President Luiz Inácio Lula da Silva in October 2022.

Karl Marx once said that history repeats itself, first as tragedy, then as farce. Donald Trump's supporters storming the US Capitol after he lost the 2020 presidential election was a tragedy. In January 2023, Bolsonaro's supporters storming Brazil's Congress and other government buildings, including the presidential palace, was a farce. It is not clear what Bolsonaro's supporters wanted to achieve, but they claimed that the election was fraudulent, and some wanted the armed forces to intervene. In other words, they pushed for a violent coup

---

* Disclaimer: I voted for him and was even quoted in the article unveiling his prize.

d'état. A coup did not happen, but their efforts illustrated the populist and anti-democratic tendencies of Bolsonaro's supporters.

Argentina: The Kirchners, the Nukeless Putins of the Patagonia

My view is that the international press, markets, and even democracy watchers such as Freedom House, V-Dem, and the EIU have overlooked the extent of the Kirchner family's attack on Argentina's democracy. This neglect may be because Argentina still has a working democracy, with free elections and freedom of the press. But as I will demonstrate, this is not because the Kirchners didn't attempt to undermine democracy and perpetuate themselves in power. Instead, it's because of their sheer ineptitude in managing the economy, and because of the strength of the country's civil society.

The late Néstor Kirchner's presidency, his wife Cristina Kirchner's two terms as president and one term as vice president bear some resemblance to Vladimir Putin's, save for the atrocities Putin committed in his invasion of Ukraine. Laura Di Marco, a journalist for the newspaper *La Nación* who wrote a biography of Cristina Kirchner, believes Cristina is a Putin admirer.[75,*] Similar to how Putin brought his corruption, undemocratic practices, and close aides from his government days in Saint Petersburg to the national political scene in Moscow, the Kirchners brought their friends, their corruption schemes, and tried to bring their brutal government practices from Santa Cruz to Buenos Aires.

A windy province in the southernmost part of the continent, Santa Cruz lives on oil and tourism. In 1991, when Néstor Kirchner was elected governor, Santa Cruz had only 159,839 inhabitants, or 0.5

---

* They are in fact close. Cristina Kirchner's administration first supported Ukraine in the United Nations (UN) Security Council when Russia invaded Crimea in 2014, but after a call she had with Putin, Argentina abstained in the UN's General Assembly vote. She also questioned the sanctions imposed by the United States and the European Union on Russia. Putin visited Buenos Aires in July 2014, and then Kirchner visited Moscow in 2015. Her proximity to Putin was also instrumental in Argentina receiving the Sputnik V Covid-19 vaccine. The government's decision to accept Russia's vaccine was widely viewed in geopolitical terms, by the opposition especially. Argentina sidelined American-made Pfizer and other Western countries' vaccines and preferred to distribute the Sputnik V first.

percent of Argentina's population. Totaling 243,943 square kilometers, the province's population density was only 0.7, versus 11.7 at the national level. Mariana Zuvic, a politician from Santa Cruz, wrote a book called *El Origen*, chronicling the origins of the Kirchners' corruption. Zuvic said that after the Kirchners' decade-plus reign in Santa Cruz, "my province was, due to their merit, an oppressive place, where fear and silence reigned supreme and where giving a different opinion implied a risk that very few were encouraged to take." She added that "in the province they exercised structural and systematic violence" and that "when the Kirchners arrived at the Casa Rosada [the presidential palace], everything had already been invented in Santa Cruz."[76]

I had an unusual preview of their method of terror. In December 2001, recently returned to Argentina from earning my PhD at the University of Pennsylvania, an American professor from UPenn invited me to a social gathering in an apartment he had in Buenos Aires. Unknown to me at the time, his wife was from Santa Cruz, and her family had been involved in local politics. Fear was pervasive among her friends from Santa Cruz. Their stories were frightening, and many of them told me that they could not return to Santa Cruz. They were, for all practical purposes, exiled from their land. Few in Argentina knew about this, as at that time the Kirchners were mostly unknown outside their distant province. I was baffled: I could not believe this was happening in my country.

I would have been more scared had I known that Néstor Kirchner was about to become president in May 2003. Kirchner, who governed Santa Cruz from 1991 to 2003, deployed in his province the full arsenal used by petro-autocrats. He co-opted the judiciary, including the Supreme Court and the Consejo de la Magistratura, the body that appoints judges.[77] He named family members to key posts. He fired the attorney general, Eduardo Sosa, after Sosa tried to investigate corruption related to the YPF privatization funds that Santa Cruz received. The Supreme Court of Argentina ordered the government of Santa Cruz to reinstate Sosa, but the order was ignored. Néstor Kirchner removed term limits and co-opted the bureaucracy, the independent media, and even most of the opposition.[78] The Kirchners' accomplices bought almost all the local newspapers and radio stations, and they received substantial government advertisements to stay afloat.

In Santa Cruz, the Kirchners also showcased their ruling strategy: divide society between "us" and "them." According to Zuvic, "the Kirchners were always the generators and managers of the conflicts in the province."[79]

The most significant practice that they started in the province and then brought to the national arena was a massive corruption network. The Kirchners, like Putin, are kleptocrats. Speaking of Néstor, who died in 2010, "Money in cash would be one of Kirchner's most notable obsessions," according to Luis Majul in his 2009 book *El Dueño* (in English: *The Owner*).[80] To that end, they used the same aides that helped them in Santa Cruz to orchestrate the biggest corruption scheme ever in Argentina. And believe me, the corruption bar is very high in Argentina.

The privatization of YPF, the state-owned oil company, offers a prime example of the Kirchners' ways. In 1993, as part of the agreement between the federal government and the provinces to privatize YPF, Santa Cruz received $535 million of unpaid royalties, of which 40.1 percent was paid in cash and 59.9 percent in newly issued YPF stock. The shares were later sold in 1999 for three times their original value, generating an additional $660 million for the province.[81] But Néstor managed this bounty as his own, without any accountability of its whereabouts.

In a famous video in which he is unaware that the cameras are still on, Kirchner says with a smile: "*I* [emphasis added] have 600 million pesos." (At that point, 1 Argentine peso equaled 1 US dollar).[82] He took the money out of Argentina and moved it through different banks until it ended up in an account at Credit Suisse. Then, the funds simply disappeared. In 2018, only $10,000 was left in the account.[83]

Like other autocrat wannabes, the Kirchners were lucky with the situation that they inherited. The previous government implemented harsh macro adjustment policies, including a devaluation of the peso from 1 per USD to 3.7 in October 2002, an unprecedented fiscal adjustment, and a debt moratorium. When Néstor became president, the economy was growing again, quickly, aided by a weak peso and soaring commodities. The price of soybeans, Argentina's main export, was 85 percent higher at year-end 2003 than at its trough in April 2001. By December 2007, when Cristina Kirchner succeeded her husband as president, soybean prices were 54 percent higher than in December 2003.

This manna from heaven—or better said, from Chinese buyers—allowed the Kirchners to expand fiscal spending briskly, making them highly popular among low-income Argentines. It was not only about money, but it was also about the message. The 2001–2002 financial crisis shattered Argentina, and the unemployment rate soared to 24 percent. The population questioned the market-driven model of the Washington Consensus implemented in the 1990s by President Carlos Menem and his finance minister, Domingo Cavallo. Dissatisfied with the plan that gave more power to markets, voters questioned Argentina's traditional power players, including the political parties, the unions, and the military.

The Kirchners were adept at reading the room and interpreting the mood of the populace, and they were calculating in choosing their battles with perceived enemies. Their enemies were similar to Putin's: the United States, the IMF, and Wall Street. In January 2006, Néstor Kirchner used the country's international reserves to wholly pay the $9.8 billion debt to the IMF, "recovering freedom for national interest decisions."[84] When President George W. Bush visited the Argentine coastal city of Mar del Plata in November 2005 for the Fourth Summit of the Americas, Hugo Chávez and Kirchner held a counter-summit at the same time, targeting the Free Trade Area of the Americas (FTAA), which the United States sponsored.

In Putin's mind, Russia is constantly under threat from the West. To unify the country and garner support for his views, he embraced the Orthodox Church, despite there being no trace of religion in his life prior to becoming president. Like Putin, the Kirchners reinterpreted history to consolidate their base and signal their enemies. For the Kirchners, the watershed moment in Argentina's history was the 1976 military coup d'état, which introduced repression and "neoliberal" policies in the country.

This view led them to embrace the cause of human rights, which was a rather significant shift for them. In Santa Cruz, they could not be bothered to receive the leader of the Madres de Plaza de Mayo, or the Mothers of the Disappeared, a human rights organization formed following Jorge Rafael Videla's military dictatorship.[85] But once in the national government, they made human rights a cornerstone of their government. When asked by former President Ramón Puerta, "Why are you on the left now if we were both great pimps of Cavallo, you first and me second?" Néstor Kirchner allegedly replied, "Being from the left gives you privileges."[86]

Their economic success, their fight for human rights, and their fights against the United States and other declared enemies gave the Kirchners leeway to take their corruption and state-capture scheme to the national level. Luis Majul summarized it well:

> From 2003 until now he took on his own the sum of the State's patrimony, he distributed among his friends the great business of public works, he made sure that an allied businessman bought part of the oil company that at the same time is the largest company in Argentina, he managed the cash from the public transport subsidies, he got into public and private banks, he interceded so that another friend of his multiplied his interests in the casinos business and broke into the media to hit Clarín [the biggest media company] and manage part of the information of all Argentines. In addition, through unconditional officials, he took control of the Post Office, Aguas Argentinas [the water company], and Aerolíneas Argentinas [the national airline], as well as the money from private pensions, among other sources of political and economic power. But that was not all. He also took control of the federal judges through the Council of the Judiciary, . . . invaded the Institute of Statistics and Censuses (INDEC) to manipulate the inflation and poverty rates, and penetrated the Federal Administration of Public Revenues (AFIP) [the local IRS], to prevent further investigation of his friends in business.[87]

The Kirchners' main corruption scheme involved shady public works auctions. The family's main accomplice and front man was Lázaro Báez, whom Néstor met when Báez lived in a social housing complex. They got close quickly, likely because Mr. Báez was a teller at the Bank of Santa Cruz, the state-owned provincial bank.[88] Báez provided Kirchner with something the former president always valued: private information about his opponents and his targets. In this case, Báez had information about debtors to the Bank of Santa Cruz.[89]

When Néstor became governor of Santa Cruz, Báez's career at the bank skyrocketed, and it wasn't long before he rose through the ranks to become the bank's de facto CEO. Under his control, the bank extended suspicious credits, including politicized credits—that is, easy credit for friends, no credit for adversaries. By the time the bank was privatized and sold to the Eskenazi family's Grupo Petersen in 1998, the bank was under water. The province kept its bad loans for $180 million.[90]

When Néstor became president in 2003, Báez essentially won the lottery. On May 8, 2003, a mere 17 days before Kirchner assumed the presidency, Báez incorporated a construction company, Austral Construcciones, although he had no previous experience in the construction business. Through Austral Construcciones, Báez won 78.4 percent of the public works allocated to Santa Cruz. The province, with just 0.5 percent of the population of Argentina, received an astounding 12 percent of the national public work contracts during Néstor and Cristina Kirchner's administrations.[91]

With such capital deployment, it would be reasonable to expect Santa Cruz to be a model of best-in-class infrastructure, but it is not. Of the 51 public works contracts awarded to Báez's companies, only 27 were finished, and only three were completed on time and on budget. Coincidentally or not, Austral Construcciones, Báez's main construction company, closed shop when Cristina Kirchner's second term ended in 2015.[92] At that point, it was the only construction company to which the federal government owed no money.

Báez became a multimillionaire, if not a billionaire. With his windfall, he purchased 25 estates totaling 427,037 hectares in Santa Cruz.[93] This land is desert-like and very windy, but some of the estates are close to the Rio Santa Cruz. According to Mariana Zuvic, it is land that will be used to construct two hydroelectric dams,[94] and Báez will be compensated by the national government for the expropriation of this land.[95] Báez, like many of Kirchner's friends and family members, was able to purchase land in El Calafate, Santa Cruz, one of the top tourist destinations in Argentina, at well below market prices.[96]

Báez also returned money to the Kirchners. Báez rented several properties owned by the family, purchased some of them, and loaned money to them at a 0 percent interest rate for several years, which is a gift in a country with double-digit inflation.[97] His biggest deals were with the hotels owned by the Kirchners in Calafate. They have two: Los Sauces, a posh boutique hotel, partly built on Báez's cheaply purchased land, and Alto Calafate, which sits on a hillside overlooking Lake Argentina.

Hugo Alconada Mon and Mariana Arias, investigative journalists from the newspaper *La Nación*, discovered that for years eight companies owned by Báez rented 1,100 rooms per month at Alto Calafate without using them.[98] Croissants, or lack thereof, was one of the several clues that led Alconada Mon and Arias to this; they realized that the hotel's croissants order was much smaller than what a hotel of that size would require had the rooms been occupied. Other companies owned by Néstor's friends and the state-owned airline company, Aerolíneas Argentinas, had similar deals. Simply put: it was money laundering at its best.

Like Putin, the Kirchners aimed to create a "national bourgeoisie" of businessmen that they could control by taking stakes in the energy and the media sectors. A notable example is the Eskenazi family. In 2007, the Eskenazis' Grupo Petersen bought 14.9 percent of YPF, the biggest company in Argentina, and managed to do so by barely putting $100 million of their own into the deal.[99] They later bought an additional 0.1 percent stake and took over the company's management. Before this transaction, the Eskenazis had almost no experience in the oil business, but Néstor Kirchner wanted to have a local businessman in charge of YPF.

The memorandum of understanding of the purchase argued that Repsol, the Spanish oil company selling the stake to Grupo Petersen, was adding "a prestigious partner with *experience in the management of companies with high regulatory requirements* at the federal, provincial and regional levels in Argentina"[100] (my emphasis). My translation: they were buying access to the most powerful person in Argentina, Néstor Kirchner. Of the $2,235 million that Petersen paid for 14.9 percent of YPF, $1,026 million was loaned by a group of banks that included Credit Suisse, Goldman Sachs, and BNP Paribas, and $1,015 million were loaned by Repsol itself.[101] How would the Eskenazis repay such big loans, given the small size of their other companies? The answer is with YPF's dividends.

The Eskenazis were not the only friends of Néstor Kirchner trying to get control of oil companies. Lázaro Báez tried to purchase Shell's assets in Argentina at the end of 2007, but he couldn't, according to Alconada Mon.[102] Cristobal López's story provides another successful example of the Kirchners' "national bourgeoisie." López's Indalo group is one of the most important private conglomerates in Argentina, with interests including oil, media, casinos, financial services, and hotels. He started with one casino in 1992 in Comodoro Rivadavia, in the province of Chubut, but then got the concession for casinos in Santa Cruz when Kirchner was governor.[103] López expanded his franchise through partnerships, and Casino Club grew to become the biggest casino franchise of Argentina.[104]

López is the right man to own casinos: He's a very lucky guy. Right before he left office in December 2007, Kirchner extended the concession of Buenos Aires' racetrack and casino, the most important of the country. The concession was set to expire in 2017, but Kircher extended it by presidential decree until 2032 in exchange for the installation of 1,500 additional slot machines, to be run by the Casino Club.

Through his oil company, Oil M&S, López received half the oil concessions in the province of Santa Cruz, and then bought Argentina's assets of Brazilian oil company Petrobras.[105] He acquired the assets using unpaid taxes on gasoline, totaling between $218 million and $319 million.[106] To get away with this scheme, López had the help of officials from the AFIP, the federal government tax agency, which was lenient not only with López but also with the Kirchners. According to Luis Majul, Kirchner "corrected his tax declaration with the complicity of the AFIP officials."[107] Several officials tracked the "inconsistencies" in the presidential couple's tax declaration, but these officials were removed and transferred to completely unimportant jobs.[108]

Just as Putin and other wannabe autocrats, the Kirchners tried to control the media. From day one, they used state-owned media to disseminate government propaganda and attack opposition members, including the state-run TV channel, Canal 7. At the beginning of Néstor Kirchner's first term, the government was on good terms with Grupo Clarín, by far the biggest media conglomerate in Argentina. Alberto Fernández, then Kirchner's chief of staff, phoned one journalist every night to ask about the next day's cover of *Clarín*, Argentina's biggest newspaper.[109]

About a month before leaving power, Kirchner allowed Cablevision, Grupo Clarín's cable company, to merge with Multicanal, giving Clarín more than 50 percent of the Argentine market. The move likely would have been blocked if Argentina had an independent competition regulatory agency. Néstor Kirchner offered this candid statement to a select group of his acolytes before the deal: "With Magnetto (Clarín's CEO) everything is fixed. We have 20 years ahead."[110]

A few months later, however, the government began waging war against *Clarín*, headlined by a campaign featuring the slogan "*Clarín* miente," or "*Clarín* lies." The government passed a media law under the guise of "democratizing the media," but instead tried to control it. The government pulled its advertisements from *Clarín* and put undue pressure on private supermarket chains, the biggest advertising spenders in Argentine newspapers, to remove their ads in *Clarín*, *La Nación*, and other independent newspapers. The pressure included the government's attempt to control Papel Prensa, the largest producer of newsprint in the country, which major newspapers *Clarín* and *La Nación* owned. Ernestina Herrera de Noble, the owner of *Clarín*, and her family faced personal attacks. The attempt to control the media also included pressures to fire journalists.

Another tactic involved businessmen close to the Kirchners simply buying TV and radio stations and newspapers. Cristobal López bought cable news channels C5N and Radio 10, which allowed him to fire their most prominent morning journalist, Marcelo Longobardi. López also bought *Infobae* and *Ámbito Financiero*, two important newspapers. Rudy Ulloa, who once ran errands for Néstor Kirchner and served as his chauffeur when the former president established his law practice in Santa Cruz in the 1970s, tried to buy Telefe, the biggest broadcast TV channel by audience.[111]

Like Putin, Néstor Kirchner also had an affinity for illegally taped conversations. Although he did not emerge from Argentina's version of the KGB, called the AFI, Kirchner did use intelligence services against his adversaries and to control his partners in government. According to *La Nación's* Alconada Mon, "if Kirchner criticized someone—politician, businessman, journalist, it doesn't matter—a dossier of the current victim would immediately appear. And, suddenly, the wiretaps that 'Lupo' (Néstor's nickname) enjoyed at siesta time began to appear."[112]

To control the judiciary, the Kirchners sought to steer in their favor the Consejo de Magistratura, the institution in charge of naming federal and national judges, removing magistrates, and administering the resources of the Judicial Council.[113] In 2006, the Kirchners pushed for a law changing the Consejo de Magistratura's composition, lowering the number of members but increasing the percentage of them coming from the legislative and executive branches. The law passed, but after many years of review, the Supreme Court declared the law unconstitutional, arguing it broke the equilibrium between the political and the technical members of the Consejo de la Magistratura required by article 114 of the Argentine Constitution.[114] In 2022, the government coalition, the Frente de Todos (FdT), tried to pass a bill changing its composition again, but this time they did not have a majority in the Senate.[115]

Previously, the Supreme Court established that a new law related to the composition of the Consejo de Magistratura had to be sanctioned before April 15, 2022; if not, the previous legislation from 1997 would be in force.[116] Not happy with this option, the FdT made a dubious and unexpected maneuver: it split its caucus in the Senate so that it could count one more representative in the Consejo de la Magistratura. This maneuver left the FdT coalition with three out of four seats of the Senate's representation in the Consejo de Magistratura, which did not reflect their real representation in Congress. Ricardo Gil, a constitutional lawyer and a member of the panel of judges that tried the military Juntas, called this maneuver "an erosion of the democratic form."[117] When the Supreme Court dictated that this maneuver was unconstitutional in October 2022, Cristina Kirchner, the head of the Senate then, simply ignored the ruling.

Investigating the Kirchners proved to be risky for prosecutors. Alberto Nisman, as discussed earlier in this book, was killed one day before testifying in Congress against Cristina Kirchner. When the first case alleging the Kirchners' illicit enrichment hit the federal courts in 2005, and prosecutor Eduardo Taiano had to decide whether to indict Néstor Kirchner, his 19 year-old son was briefly abducted.[118] When he had to decide whether to appeal a related case against the Kirchners in 2008, Taiano needed no such warning; he did not appeal.[119]

In August 2022, prosecutor Diego Luciani indicted Cristina Kirchner in the "Vialidad" (Road Works) case. She and other government officials were accused of having set up an "illicit association" by which most public tenders for road works in Santa Cruz were given to construction companies owned by Lázaro Báez. In response, President Alberto Fernández said, "Nisman committed suicide, I hope Luciani doesn't do something like that."[120] Many interpreted the statement as a warning to Luciani. Kirchner was sentenced in March 2023 to six years in prison by a three-member penal court, although she will not serve in jail given her immunity as a vice president.

An argument can be made that international markets did not finance the Kirchners' attempt to undo Argentina's democracy because the Kirchners did not tap voluntary debt markets. Wall Street and the IMF were the declared enemies, so Néstor and Cristina Kirchner's governments, as well Alberto Fernández's, avoided being seen as sympathetic to the markets. They even went through the pain of depleting almost all the central bank's international reserves, $64.5 billion in total, to repay the $9.8 billion debt with the IMF in 2006 and to pay other foreign currency debt services without tapping voluntary debt markets.

On the other hand, markets were quite lenient with the timing of payments in the three debt restructurings during the Kirchner administrations (2005, 2010, and 2020). Public declarations aren't always a Fernández strength, but he was cunning when he announced the result of the $66.1 billion foreign currency sovereign debt restructuring in August 2020. During the announcement, he intentionally folded the page that compared the yearly debt services of the new debt and the old debt. He only showed the years under his mandate, in which Argentina's government would save $23.3 billion.[121] He intentionally avoided indicating that the next administration would face substantially higher debt services, so much higher that the market did not react very well to the proposal. From the outset, the market priced that the next administration may be forced to restructure the debt again, given that the government likely would not have the capacity to service it.

In sovereign debt restructurings, the deals fulfill two objectives: to give the borrower relief, while allowing it to regain market access as soon as possible. The Kirchners only wanted debt services relief for their terms, not for future administrations, and the markets accommodated them more than once. The relief would be used to pursue expansionary policies that bought them popularity. The tab would have to be picked up by non-Peronist administrations in the future.

The IMF was also oblivious to Kirchner's attempt to undermine democracy, in a way that supports the claim that international financial institutions (IFIs) do not consider democracy in their decision making, as I argued in Chapter 1. Although the IMF gave non-Peronist President Mauricio Macri the biggest loan in its history in 2018, it imposed on him such a harsh fiscal and monetary adjustment that it handed Cristina Kirchner the vice presidency in the 2019 election.

I do not make this argument with the benefit of hindsight; I stated that this would happen in an op-ed published in *La Nación* just as the program was unveiled in October 2018. I sarcastically referred to IMF Chief Christine Lagarde as "compañera," a version of "comrade," which is what Peronist women often call each other.[122] In my view, Lagarde and the IMF imposed such a harsh fiscal and monetary adjustment on Macri's government that she seemed to be working for Cristina. And I was proved correct.

When the new Peronist administration assumed power in 2019, the IMF signed a new program imposing scant fiscal and exchange rate adjustments for the final two years of its term in 2022 and 2023. Moreover, the IMF looked the other way when the administration fudged the fiscal, monetary, and reserve numbers to pretend it was meeting the program targets. The IMF program ended up being so lenient on the Fernández-Kirchner government that by November its candidate Sergio Massa had real chances of winning the presidential election; in any case the next administration will have no other option than to adjust fiscal and monetary policies harshly again. It will also have to devalue the peso against the US dollar. A weakened government may help Cristina Kirchner to return to power in 2027.

That the IMF does not consider democracy standards is evident from its loan portfolio. In March 2023, 44.7 percent of the countries under its programs were labeled Partly Free by Freedom House, and 30.8 percent Not Free.[123] That is, only 24.5 percent of the countries under an IMF program were considered Free by Freedom House. When looking at the amounts loaned, a bigger share of the total loans is directed to Free countries, 41.2 percent, as Argentina is the IMF's biggest debtor by far, and it is classified as s Free country by Freedom House. In the case of the World Bank, 55 percent of the countries receiving some World Bank financing in 2023 are Partly Free or Not Free according to Freedom House,[124] but 67.5 percent of its loan portfolio is directed to Partly Free and Not Free countries. Argentina is the seventh-largest World Bank debtor.

In 2023, Cristina Kirchner remained the central figure in Argentina's politics. When the "Vialidad" cases against her advanced in court, she managed to mobilize one part of a divided country behind her cause. She attacked court members repeatedly. The phones of the judges that condemned her to six years in prison, among many other judges, were hacked. That Argentina is not an autocracy is due to civil society's resilience, including the work of investigative journalists, what is left of the independent media, massive street demonstrations by its middle class, and to her incompetence in managing the economy. When Néstor Kirchner assumed the presidency in May 2004, the economy was booming, inflation was below 5 percent, and the government ran a surplus. When Cristina Kirchner left government in December 2015, the economy had been stagnant for four years, there was a fiscal deficit of more than 4 percent of GDP, and inflation was at 27 percent. During that time, INDEC, the statistical agency, intervened and reported much lower inflation and higher-than-real growth figures. Her stint as vice president was no better; by September 2023, inflation exceeded 136 percent, the economy was contracting more than 3 percent, and more than 40 percent of the population was poor.

Investors lost dearly under Cristina Kirchner's populist regime, a theme that I will revisit in Chapter 8. In this case, markets did not wait for her to take power. On August 11, 2019, the day after a primary election in which it became clear that she would rule Argentina again, this time as vice president, markets had one of the biggest falls in recorded history by any country in the world. The local equity market index MERVAL dropped 48 percent measured in US dollars, the currency slipped 22.5 percent against the USD, and USD denominated bonds plunged by as much as 32 percent. For perspective, markets in Argentina fared much worse when populism's return to power was seen as a given than markets in Ukraine fared after Russia's invasion. The markets were right; under Alberto Fernández and Cristina Kirchner's government, external bond prices remained close to 25 cents to the USD three years after being restructured. The MERVAL index only started to rise in 2022 once it became clear that Cristina would not be reelected in 2023.

KEY TAKEAWAYS OF CHAPTER 7

This chapter:

- Underscores another trait of autocratic and populist governments: they tend to manage their economies dismally. Latin America's brand of populism provides an extreme example. The region's populists have a long track record of expanding spending when commodity prices rise, and then sending their economies into a tailspin of inflation and debt defaults when commodity prices drop.

- Highlights how this scenario is not good for equity and bond investors. Latin America is full of serial defaulters, notably Argentina and Ecuador but also Brazil, Chile, and others. This characteristic is one reason why Latin America's equity markets are small and trade at big discounts compared to other equity markets.

- Discusses how Latin America also provides extreme examples of another common trait of populist and autocrats: corruption. When investors finance countries run by wannabe autocrats, they are pouring money into the pockets of people like Néstor and Cristina Kirchner in Argentina.

- Provides another example of how investors' money can indirectly finance wannabe autocrats or autocrats through supra-national institutions, in this case the IMF. The IMF proved too lenient with Cristina Kirchner's government just as she was attacking the judiciary.

CHAPTER 8

IS INVESTING IN MORE DEMOCRATIC COUNTRIES THE RIGHT INVESTMENT DECISION?

Democratic countries grow faster and are subject to fewer downside risks.

Investing in Autocracies Carries Many Downside Risks

The day Russia invaded Ukraine in 2022, markets panicked. Moscow's stock market suffered one of the biggest collapses in financial history as the RTS Index dropped 38 percent in US dollars on Thursday, February 24.[1] Russia's government bonds didn't fare any better, dropping 45 percent the same day.[2]

The reaction of market participants was swift. Most institutional investors suspended their Russian bond and stock purchases immediately.[3] A few days after the war began, Norway's $1.3 trillion sovereign wealth fund announced that it would sell all its Russian assets, a total of $3.3 billion in stocks and bonds, as part of a wider support package for Ukraine.[4] Rating agencies downgraded Russia's government bond ratings. By February 25, Fitch had cut Russia's credit two notches to CCC, and Moody's warned that it could strip Russia of its investment grade status,[5] which it did on March 6.[6]

It was too late; investors were hit hard. BlackRock, the biggest asset manager in the world, took a $17 billion loss as a result of its Russian exposure.[7] Its Russia-dedicated ETF, the iShares MSCI Russia ETF, plunged from $600 million at the end of 2021 to $1 million a week into the war. Combined, BlackRock and asset managers Allianz, Capital, Western Asset Management, and Vanguard owned $7.4 billion of Russian bonds.[8] In total, global investors, pension funds, hedge funds, and allocators of sovereign wealth had $170 billion of exposure to Russia at the end of 2021.[9] Western banks had a total exposure of $91 billion to Russia, according to the Bank of International Settlements (BIS), an organization owned by 63 central banks.[10] The war not only affected Russian markets and entities directly exposed to Russia, but it also rattled the global economy, sending food and energy prices, among others, skyrocketing.

But autocratic governments don't need to resort to war to bring substantial downside risks for investors. Sometimes, a slow slide toward autocracy and economic mismanagement can suddenly become too much for investors and market watchers. When Goldman Sachs Asset Management (GSAM) bought Venezuela national oil company PDVSA's bonds in May 2017, Venezuela bonds had returned 8.5 percent year-to-date, and were a major contributor to emerging market gains that year.[11] High returns tend to attract more flows, and this case was no different. For example, for those five months, Venezuela debt accounted for 2.4 percent of the iShares J.P. Morgan USD Emerging Markets Bond ETF (EMB), and its assets increased by 45 percent to $11.6 billion.[12]

Since then, Venezuela's bonds have done nothing but cause investors pain. In August 2017 the US government imposed sanctions, effectively banning any institution within arm's length of US government regulators from trading the bonds. In late 2017, Venezuela's government and PDVSA defaulted on their bonds. At the beginning of 2022, the government and PDVSA bonds were trading below 5 cents to the dollar.[13] The bonds only started to rise toward the end of 2022, driven by speculation that the Biden administration might lift some of the sanctions, but they remained below 10 cents to the dollar.

Other times, all it takes is a political show to bring substantial downside to investors. On October 22, 2022, the world watched with astonishment as Hu Jintao, former general secretary of the Chinese

Communist Party, was escorted out of the 20th Communist Party Congress.[14] His removal seemed to be another display of Xi Jinping's consolidation of power as he was elected for a third term. Xi's power moves also included packing the Politburo Standing Committee with loyalists.

Chinese stockholders were not surprised; they were scared. The next day, the Hang Seng China Enterprises Index, which includes stocks listed in Hong Kong, tumbled 7.3 percent. Chinese technology stocks fared worse. The Nasdaq Golden Dragon China Index, which includes 65 Chinese stocks listed in the United States, dropped a record 14 percent, wiping out $93 billion in market value in one day.[15] Those who believe that markets like autocracies should take a careful look at this index: during the week Xi Jinping secured his third term, the index was at its lowest level since 2013, when Xi Jinping assumed power. That is, investors had a 0 percent return in one decade.

The brutal market reaction on October 23 reflected concerns that Xi would strengthen his hardline approach toward the private sector and tech entrepreneurs. Based on the government's clampdown on the tech and the education sectors, discussed in Chapter 6, the market's fear was unsurprising. The total market rout that week was a stunning $6 trillion.[16] In the weeks that followed, investors pulled money from China in scores, including $2.4 billion on October 24 alone.

The destruction of value was massive. The Emerging Markets Internet & Ecommerce ETF (EMQQ), which offers investors exposure to internet and Ecommerce activities in the developing world, went from a peak of about $80 in February 2021 to near $30 at the beginning of September 2022. By October 28, EMQQ was down to $22.59, at which point the fund had 51.6 percent of its assets invested in China.[17]

Certain sectors make up the usual prey for autocrats or wannabe autocrats, as the stories of energy companies in Russia (Chapter 5) and Argentina (Chapter 7) illustrate. Other frequent targets are the infrastructure, media, and telecommunications sectors.

Banks are another target, and Poland's banks offer a good example. There are many similarities between Poland's and Hungary's populist experiments. Law and Justice (PiS) party leader Jaroslaw Kaczyński, the in-the-shadows leader of Poland from 2015 to 2023, claims he speaks for "true Poles,"[18] and in 2020 he declared that the elections held that year were a "civilization clash."[19] This conservative nationalistic brand of populism is one of the many similarities between Poland and Hungary. Viktor Orbán has been a role model for Kaczyński, who said his goal was "Budapest in Warsaw."[20]

When the PiS came to power, foreigners owned 60 percent of Poland's banking sector. The "repolonization" of the banking sector became a PiS goal,[21] as the party believed that "Polish banks should be in Polish hands."[22] The government already owned several banks, including a controlling stake of 31.39 percent of Poland's largest bank, PKO Bank Polski, which is listed in the local stock market, but that was not enough for the PiS. After some small takeovers, PZU, another state-owned bank, bought a stake in Pekao, owned by Italy's Unicredit.[23] Other takeovers followed, and now more than 50 percent of the banks are owned by Polish nationals, including the government.

Hungary's government was well ahead of Poland's in terms of its intervention in various sectors of the economy. I detailed Orbán's attack on media companies in Chapter 4. His government also introduced a set of "sectoral special taxes," ostensibly aimed at improving government finances, targeting financial services, energy, retail, telecommunications, cable TV, and other companies. These extra taxes were based on turnover, not profits, and were higher for the biggest companies, which in Hungary were foreign-owned. As a result, it was natural to surmise that these taxes were implemented to force foreigners to sell to local "entrepreneurs."

Companies challenged the taxes in European courts, claiming that a measure centered on turnover discriminated on the basis of nationality, given that the biggest firms were foreign owned.[24] The courts ruled in favor of Hungary. Much like the problems with the procurement of government public work contracts outlined in Chapter 4, the European Union seemed unable to defend its own principles.

Beyond Poland, Orbán's initiatives inspired governments throughout Central Europe to intervene in the media and other sectors, including the Czech Republic, Türkiye, Serbia, Slovenia, and North Macedonia.[25] In Egypt, Juhayna Food Industries shows how a company, no matter the industry, can fall into an autocrat's crosshairs. Juhayna's controlling owner, Safwan Thabet, and his son, Seif Thabet, have been in solitary confinement in Cairo's Scorpion Prison from December 2020 and February 2021, respectively, until January 2023. Their crime, according to the government: "funding terrorism, undermining the national economy and joining an unlawful organization."[26]

In truth, they refused to give up their shares in the company to a government-owned business,[27] and Human Rights Watch reports that they were jailed in violation of due process rights.[28] Juhayna, one of the most valuable companies in the Egyptian Stock Exchange, was a "darling of foreign investors."[29] Juhayna's products are everywhere in Egypt, and the Thabets were once part of the country's establishment. They fell from the establishment's good graces in a way that would not have happened in any democratic country with well-protected property rights.

In April 2021, the Thabets' case led the *Economist* to title an article "Why Egypt Isn't Open for Business. Despite Pro-business Talk, the Army Grabs Whatever It Wants."[30] In the same vein, a senior staff member at an American bank told me that the problem in these autocratic countries, referring to companies that foreign investors can access through the local stock markets, is that "they are private, until they are not."

What Does the Evidence Say About Investing in Autocracies?

I could write an entire book of stories about investors being stripped of their assets, or parts of them, in emerging market countries run by autocrats or leaders with autocratic tendencies. At the same time, I could also come up with plenty of stories about investors who did very well with their investments in these countries. For many years, Venezuela government and PDVSA bonds delivered returns well above the bond returns from more democratic countries such as Chile or Colombia. Until Xi's crackdown on the internet and education sectors, investors with exposure to China's stock market did very well for many years. If autocratic countries didn't deliver good returns, we would not get statements such as Larry Fink's, where he said that "markets like actually totalitarian governments."[31]

All this raises the question: Does investing in more democratic countries deliver higher returns? Complicating the answer to that question is that research on the topic is quite thin. While a topic like ESG has spurred vast academic literature, analyzing the performance of different ESG strategies and sustainable investing in general, research on the impact of democracy on investment returns is scant.[32]

The few papers that are available offer contradictory evidence. Results vary substantially because the studies use different time periods, alternative econometric strategies, and different countries and/or sectors, among other variables and alternatives.

In the most comprehensive study on this topic that I have found so far, Xun Lei and Tomasz Wisniewski, using a sample of 74 countries spanning from 1975 to 2015, found a positive relationship between democracy levels and stock returns.[33] Lei and Wisniewski use country data from MSCI indices and include 22 developed economies, 23 emerging markets, 19 frontier markets, and 10 "standalone" countries (those that are not in the other categories). To measure the level of democracy, they use the Polity IV project database, which is commonly used in academia.[34] Their results do not change if they use Freedom House's democracy index.

Lei and Wisniewski took their research one step further by designing and testing a trading strategy based on the democracy index. They constructed two portfolios based on the democracy level of each country: a "High Democracy Portfolio" and a "Low Democracy Portfolio." They give in each portfolio equal weights to the stock indices of the 10 percent more democratic and the 10 percent less democratic countries in their sample, based on their annual democracy rankings, respectively. These portfolios are rebalanced at the end of each year. The result is stunning: the High Democracy Portfolio's annual return was 9.83 percent, while the Low Democracy Portfolio's annual return was only 5.29 percent, a difference of 4.54 percent per year.[35]

A word of caution: the excess returns when investing in more democratic countries should not hold forever. If strategies such as the ones Lei and Wisniewski outline were to become widespread in the market, stocks in more democratic countries would outperform stocks in less democratic countries for a period of time. But, once the shift to a new equilibrium occurs, their expected returns should fall.

Stocks in more democratic countries would command higher prices than similar firms in less democratic ones, but the expected returns should be lower. In other words, if we consider the standard capital asset pricing model (CAPM), the cost of capital would become lower for firms in more democratic countries. That is, investors could not expect to receive higher returns forever. A similar discussion will arise around ESG strategies in Chapter 9.

The methodological problems are more difficult to overcome when analyzing returns in the sovereign debt market. As a result, even fewer papers estimate the returns of more democratic versus less democratic countries than in the equity market.

Governments in emerging markets often default on their debts. How much investors lose when these bonds are restructured is subject to intense debate, and in recent years efforts to estimate these losses have increased. Federico Sturzenegger and Jeromin Zettelmeyer estimate the "haircuts" that investors took on their contractually promised payments ranged from 13 percent in Uruguay's most recent default in 2002 to 73 percent in Argentina's 2002 default, which is not its most recent default.[36] But there is no unanimous answer to the question, which complicates sovereign bond return estimates over long periods.

Additionally, the nature of sovereign lending has changed over time. In the 1970s and 1980s, financing to emerging market governments was in the form of bank lending.[37] Large and global investment banks such as Citibank and J.P. Morgan recycled the "petrodollars" saved by Middle East oil-exporting countries into syndicated loans, many of them to autocratic military juntas in Latin America. More recently, as discussed in Chapter 6, China's direct lending played a more important role in the financing portfolio of emerging market countries. All these nuances complicate an accurate analysis of how profitable it is to loan funds to more democratic countries.

Some researchers take a different approach to the problem. Instead of asking which type of regime's bonds are more profitable to buy, they ask whether there is a "democratic advantage" by which democracies can sell more bonds on better terms than their authoritarian counterparts. Others arguably go too far back in researching these problems: in studying Britain's Glorious Revolution of 1688, Nobel Prize recipient Douglass North and Barry Weingast conclude that "new institutions allowed the government to commit credibly to upholding property rights. Their success was remarkable, as the evidence from the capital markets shows."[38] That is, by placing stricter limits on the executive branch, democracies' promises to repay their debts are more credible because debts cannot be unilaterally repudiated. It should then be more profitable to buy bonds of democratic governments in the long run.

Research on more recent periods yields a more ambiguous answer on this democratic advantage to sell bonds. Using data from 80 developing countries from 1971 to 1997, Sebastian Saiegh, from the University of California at San Diego, finds that democracies are more likely to reschedule their debts and that there is no significant difference in the interest rate paid by democracies and non-democracies.[39]

In a related paper, Archer, Biglaiser, and DeRouen, using a sample of 50 developing countries from 1987 to 2003, find that democracies receive no better credit ratings than otherwise similar autocracies, based on GDP per capita, for example.[40] More generally, they argue that the regime type and other political factors have little effect on the bond raters, although in interviews that they conducted, raters said that they do have an impact. This finding is not surprising. In Chapter 3, in the context of the credit rating agencies' upgrade of Türkiye's government bonds ratings when its democracy was sliding, I reviewed some of the factors that the ratings agencies consider. I argued that, while they do include some institutional factors that overlap with those present in liberal democracies, they do not consider democracy standards per se in their ratings methodologies.

However, in a more recent paper, Emily Beaulieu from the University of Kentucky, Gary Cox from Stanford University, and Sebastian Saiegh found that there is a democratic advantage when considering an additional variable to the interest rates that countries pay and the credit ratings that they receive: their ability to access the market. Their research shows that democracies have better access to the international bond market than otherwise similar autocracies.[41]

To issue debt in international markets, a country must be rated by at least two of the major rating agencies. The argument that Beaulieu, Cox, and Saiegh make is that few autocracies get rated at all: only 17 percent, compared to 67 percent of the democratic countries in their sample. The autocratic countries that are rated are either resource-rich such as Saudi Arabia, important emerging markets such as China, or dictatorships with special geopolitical interest to the West, such as Egypt. With this consideration factored in, democracies receive better bond ratings than otherwise comparable autocracies. In other words, Saiegh and others get these results because their research includes autocratic countries that did not access the sovereign debt market at all.

These results, however, do not tell us without doubt whether it is more profitable to invest in bonds of more democratic countries. If Beaulieu, Cox, and Saiegh are right, democratic countries have better ratings and pay lower yields. Bonds from less democratic countries should then offer higher yields to investors. Prima facie, they should be more profitable, as was the case with Venezuela for years, but that does not mean anything if we do not factor in defaults.

The bottom line is that there is no available comprehensive analysis of risk-adjusted returns in the sovereign debt market from which we can draw conclusions about whether it is more profitable to invest in the bonds of countries that are more democratic. This brings to the fore a related comment that I received from some readers of drafts of this book: they argued that, as autocracy advanced in countries such as Venezuela and Türkiye, investors required higher rates to buy their government's bonds. These commentators see the higher rates as evidence that investors did consider democracy. But, if this were true, investors should be demanding higher expected rates to purchase China government bonds, and as I highlighted in Chapter 6, they don't. I think that the higher rates required by investors to purchase bonds in countries such as Venezuela and Türkiye are due to their inconsistent fiscal and monetary policies, and the higher currency and/or default risks that they run in these countries, not due to the deterioration of their democratic standards.

Given the relatively ambiguous nature of this research, a natural question when assessing the bonds and stocks of more democratic versus less democratic countries is, "What do the fundamentals tell us?" Consider if there is anything inherent to one type of country or the other that should impact returns in the long run. In my view, many factors should make investments in democratic countries and their companies more profitable, at least until the strategy is widespread, and less risky than investing in non-democratic countries and their companies.

What Factors Should Make Investing in Democratic Countries More Profitable in the Long Run?

I believe that investing in democratic countries should be more profitable because their economies grow faster and are subject to more limited expropriation risks than their non-democratic counterparts' economies. If all else remains equal, it should be better to be exposed to companies that sell in faster-growing economies, and to governments whose tax base expands faster.

However, the claim that democratic countries grow faster, which seems reasonable, has been questioned by investors, commentators, and academics. Thomas Friedman, *New York Times* columnist and author of various bestselling books on foreign affairs and globalization, once said that "one-party non-democracy certainly has its drawbacks. But when it is led by a reasonably enlightened group of people, as China is today, it can also have great advantages."[42] Among the academics who sided with him is Harvard's Robert Barro, one of the most prominent researchers in the field of economic growth. Barro said that "more political rights do not have an effect on growth."[43]

Many skeptics use the spectacular ascents of economies in East Asia this century, particularly China's, for support. China was 4 percent of the global economy in 1990, but by 2022 it represented almost 19 percent of the world's total output. In 1990, the size of China's economy was 6 percent of the size of the US economy, but by 2022 it was 77 percent of the US economy. The date by which China's economy is forecast to surpass the United States' has been delayed, but some say that it may happen as soon as 2030,[44] although others believe it will be much later.[45] Such a rapid rise at such a big scale is unprecedented, and it all took place under an autocratic government.

However, for every successful autocracy there are 10 failed ones. For every CCP, there are 10 Robert Mugabe's, who ruled Zimbabwe despotically from 1987 to 2017, with horrendous consequences for the economy. Dictators who brought economic hardship to their countries abound in Asia, Africa, and Latin America. Consider China's Great Leap Forward in the late 1950s, which led to the deadliest famine in history. Nobel Prize recipient Amartya Sen once observed that a famine has never occurred in a democratic society.[46]

More generally, as Daniel Deudney and John Ikenberry argue in their piece *The Myth of the Autocratic Revival: Why Liberal Democracy Will Prevail*, "contrary to the autocratic revival thesis, there are in fact deep contradictions between authoritarian political systems and capitalist economic systems."[47] Put differently, for capitalism to be successful in sustainably raising per capita income levels, it requires several features of liberal democracy, including well-defined property systems and the rule of law, and the checks and balances that can reduce corruption and avoid predatory tax systems, among others. These features are not present in capitalist yet undemocratic countries such as Russia and China. This view is similar to the one sustained by Daron Acemoglu and James A. Robinson in their monumental book *Why Nations Fail.*[48]

It is not surprising, although never without some controversy, that the most recent research finds a positive and significant relationship between democracy and growth. The initial empirical research did not reach a firm conclusion on the link between democracy and economic growth, however. In a review of the academic literature, John Gerring, Philip Bond, William Barndt, and Carola Moreno argued in 2005 that "the net effect of democracy on growth performance cross-nationally over the last five decades is negative or null."[49]

In a more recent and influential paper, though, economic development experts Daron Acemoglu from MIT and James Robinson from Harvard University, along with Suresh Naidu from Columbia University and Pascual Restrepo from MIT, conclude "democracy does cause growth, and that its effect is significant and sizable."[50] Furthermore, they explain that their "estimates imply that a country that transitions from non-democracy to democracy achieves about 20 percent higher GDP per capita in the next 25 years than a country that remains nondemocratic," which is no small feat.

The papers studying the effect of democracy on GDP growth use standard historical GDP databases such as the World Bank's World Development Indicators. Their results in favor of democracies would be even more compelling had they considered the relatively

143

recent finding by Luis Martinez from the Harris School of Public Policy at the University of Chicago, who argues that autocracies overstate yearly GDP growth by 35 percent.[51] He came to this startling conclusion by linking nighttime lights (NTL) recorded by satellites from outer space to economic growth data. He found that "the same amount of growth in NTL translates into higher reported GDP growth in autocracies than in democracies."

What are the channels by which democracies outpace nondemocracies? According to Acemoglu et al, democracy contributes to growth by "increasing investment, encouraging economic reforms, improving the provision of schooling and health care, and reducing social unrest."[52]

Some skeptics claim that democracy increases the demand for current consumption, especially in societies with high income inequality, and works against investment, which drives development.[53] There may be some truth to this; after all, Latin America, the most unequal income region in the world, holds regular elections but it is at the same time the land of populism. However, as I argued in the Preface, populism and autocracy overlap. That is, by claiming that they alone speak for the people in their fights against the elites, populist leaders are inherently undemocratic and have authoritarian tendencies. Populist leaders circumvent the checks and balances of the judiciary and the free press, they go against a professionalized bureaucracy, and through patronage and clientelism they corrupt what nominally remain called democratic elections.

Through their actions, populist leaders also imperil growth. In a recent paper using data from 1900 to 2018 for 60 countries, Manuel Funke, Moritz Schularick, and Christoph Trebesch report that the economic costs of populism are high. After 15 years, GDP per capita of a country that falls into a populist regime is 10 percent lower compared to a plausible non-populist counterfactual.[54]

These results are interesting for investors thinking about putting money into a country that is slipping into populism. As discussed in Chapter 7, investors usually prefer right-wing populists in Latin America such as Brazil's Jair Bolsonaro over left-wing ones such as Ecuador's Rafael Correa, because the right-wing populists are usually more market friendly and are perceived to be more fiscally prudent. They privatize publicly owned companies, deregulate the economy, and run tighter budgets, which sounds, all else equal, good for equity and government bond investors alike.

However, Funke et al. challenge this assumption, as they found that the negative impact of populist governments on the economy is invariant to the region, the era, or the ideology of the populists. That means that both left-wing and right-wing populists hurt the economy in the long run, although their impact is not the same.

What are the avenues by which populists hurt economic growth, and what differentiates one type of populist leader from the other? Trade is a major focus for populists from both the left and right, with each increasing trade protection as part of their core strategies. According to Funke et al., import tariffs are significantly higher in populist regimes. For investors, these dynamics signal that under populist regimes, it is better to invest in companies that compete with imports because the government shields them from foreign competitors. Conversely, populists imperil economic development because their policies hurt the exporting sector, which is crucial to growth.

In line with what Dornbusch and Edwards argued many years ago,[55] Funke et al. report that unsustainable macro policies are a feature and not a bug of populist leaders. Populists from the left and the right run high fiscal deficits, though their financing strategies differ. Funke et al. note that the ratio of government debt to GDP expands under all populist governments, particularly under right-wing populists. This increase is a warning for sovereign debt investors who may think that their investment is safer under a right-wing populist leader. Leftist populist leaders want to remain more isolated from Wall Street, so they shun debt markets and resort to monetary financing of the deficits. In doing so, they end up with higher inflation rates. Excessive debt levels, which may end up in defaults, and excessive inflation rates both hurt economic growth.

Institutional quality declines under populist regimes, according to Funke et al. They find that judicial independence and media freedom decline the most under left-wing populists, while there are stronger limitations to electoral freedom under right-wing populists. Democracy and constraints on the executive branch are key for long-term economic growth.[56] "Democratic institutions help to foster technology adoption and innovation, educational investments, and capital accumulation, resulting in higher growth rates."[57] As a result, populist leaders, with their authoritarian tendencies, hinder economic development in their countries.

In sum, I believe that skeptics who argue that democracy runs against economic development, because it increases the demand for consumption and thus reduces investment, are missing the point. In my view, a deformation of democracy, namely populism, is what causes those undesired results.

A related way in which the deterioration of democracy affects investors is that less democratic countries tend to have higher political risk. According to Ida Nesset, Ingrid Bøgeberg, and Frode Kjærland from the Norwegian University of Science and Technology, and Lars Molden from Nord University, political risk can be broadly defined as "those events, actions, processes or characteristics of a socio-political nature that have the potential to—directly or indirectly—significantly and negatively affect the goal of foreign direct investors." Political risks can be broken down into five types: legal, tension, conflict, policy, and ethnic and religious.[58] Coups or coup attempts, sudden government changes, upheavals, ethnic and religious clashes, and sudden legal and whimsical regulatory changes, among other events, are more frequent in less democratic countries.

The Arab Spring in 2011, which started in Tunisia and then spread to Egypt and other countries in the region, illustrates the market impacts political risk can have. The EGX 30 Index, Egypt's benchmark stock index, lost almost 50 percent of its value between January 3, 2011, and January 2, 2012.[59] More recently, when it became clear to the market that populist Cristina Kirchner would return to power in December 2019, the MERVAL, Argentina's benchmark stock index, dropped 48 percent on August 11, 2019.[60]

Using a sample of 49 emerging markets from 2000 to 2012, Lehkonen and Heimonen found that political risk has a negative impact on stock returns. They argue that semi-democracies are more prone to conflicts than full autocracies or full democracies.[61] As countries transition from autocracies to semi-democracies, political risk initially increases, only to drop as countries become more democratic. However, two of my research assistants, Miranda Cortizo and Connor Fernandez, have found that the relationship between democracy—measured using Freedom House's score—and political risk—measured with the Fragile State Index compiled by the Fund for Peace—is lineal. That means that political risk decreases as the democracy level of countries increases.

Property rights is another related but more subtle channel through which foreign investors face higher risks in less democratic countries, and that also affects economic growth. Property rights protections are weaker in less democratic countries because the presidents and prime ministers in these countries are subject to fewer checks and balances, whether from the legislative branch, the judiciary, the press, or independent bureaucracy.

When expropriation risks are high, the optimal response in the private sector sets in motion a series of changes in the structure of firms that affects minority shareholders and the growth of the economy at the same time. Under the banner of "expropriation risks" we include not only when a government nationalizes a company, but also any power used by the state that reduces the return of corporate investors through regulations, taxes, special benefits, preferences in government auctions, preferences when there are government restrictions (e.g., import permits), and others.[62]

The "optimal" response when property rights are insecure is to increase the opacity of the operations and the discretion of the managers, or let's call them, "controlling shareholders." For example, as inflation increased in Argentina under Alberto Fernández and Cristina Kirchner (2019–2023), government cronies went viral on social media by blaming inflation on "excessive profits" of companies with bonds in the market, such as Arcor. A confectionery company, Arcor is the largest producer of processed foods in Argentina, has 39 plants across Latin America, and is the world's top producer of hard candies.

In this situation, it would be optimal for companies to keep a low profile by "hiding" profits through perks to its insiders and reporting low profits. But once controlling shareholders make the company's operations harder to monitor, they can take advantage of minority shareholders,[63] including foreign investors. To reduce the incentive for controlling shareholders to take advantage of minority shareholders, the controlling shareholders must put more skin in the game.

The result is also that ownership is concentrated in countries with weaker property rights protections.[64] For example, the stock markets in countries such as Mexico mostly include companies run tightly by big shareholders, such as Carlos Slim with América Móvil. For the same reason, fewer companies are publicly listed; Arcor, for instance, is not listed. Conversely, in countries where property rights are better protected, such as the United States and the United Kingdom, more companies are publicly listed, and the ownership of listed companies is diffused among thousands of investors.

At the same time, increased expropriation risks mean the private sector is less dynamic, for at least three reasons. First, the governance structure gets more opaque when expropriation risks are high. Transparency, which tends to increase the value of firms in countries with well-protected property rights, may be a hindrance when expropriation risks are high.

Second, in these settings, companies engage in projects to gain the favor of the autocratic or populist ruler, and many of these projects have negative net present values (NPV). "Greater disclosure makes expropriation by the state easier, but it also makes transfers that benefit state rulers easier to observe."[65] Companies often hire the heirs of the political leaders, subcontract firms linked to them, and use their banks and financing channels.

Third, there is less capital available to expand into profitable ventures, as the non-controlling shareholders will not want to participate as much in companies with opaque governance, negative NPV projects, and substantial expropriation risks. As fewer companies are publicly listed, the amount of capital to invest is smaller. Therefore, it is not surprising that public equity markets are smaller in GDP terms in countries where property rights protections are weak.

In summary, there are many fundamental economic and institutional reasons to believe that stocks in more democratic countries should perform better in the long run than stocks in nondemocratic countries. Democratic countries tend to grow faster and to have lower political risk and lower expropriation risks, which should bode well for stock returns. A similar logic applies to sovereign bonds: the government of a country that grows faster should have a better repayment capacity over time.

KEY TAKEAWAYS OF CHAPTER 8

This chapter:

- Cites many examples of the downside risks that equity and bond investors face when investing in nondemocratic countries.

- Discusses academic literature on whether investing in democracies brings higher returns. The evidence is mixed because it is plagued by methodological problems, though a recent and comprehensive paper argues that investing in stocks of democratic countries is a profitable strategy.

- Goes a step further to look for a key underlying factor of country returns, GDP growth. The evidence suggests that democratic countries tend to grow faster than nondemocratic countries, which should be good for stocks because companies in countries that grow faster can expand quicker.

- Counters some common views that democracy fosters consumption against investment, and thus reduces GDP growth. Argues instead that a deformation of democracy, namely populism, is what causes these results.

- Analyzes other avenues by which nondemocratic countries hurt investors, such as lack of protection for minority investors.

CHAPTER 9

DO ESG METRICS ACCOUNT FOR DEMOCRACY STANDARDS?

ESG is incapable of stopping investors' money from financing dictators and aspiring autocrats.

ESG: A Meteoric Rise Subject to Increasing Criticism

The growth of investments into funds with sustainable objectives has been so brisk in recent years that it has been difficult to keep track of it all. In the first half of 2021, sustainable investments totaled approximately $25 trillion, according to investment research provider Morningstar.[1] That robust figure came on the heels of a Global Sustainable Investment Alliance estimate that put sustainable investments for 2020 at a whopping $35.3 trillion. For perspective, that figure represents more than a third of assets under management in the major economies that it covers.[2]

Although it is not easy to agree on the exact size of the sustainable investments market, its impressive growth is undeniable. In 2022, ESG investments accounted for one in three dollars under professional management in the United States and one in two in Europe.[3] Retail investors can also access ESG investment funds directly, and they have no shortage of options. In 2022, US investors could choose from more than 400 ESG funds and ETFs across different asset classes, of which 70 were launched in 2022 alone.[4]

ESG investing's actual impact is the subject of rising debate, but it is bound to grow with investor preferences shifting significantly. According to a 2019 Morgan Stanley survey, 49 percent of investors polled said that they were "very interested" in sustainable investing, and 36 percent were "somewhat" interested, up from 19 percent and 52 percent respectively in 2015.[5] Interest was much higher among millennials in 2019, at 70 percent and 25 percent, respectively. Given that millennials and Gen Z will be the ones building their retirement funds in the coming decades, what they value is critical for the future of the financial industry.

Burton Malkiel, Princeton professor and author of *A Random Walk Down Wall Street*, argued that "people want to align their investment strategies with their societal values."[6] With global warming and environmental destruction immediate threats, it is not surprising that the younger generations want to align their investments with their perceptions of what is sustainable for the global economy in the long run. In that sense, sustainable investing is about the emotional benefits that promoting a better world brings to a growing segment of investors.

There are many ESG strategies available for investors. The most common one, called ESG integration, is about integrating extra-financial criteria into the analysis of companies and sovereign bonds.[7] The environmental factor captures data on the natural resources that a firm consumes and how much it pollutes. The social factor looks at how well companies manage their relationships with employees, consumers, and suppliers. The governance factor captures issues such as board independence and executive pay.[8] Part of ESG's mission is to make negative externalities measurable and visible, and to flag potential reputational risks that could arise from them.[9] In that sense, many view ESG as a risk-reducing strategy.

ESG can also be thought of as a brand of ethical or socially responsible investing (SRI). SRI avoids investing in certain companies due to religious and other ethical considerations. Catholics, for instance, have funds that avoid companies involved in abortion or contraception. Other exclusions include "sin stocks," such as those in the alcohol, gambling, pornography, or tobacco industries.

Other ESG strategies are related to stakeholder capitalism, which aims for companies to serve not just shareholders but also their customers, employees, and the wider community in which they operate.

From these definitions, we can identify some of the problems that plague ESG investing. First, ESG considerations are broad, with many different factors included under one roof, which makes its measurement complicated. Controversial ESG ratings are common. One famous case is electric car, solar panel, and battery maker Tesla, which has a worse ESG score than some oil companies according to Sustainalytics, an ESG score provider. The poor rating derives from Tesla's exposure to "material ESG issues" and "management."[10]

The second problem is that ESG is, in part, about internalizing into the analysis of a company or a bond the externalities that the issuer produces. Externalities are costs that are not internalized by companies, such as pollution or congestion. In truth, these externalities should be addressed through taxes and regulations, but how governments around the world address them is inconsistent or incomplete. It therefore makes sense to take these externalities into consideration for investment decisions to achieve sustainability goals, but we should not be surprised that doing so sometimes comes at a cost.

For these and other reasons, ESG's merits have been under attack recently. Tariq Fancy, former chief investment officer for sustainable investing at BlackRock, called today's approach to ESG issues a "dangerous placebo that harms the public interest."[11] The *Economist*'s July 23, 2022, edition was titled "ESG: Three Letters That Won't Save the Planet," and its editorial argued that ESG is "in danger of standing for exaggerated, superficial guff." That edition included a special report that highlighted the three most important problems ESG faces. The first is that by lumping together too many objectives, it provides no coherent guide for investors. The Tesla example highlights this problem well and raises an important question: Should investors care more about a company's governance, the rotation of its labor force, or its impact on the environment?

In the same vein, some argue that ESG should be streamlined. Aswath Damodaran, a Stern Business School finance professor, who is sometimes called "the dean of valuation,"[12] argues that the G in ESG is redundant. Damodaran and valuation theory expert Bradford

Cornell wrote that they "question why governance, a measure that has historically been defined in research in terms of responsiveness of managers at publicly traded companies to their shareholders, is bundled with environmental responsiveness and social consciousness, two concepts that often require managers to put the interests of other stakeholder groups ahead of shareholders."[13]

The *Economist*'s special report goes one step further and suggests that it should also exclude S and concentrate only on E, and more specifically on emissions. The argument to exclude S is similar to Damodaran's argument to exclude G: in a market economy, companies will take care of the S and the G in their own interest.[14]

The second problem ESG faces according to the *Economist*'s report is that there are serious measurement problems. Li and Polychronopoulos report that by year-end 2019 they had identified 70 firms that provided ESG ratings.[15] Meanwhile, the *Economist* had that number at 160 worldwide.[16] More worryingly is that these firms do not provide coherent ratings.

In a paper titled "Aggregate Confusion: The Divergence of ESG Ratings," Florian Berg, Julian Kobel, and Roberto Rigobon estimated the correlation between ESG scores ranges from 0.38 to 0.71 for the six main ESG score providers: KLD, Sustainalytics, Moody's ESG, S&P Global, Refinitiv, and MSCI. That is, the correlation among their ESG scores is very low. For comparison, the correlation between the credit ratings of S&P, Moody's, and Fitch is 0.99. ESG scores vary due to differences in scope—or the attributes measured, in measurement—or how they measure these attributes, and in weightings—or the relative importance of the attributes. Measurement accounts for 56 percent of the divergence among ESG score providers, scope accounts for 38 percent, and weight only 6 percent. The divergence in ESG scores is problematic on several levels, but primarily because it makes it difficult to evaluate a company's ESG performance and it reduces the incentives of companies to improve their ESG performance given the mixed signals.[17]

The third problem that ESG faces, according to the *Economist*'s report, is that its incentives aren't straightforward. The evidence that ESG funds outperform non-ESG funds is mixed at best. It would be natural to assume that as investors pour more money into stocks with high ESG ratings these stocks would outperform ESG stocks with low scores. Then when ESG strategies become widespread, green stocks should be pricier, and therefore have lower expected returns. Ľuboš Pástor, Robert Stambaugh, and Lucian Taylor argue and test this assumption in a technical but influential paper titled "Sustainable Investing in Equilibrium."[18] To think of it another way, if ESG is a risk-reducing strategy, in equilibrium, lower risk should be compensated with lower expected returns. But this trade-off is not often mentioned in the ESG world, which instead conveys the idea that investors can have their cake and eat it too.

The overselling of ESG benefits, including at times dubious data on expected returns, has spurred accusations that ESG investing is mere greenwashing, even sometimes from environmentalists. Yan Swiderski, cofounder of the Global Returns Project, which selects and finances the most effective not-for-profits tackling climate change, said that "ESG often means 'Expect Serious Greenwash.'"[19] Research confirms that this argument has some merit. Soohun Kim and Aaron Yoon examined the commitment of active funds that sign the United Nations Principles for Responsible Investment (PRI), finding that "signatories vote less on environmental issues and their stock holdings experience increased environment related controversies."[20] Relatedly, Rajna Gibson, Simon Glossner, Philipp Krueger, Pedro Matos, and Tom Steffen found in a 2020 paper that "U.S. institutions that publicly commit to responsible investing do not exhibit better ESG scores."[21]

Findings like these have spurred something of a regulatory crackdown. In May 2022, the US Securities and Exchange Commission (SEC) fined a Bank of New York Mellon Corp. investment unit, for "misstatements and omissions about Environmental, Social, and Governance (ESG) considerations in making investment decisions for certain mutual funds that it managed."[22] The SEC also looked into whether Goldman Sachs Group Inc.'s mutual funds met the ESG metrics proclaimed by its marketing materials.[23] American and German authorities previously investigated DWS, a German asset manager related to Deutsche Bank, after its former head of sustainability, Desiree Fixler, alleged DWS may have misstated the use of ESG criteria in its investment portfolio.[24]

The regulatory crackdown has been rather sporadic, but stricter regulations and international standards are expected to come over time. The SEC proposes enhancing and standardizing climate-related disclosures for companies.[25] The International Sustainability Standards Board (ISSB) intends to deliver a "comprehensive global baseline of sustainability-related disclosure standards."[26] The European Union plans to set its own criteria.[27] Climate disclosures are in all these plans, but they differ on other issues. Although these regulatory bodies may bring more clarity than the Tower of Babel of ESG scores, at this point they are unlikely to provide uniform measuring standards. This expected shortfall contrasts with accounting standards set by the Financial Accounting Standards Board (FASB), whose Generally Accepted Accounting Principles (GAAP) have been adopted globally.

Yet amid all this noise about what ESG is and how to measure sustainability, even the critical *Economist* argues that it is better to overhaul ESG than to get rid of it. In my view, any overhaul of ESG should include another factor: democracy.

ESG Does Not Account for Democracy, but It Should

By the time Russia invaded Ukraine, Russia's government bonds had a bigger share in J.P. Morgan's ESG version (JESG EMBIG) of the EMBI Global Diversified Index than in its non-ESG-corrected version. That is, in February 2022, a sovereign bond investor who tracked the EMBI Global Diversified Index would have had roughly 0.89 percent of her portfolio in Russian sovereign bonds, compared to 1.03 percent if she tracked the ESG-corrected version.[28] To understand how this incongruity was possible, it is interesting to try to understand the ESG-corrected version's construction.

The J.P. Morgan JESG EMBI Index applies issuer scores to adjust the shares of the baseline index.[29] Its issuer scores are a 0 to 100 rank calculated from ESG scores provided by Sustainalytics and RepRisk. With these ranks, it constructs five bands with which they adjust the weight of the sovereign bond issues included in the EMBI Diversified index. For example, if the score is more than 80, then the bond is in band 1, and it enters the JESG with its full baseline index market value. If the score is more than 60 and lower or equal to 80, it is in band 2, and it enters with 80 percent weight of its baseline index market value, and so forth. Bonds in band 5 (rank lower or equal to 20) are excluded from the index. Green bonds receive a one-band upgrade, except in cases they were already in band 1.

As neither Sustainalytics nor RepRisk takes democracy into consideration, Russia's government bonds were likely not weighted down, whereas countries that issued green bonds, be they democratic or not, probably received higher weights. Although I could not access the exact weights of each country, I can easily imagine that Poland, called by the *Financial Times* in 2019 "the most frequent sovereign issuer of debt linked to climate and environmental projects,"[30] had a much higher weight in the JESG EMBI Index than in the EMBI Index.

By the beginning of March 2022, J.P. Morgan announced that it would exclude Russia from all its fixed-income indexes on March 31, following similar actions by other index providers.[31] It was already too late; the ESG correction had not prevented investors from the downside of being exposed to an autocratic government. In fact, they were overexposed to it.

The same happened in the equity market. Before February 24, 2022, Sberbank, a Kremlin-backed bank already subjected to sanctions, had higher ESG ratings than some Western banks, according to a Reuters report.[32] MSCI and Sustainalytics had improved their ESG scores for Sberbank as late as December 2021, according to the same article. Although Russia's invasion has some ESG raters making methodological revisions, Meggin Thwing Eastman, head of ESG Research at MSCI, said that "many emerging markets (EM) investors still want exposure to countries despite their sometimes poor human rights records."[33]

ESG scores pay little to no attention to democracy. I reviewed several popular books on the subject, including *Your Essential Guide to Sustainable Investing* and *The ESG Investing Handbook*, and they do not so much as mention the word *democracy*, though they do include some cousins of democracy, such as human rights in one case and corruption in the other. The same pattern emerges for the methodologies of the main ESG score providers. Miranda Cortizo and Connor Fernandez, from my research team, found that S&P Global mentions corruption, bribery, and human rights as part of the S of ESG.[34] RepRisk mentions human rights abuses and corporate complicity in S, and corruption, bribery, extortion, and money laundering in the G.[35] MSCI mentions corruption and human rights, but does not include them in their ESG key issues.[36] Sustainalytics does not mention any of these.[37]

The authors of the "Aggregate Confusion" paper went through the pain of deconstructing ESG ratings. For the six ESG score providers that they analyzed, the authors looked at the combined 709 indicators used and grouped them into 64 different categories. Among the categories are Access to Basic Services, Unions, and Water, as well as Human Rights and Corruption. We found no mention of the word *democracy*.[38]

That democracy is not an essential part of ESG is clear from the creation of the One Planet Sovereign Wealth Funds Group in 2017.[39] Founded by the sovereign wealth funds (SWF) of Abu Dhabi, Kuwait, New Zealand, Norway, Saudi Arabia, and Qatar, this coalition's goal is to "accelerate efforts to integrate financial risks and opportunities related to climate change in the management of large, long-term asset pools." As it happens, four out of these six countries are autocratic.

To argue that ESG investing completely excludes democracy would not be entirely fair, as there are many ways to implement sustainability and ESG strategies. For example, some participants in the sovereign bond market use the World Bank's World Governance Indicator (WGI) to measure governance. The Chartered Financial Analysts (CFA) Institute "Guidance and Case Studies for ESG Integration: Equities and Fixed Income" report of 2018 offers insights on how ESG is implemented in practice in the fixed-income market.[40]

In two cases, those of PIMCO, the biggest bond house in the world, and global government bond manager Colchester Global Investors, portfolio managers use the WGI to approach the G of ESG. The WGI includes a set of six indicators: voice of accountability, political stability and absence of violence/terrorism, government effectiveness, regulatory quality, rule of law, and control of corruption. While not measuring democracy directly—for instance, there is no measure linked to the sanctity of the electoral process—the WGI includes many factors that are concomitant with more democratic countries.

However, Franco Nuñez, one of my research team members, estimated that the correlation between the WGI and the three main democracy indexes, Freedom House, V-Dem, and the Economist Intelligence Unit, is relatively low, ranging between 49.7 percent and 56.9 percent. That is, the WGI is not only an imperfect indicator of democracy on paper because it does not include measures of freedom, the quality of the electoral process, the division of powers, and other hallmarks of liberal democracy, but it is also not a good indicator in practice.

This deficiency aside, the case studies included in the CFA's report indicate that this approach decreased the exposure of these asset managers to nondemocratic government bonds. Colchester Global Investors, for instance, decreased its exposure to Russian bonds due to Russia's low rank in the WGI, despite considering that it had a strong balance sheet. In this case, governance considerations led them to reduce their exposure to Russia.

Some financial institutions and market participants include measures more directly linked to democratic standards, such as press freedom. Examples include German insurer Allianz GE, which incorporates press freedom in its ESG framework for emerging markets, according to a report in Bloomberg. International bank BNP Paribas SA also includes press freedom among its ESG criteria.[41] Nordic countries' asset managers seem to be at the forefront of including democracy in their investment decisions. For example, public pension Industriens Pension from Denmark sold its Myanmar and Belarus government bonds at the beginning of 2021 over human rights considerations, according to a *Responsible Investor* report.[42]

In my view, these actions are not enough and more needs to be done. Investors have committed billions, if not trillions, of dollars into financing dictators or wannabe autocrats, or to companies connected to them, sometimes unknowingly or unwillingly, because the countries and companies in question are part of benchmark indices. ESG can't stop investors' money from financing dictators and aspiring autocrats, but inasmuch as protecting the environment is now a core value for Western countries, democracy is also a core value of these countries.

Despite democracy's recent backslide around the world, even in Western countries, polls from the Pew Research Center show that "public commitment to representative democracy is highest in countries that have a well-functioning democracy."[43] Pew found that the percentage of the population committed to representative democracy closely correlates with the Economist Intelligence Unit's Democracy Index.

According to Pew's research, the countries classified as more fully democratic and with higher commitment to representative democracy are also wealthier countries, such as the Western developed countries and Australia. Most of the pools of money that have been financing autocracies and wannabe autocrats, from pension funds to individual investors, originate from these countries. The irony cannot be lost: investors in democratic countries are financing the undermining of democratic standards elsewhere. I do not think this is what investors want.

Moreover, Russia's invasion of Ukraine shows that the danger of autocrats is not restricted to the populations in their own countries. The rise in food and energy prices around the world following the invasion brings the impact of autocracy closer to home. Something must be done about this, and in my view, it can be done in the context of ESG standards.

How to Add Democracy's D to ESG

To add a D to ESG, we first need reliable measures of democracy, or else we would only add noise to already noisy ESG scores. Box 9.1 includes my summary of how three of the main democracy indices that are publicly available are constructed: Varieties of Democracy (V-Dem), the Economist Intelligence Unit (EIU), and Freedom House (FH).

Democracy indices start from a conceptualization of democracy that draws from the insight of one of the most prominent political scientists of all time, Robert A. Dahl of Yale. Essentially, Dahl argues that "democracy consists of two attributes—contestation or competition and participation or inclusion."[44] Democracy indexes rely on tens of indicators to measure these two attributes of a democracy. The differences between them are in the measurement and aggregation of these attributes; the Economist Intelligence Unit, for instance, uses public opinion surveys, mainly the World Values Survey, in addition to expert assessments. The indexes also differ on whether additional attributes are included, such as property rights, which the EIU and FH include.

BOX 9.1 How the Three Main Democracy Indexes Are Constructed

The Economist Intelligence Unit's (EIU) Democracy Index[45]

Scope: 164 countries.

Since when and how often: Every two years since 2006, and then annually since 2010.

Measured categories: Democracy is measured by the level of fulfillment of five interrelated categories: electoral process and pluralism, civil liberties, the functioning of government, political participation, and political culture.

Number of indicators used: 60, which take the form of a 60-question survey where the possible answers are 1, 0.5, or 0.

Aggregation rules: Each category receives a score from 0 to 10, with 0 being the least democratic score and 10 the most democratic score. Four indicators have more influence on the final score of each category: whether national elections are free and fair, the security of voters, the influence of foreign powers on government, and the capability of the civil service to implement policies. If the answer to one of these questions is 0, a full point is subtracted from the corresponding category's score; if an answer is 0.5, a half point is subtracted. The overall democracy score comes from the average of the five categories.

Democracy scores: 0 to 10, with higher scores meaning a more democratic country.

Country classification: Countries that score between 0 and 3.99 points are classified as Authoritarian Regimes; those that score between 4 and 5.99 are Hybrid Regimes; those between 6 and 7.99 are Flawed Democracies; and those that score 8 points or more are considered Full Democracies.

(continued)

Freedom House's Freedom in the World Index[46]

Scope: 195 countries and 15 territories (as of 2022).

Since when and how often: Annually since 1973.

Measured categories: Two categories are measured: political rights and civil liberties. Inside the political rights category there are three subcategories: electoral process, political pluralism and participation, and functioning of government. Civil liberties has four subcategories: freedom of expression and belief, associational and organizational rights, rule of law, and personal autonomy and individual rights.

Number of indicators used: 26, including 10 indicators to measure political rights, 15 indicators to measure civil liberties, and 1 discretionary question that addresses forced democratic change, which is added to the political rights category.

Aggregation rules: Each indicator can rank between 0 and 4 points; therefore, the maximum score for political rights is 40, and the maximum score for civil liberties is 60. Up to 4 points may be subtracted from the political rights, depending on the gravity of the situation in the forced democratic change question. The total score is the addition of the political rights and the civil liberties scores.

Democracy scores: 0 to 100, with 100 being the maximum degree of freedom possible.

Country classification: Freedom House classifies countries as Free, Partly Free, or Not Free, depending on combinations of the two main scores. To construct these combinations, each category is divided into seven; for example, the civil liberties score runs from 0 to 7, 8 to 16, 17 to 25, and so on. Ten combinations of political rights (PR) scores and civil liberties (CL) scores classify a country as Not Free: CL 7 or lower and PR 23 or lower (four combinations), CL 8 to 16 and PR 17 or lower (three combinations), CL 17 to 25 and PR 11 or lower (two combinations), and CL 26 to 34 and PR 5 or lower (one combination).

Varieties of Democracy (V-Dem) Index[47]

Scope: 202 countries (as of 2022).

Since when and how often: Annually since 1789.

Measured categories: Five categories of democracy are measured through different indices: a liberal democracy index (LDI), an electoral democracy index (EDI), an egalitarian component index, a participatory component index, and a deliberative component index. This book mainly considers the LDI.

Number of indicators used: 470, of which 369 are coded from 1900 to date, and 260 are coded from 1789 to 1900.[48] The index uses 3,700 country experts. The LDI is based on 71 indicators, which include those measured in the EDI and others which determine the liberal component index (ex: judicial and legislative constrains on the executive, equality before the law and individual liberties).

Aggregation rules: A complicated formula that includes additive and multiplicative factors. The multiplicative factors are included to take into account that without elections there is no democracy.

Democracy scores: 0 to 3 in the LDI, with 0 being a closed autocracy and 3 being a liberal democracy.

Country classification: Based on the Regimes of the World (RoW) categorization: Two forms of democracy (Liberal and Electoral) and two types of autocracies (Electoral and Closed).

The measurement of democracy is not without controversy. In a paper published in 2002, Gerardo Munck and Jay Verkuilen analyzed nine democracy indexes, including the one issued by Freedom House. The authors concluded that "no single index offers a satisfactory response to all three challenges of conceptualization, measurement, and aggregation" (of democracy.)[49] The authors have a particularly harsh review of Freedom House's index, which I use extensively in this book. They criticize the index's conceptualization of democracy, its measurement of the attributes of democracy, and its aggregation rule.

Importantly, though, the authors find that the correlation between the nine indexes they analyze is very high; "they seem to show that the reviewed indices are tapping into the same fundamental underlying realities."[50] My research team calculated the correlation for the three indices used in this book and reached the same conclusion: it is very high, between 87.2 percent and 94 percent.

We can then rest assured that the most-often-used democracy indices are very consistent in measuring the level of democracy around the world. Consistency extends to one crucial aspect for investors: The three democracy indices are highly consistent when they single out a country as nondemocratic.

I consider nondemocratic countries those that are labeled in the two lowest categories: Electoral Autocracies and Closed Autocracies by V-Dem, Partly Free and Not Free by FH, and Hybrid Regimes and Authoritarian Regimes by EIU. Given that FH has three categories and V-Dem and EIU have four each, this division is somewhat unfair to some countries that FH labels Partly Free. The distribution of countries in their samples illustrates why: while FH includes 57.4 percent of the countries covered in the Partly Free and Not Free categories, V-Dem includes 50.3 percent of the countries covered in the Electoral Autocracies and Closed Autocracies categories, and EIU includes 55.1 percent of the countries covered in the Hybrid Regimes and Authoritarian Regimes categories. This divergence does not change the usefulness of these indices.

The resemblance in how the three indices categorize countries as nondemocratic is striking. The categorization is clear-cut for countries such as China, but importantly, also where forces are in the process of undermining democracy. Let's consider the classifications of the countries included as examples in this book: Argentina, Bolivia, Brazil, China, Ecuador, Hungary, Russia, Türkiye, and Venezuela, using data from 2006 to date:*

- **Argentina:** Considered an Electoral Democracy by V-Dem, a Free country by FH, and a Flawed Democracy by EIU

---

* In all cases the years indicated correspond to the year of the publication of the reports by FH, EIU and V-Dem."

from 2006 to 2022. Though I think the indices missed the deterioration of democracy under the Kirchners' rule, they are consistent.

- **Bolivia:** Considered an Electoral Democracy by V-Dem from 2006 to 2018, an Electoral Autocracy in 2019 and 2020, and an Electoral Democracy again in 2021. It was considered Partly Free by FH since 2006, and a Hybrid Regime by EIU in all years since 2006, except for 2008 and 2009, when it ranked it as a Flawed Democracy.

- **Brazil:** Considered an Electoral Democracy by V-Dem, a Free country by FH, and a Flawed Democracy by EIU from 2006 to 2022. The same considerations as Argentina apply here. The scores dropped in all indices, but the categorizations did not change under Bolsonaro's rule.

- **China:** Considered a Closed Autocracy by V-Dem, Not Free by FH, and an Authoritarian Regime by EIU since 2006.

- **Ecuador:** Considered an Electoral Democracy by V-Dem since 2006, although its Liberal Democracy Index declined significantly during Correa's term. It was considered Partly Free until 2021 by FH, and Free since then. It was considered a Hybrid Regime until 2016 by EIU, a Flawed Democracy from 2017 to 2020, and then a Hybrid Regime again in 2021 by EIU.

- **Hungary:** Considered a Flawed Democracy by EIU since 2006, albeit with lower scores over time. It was ranked as Free by FH until 2018, and Partly Free since then. In the same year, V-Dem downgraded it from an Electoral Democracy to an Electoral Autocracy.

- **Russia:** Considered an Electoral Autocracy by V-Dem since 2006, Not Free by FH since 2006, a Hybrid Regime by EIU from 2006 to 2010, and since then an Authoritarian Regime.

- **Türkiye:** Considered an Electoral Democracy by V-Dem until 2012 and then an Electoral Autocracy, Partly Free by FH until 2017 and Not Free since then, and a Hybrid Regime by EIU since 2006.

- **Venezuela:** Considered an Electoral Autocracy by V-Dem since 2006, Partly Free by FH until 2016 and then Not Free, and a Hybrid Regime by EIU until 2016 and then an Authoritarian Regime.

I propose the following rule: if at least two of the three democracy indices give a country one of their two lowest rankings, the country should be labeled as "Nondemocratic." Based on the examples that I have included in this book, I believe we can be confident that the classification is correct. This guidance resembles the rules of inclusion into the Bloomberg Barclays Global Aggregate Index, which requires countries to have IG status based on the middle rating of Fitch, Moody's, and S&P, and by the FTSE World Government Bond Index (WGBI), which requires countries to be at least A– by S&P and A3 by Moody's (see Chapter 3).

If we followed this rule, of the countries included previously, the ones that would be considered Nondemocratic, or Autocratic, are Bolivia since 2010, China since the beginning of the indices' measures (2006 is the earliest year in which the three democracy indices were available), Ecuador from 2006 to 2020, Hungary since 2018, and Russia, Türkiye, and Venezuela since 2006. If a rule like this one had been applied since 2006, markets would have refrained from helping to consolidate the power of Chávez, Orbán, Erdoğan, Putin, Correa, and Morales.

If we consider all the countries that are part of the Emerging Market Bond Index Global (EMBI)[*,51] and the Morgan Stanley Global Emerging Markets Equity Index[†,52] the countries that would meet our criteria of being labeled autocratic, besides those previously mentioned, are: Saudi Arabia, United Arab Emirates, Kuwait, Qatar, Côte d'Ivoire, Thailand, Pakistan, Nigeria, Morocco, Malaysia, Lebanon and Egypt since 2006, Tunisia from 2006 to 2013 and in

---

* Argentina, Brazil, Bulgaria, Chile, China, Colombia, Côte d'Ivoire, Croatia, Dominican Republic, Ecuador, Egypt, El Salvador, Hungary, Lebanon, Malaysia, Mexico, Morocco, Nigeria, Pakistan, Panama, Peru, Philippines, Poland, Russia, South Africa, Thailand, Tunisia, Türkiye, Ukraine, Uruguay, and Venezuela.
† Brazil, Chile, China, Colombia, Czech Republic, Egypt, Greece, Hungary, India, Indonesia, Korea, Kuwait, Malaysia, Mexico, Peru, Philippines, Poland, Qatar, Saudi Arabia, South Africa, Taiwan, Thailand, Türkiye, and United Arab Emirates.

DO ESG METRICS ACCOUNT FOR DEMOCRACY STANDARDS?

2021, Ukraine since 2010, Philippines since 2018, El Salvador since 2019, India since 2020, and Mexico in 2021. If we analyze Morgan Stanley's Frontier Market Index,* the countries that are considered autocratic are Kazakhstan, Kenya, Bahrain, Morocco, Jordan, Oman, Bangladesh, Pakistan, Nigeria and Vietnam since 2006, Serbia since 2018, Tunisia from 2006 to 2013 and in 2021, and Sri Lanka from 2006 to 2014.

Thus, one way to add the D of democracy to ESG would be to exclude those countries that are labeled as nondemocratic by at least two of the three main publicly available democracy index providers from bond and stock indices, such as the EMBI Global, the EMBI Global Diversified, and the MSCI Emerging Markets Stock Index, or at least of their ESG versions. Implementing what I call DESG indices, with ESG criteria augmented to include democracy considerations, would generate more alternatives for investors. Some readers of this book saw what I am proposing as a strengthening of the S factor (for companies) and the G factor (for sovereign issuers) in ESG; I could rephrase my proposal as creating ESG+ indices, with the S and the G enhanced to include democracy considerations.

As I stress in several parts of this book, a big part of the individual's and institutional investor's money deployed into nondemocratic countries is by way of their adherence to benchmark portfolios like these. I explore this and more options to avoid this pitfall in the next and final chapter.

---

* Croatia, Estonia, Iceland, Lithuania, Kazakhstan, Romania, Serbia, Slovenia, Kenya, Mauritius, Morocco, Nigeria, Tunisia, West African Economic and Monetary Union, Bahrain, Jordan, Oman, Bangladesh, Pakistan, Sri Lanka, and Vietnam.

KEY TAKEAWAYS OF CHAPTER 9

This chapter:

- Reviews the impressive growth of ESG investing and discusses its drivers and controversies, including why many participants want it overhauled.

- Argues that ESG criteria do not account for democracy standards and why they should.

- Shows that major democracy index providers, namely Freedom House, the Economist Intelligence Unit, and V-Dem, are very consistent in their rankings of nondemocratic countries.

- Proposes a rule to add the D of democracy to ESG and create DESG or ESG+ indices by excluding countries that receive one of the two lowest possible democracy ratings from at least two of the major democracy index providers.

CHAPTER 10

WHAT CAN BE DONE TO ADD A D TO ESG?

Individual investors, financial advisors, portfolio managers, index and ESG providers, rating agencies, and regulators have a job to do.

What Can Index Providers and ESG Score Providers Do?

Individual investors, financial advisors, and portfolio managers would have a much easier time avoiding pouring their money into autocratic governments and firms in autocratic countries if the equity and bond index providers introduced democracy consideration to their indices. An important step in that direction would be to amend or to expand the ESG-adjusted bond and stock indices to take democracy into account, introducing DESG or ESG+ indices. J.P. Morgan's bond index suite, for instance, has an incredible number of bond indices, with varying types of countries (developed, emerging), bonds (local currency, foreign currency), geographies (China, Asia, United Kingdom), and issuers (governments, corporations). In total, J.P. Morgan's index composition page lists 83 indices.[1] Of these, 35 are ESG versions of the original indices. The suite includes the EMBI Global Diversified and the ESG EMBI Global Diversified, the GBI-EM Global Diversified, and the ESG GBI-EM Global Diversified indices, and so on. There are green bond indices as well. J.P. Morgan created the ESG Index Suite (JESG; see Chapter 9) in April 2018 by introducing the JESG suite of emerging market bond indices.[2] Later, the firm added other ESG indices to its product suite. Altogether, by January 2021 they covered 6,000 global corporate and quasi-sovereigns and 173 sovereigns.

As a reminder, J.P. Morgan's EMBI Global Diversified, the most widely followed emerging markets government bond index with $306 billion of AUM tracking it as of April 2018,[3] is heavily weighted toward nondemocratic countries. In Chapter 9, I defined nondemocratic countries as those that are classified in the lowest two democracy categories by at least two democracy indices. In June 2019, of the 67 countries included in the index,[4] 35 were nondemocratic, and they represented 45.2 percent of the index. Moreover, 16 of them were rated in the worst category by at least two of the three main democracy index providers, and they represented 24 percent of the index.[5]

It's a similar story elsewhere, including MSCI's equity and bond indices. By the end of 2022, MSCI had five ESG integration equity indices and five ESG integration fixed-income indices, two of which were in partnership with Bloomberg and Barclays. In addition, MSCI had 10 equity indices in the "ESG Values" and "Screens and Impact" categories, and three indices in the fixed-income market in these same categories.[6] Yet, to the best of my knowledge, none of these factor in democracy.

As a consequence, many popular Emerging Market ETFs that track these indices are full of nondemocratic countries in their portfolios. As for some of the most popular ETFs in this segment, BlackRock's iShares J.P. Morgan USD Emerging Market Bonds ETF (EMB) was the largest by AUM as of year-end 2022, according to ETF.COM.[7] The fund's biggest holdings in December 2022 were Türkiye (4.28 percent), Saudi Arabia (4.09 percent), Brazil (3.69 percent), Qatar (3.59 percent), Philippines (3.58 percent), Dominican Republic (3.28 percent), Mexico (3.2 percent), Indonesia (3.16 percent), Colombia (3.21 percent), and the Sultanate of Oman (2.94 percent).[8] Of these 10 countries, which represented 34.93 percent of the portfolio, five were ranked as nondemocratic, representing more than half of the 34.93 percent.

Another popular emerging markets government bonds ETF, according to ETF.COM, is Vanguard's Emerging Markets

Government Bond ETF (VWOB).[9] It tracks the performance of Bloomberg USD Emerging Markets Government RIC Capped Index. As of mid-2022 it had 59.7 percent of its portfolio invested in 10 countries, of which 6 were nondemocratic (Saudi Arabia, Türkiye, United Arab Emirates, Qatar, China, and the Philippines), representing 60 percent of the 59.7 percent.[10]

In my view, index providers should let investors decide whether they want to add a D to the ESG portfolio. In the sovereign debt market, index providers should add DESG or ESG+ indices to their product suites. These indices could replicate their ESG indices except for the exclusion of autocratic, or at least of highly autocratic countries, as I will define below. In the equity market, they could exclude companies of highly autocratic countries and quasi-sovereign companies of autocratic and highly autocratic countries. Quasi-sovereigns, as we saw in the cases of Venezuela and Russia, are pawns used by their governments to achieve certain domestic or international political goals often not in the best interests of a healthy democracy.

Index providers, in turn, would have it much easier if ESG score providers accounted for democracy in their scores. They could, in addition to their ESG scores, provide DESG or ESG+ scores. For sovereign bond DESG or ESG+ scores they could supplement the use of the World Bank's World Governance Indicators (WGI) with a democracy measure. One way to do this could be to imitate J.P. Morgan's rule for its ESG corrected indices (JESG; see Chapter 9). As a first step, they could build five bands according to the G score, as indicated by the WGI index. Then, autocratic countries could be lowered by, say, one band, and highly autocratic countries by two bands. Countries in the lowest G band would be given the lowest total ESG scores. Let no good performance in the E and the S compensate for the fact that they are autocratic or highly autocratic countries.

In terms of DESG or ESG+ scores for companies, the methodology needs to much be more elaborate. Asking companies in sectors such as energy and mining to avoid nondemocratic countries would be naive. However, sectors like consumer staples may have more potential to be dissuaded from activities such as expanding into nondemocratic countries just because sourcing there is cheaper or because they offer large captive markets. The case is even more compelling in sectors such as electronics and technology, which pose potential security threats. One first step could be that DESG and ESG+ score providers display information about the percentage of sales and investment made by each company in democratic, autocratic, and highly autocratic countries. As Jianli Yang, president of Citizen Power Initiatives for China, and Alvaro Piaggio, Senior Policy Officer at the Human Rights Foundation, stated, "Providing consumers and investors an independent, systematic rating of companies and their commitment to human rights will empower people to effect meaningful change around the world."[11]

What Can Governments and Regulators Do?

Governments and regulators can also play a bigger role in deterring investors from financing autocrats, or at least the worst democracy offenders among them. One way is through sanctions. The United States and Europe increasingly rely on sanctions to deal with autocratic regimes, but sanctions packages are often sparse in their bans on bond and equity issuance and investment. Even when more restrictive bans are included, they always seem to be added to sanctions packages after it's too late.

Sanctions, boycotts, and embargoes have been part of US history since the American Revolution. In 1774, the First Continental Congress met in Philadelphia and pushed for a strong response to the British Parliament's Coercive Acts. The acts consisted of four laws following the Boston Tea Party, where protesters gathered to protest the British imposing "taxation without representation." To show their opposition, protesters dumped tea imported from the British East India Company into Boston Harbor. The 12 delegations participating in Philadelphia pledged to prohibit popular consumption of British goods, followed by nonexportation of American commodities to Britain in 1775.[12] Soon after what became the United States won its independence, President Thomas Jefferson blocked British and French imports to push back against their interference in trade with the Embargo Act of 1807.[13] All this is to say that sanctions, boycotts, and embargoes are ingrained in the US political and foreign policy traditions, and as such it is not surprising to see that their use is rising, regardless of their efficacy.

During the 1990s, the United States used some form of unilateral sanctions against 35 countries, compared to 20 in the 1980s.[14] According to Daniel W. Drezner, professor of International Politics in the Fletcher School of Law and Diplomacy at Tufts University, sanctions have become the United States' most important tool in the last decade.[15] President Barack Obama designated an average of 500 entities for sanctions per year during his first term, which President Donald Trump then nearly doubled during his term.[16] The 2021 US Treasury Sanctions Review identified 9,421 sanction designations in 2021, compared to 921 in 2000.[17]

Sanctions applied by the United States and other governments can take many forms. Broad-based or country-based sanctions prohibit transactions with an entire country and its people. Targeted sanctions, which are much more popular today, are aimed at specific actors.[18] Examples are the visa bans and asset freezes authorized by the Magnitsky and the Global Magnitsky laws (see Chapter 5). Commercial sanctions restrict trade. Financial sanctions restrict financial flows and/or freeze assets. Personal sanctions restrict people. Additionally, primary sanctions restrict citizens and companies of the country imposing sanctions from doing business with sanctioned companies or individuals. Secondary sanctions also prohibit doing business with any third party doing business with the sanctioned companies and individuals.[19]

As the use of sanctions has become more prevalent, so have concerns about their efficacy. Experts argue that they are used too often,[20] that they are used in "aggressive and counterproductive ways,"[21] that they are ineffective,[22] and that they cause excessive harm to the local population,[23] among other critiques.

One key issue to assess the efficacy of sanctions is to discuss what they are aimed at. Are they imposed for containment, to limit the power of another state, or are they imposed for compellence, to change the other state's behavior? That is, are they imposed to make the life of the sanctioned persons or countries more difficult, or are they imposed to spur the sanctioned to act in a different way? In general, sanctions seem to be more effective in making life more difficult, rather than in altering the behavior of the sanctioned. There is unanimity, though, that when taken in a coordinated global manner, they are significantly more effective, as they are more difficult to eschew.

In any case, what is clear is that sanctions that restrict the sale and/or the trading of government bonds of countries that slip into autocracy are seldom implemented or are imposed when it is too late. I discussed Venezuela's case in Chapter 2 and Russia's in Chapter 5.

Executive Order 13808, which prohibited the purchase of Venezuela's sovereign and quasi-sovereign bonds, was issued in August 2017. At the time, V-Dem had considered Venezuela an Electoral Autocracy since 2003, Freedom House had it as Partly Free since 1999, and the Economic Intelligence Unit had it as a Hybrid Regime since the beginning of the index in 2006. In 2016, Freedom House changed Venezuela's status to Not Free, and the EIU changed its status to an Authoritarian Regime in 2017. In addition, since 2006, the top echelons of Venezuela's government were subject to sanctions due to drug trafficking, anti-terrorism efforts, and anti-democratic actions.

In Russia's case, in April 2021 the Department of the Treasury Directive 1, issued under Executive Order 14024, prohibited US financial institutions from "participation in the primary market for ruble or non-ruble denominated bonds issued after June 14, 2021 by the Central Bank of the Russian Federation, the National Wealth Fund of the Russian Federation, or the Ministry of Finance of the Russian Federation."[24] The primary market refers to the issuance and sale of securities to purchasers directly by the issuer, in which the issuer receives the proceeds of the bond sale from the purchaser. That is, Directive 1 still allowed trading in the secondary market, the market for the purchase and sale of securities that are already in the market, by any party. The prohibition of participation of US financial institutions in the secondary markets of the same bonds was only implemented by Directive 1A in March 2022, after Russia's invasion of Ukraine.[25]

Belarus is another case. Highly autocratic, V-Dem has rated Belarus as an Electoral Autocracy since 1996, Freedom House has rated it Not Free since 1996, and EIU has rated it an Authoritarian Regime since it started its ratings in 2006. Aleksandr Lukashenko, called "Europe's last dictator,"[26] won free and fair elections in 1994. Following the autocrat script seen repeatedly in this book, two years later he proposed changes to the constitution that would have given him unlimited powers. Parliament resisted his move, and Lukashenko answered by dissolving it, after which he removed presidential term limits by (a rigged) referendum.[27] He then stuck to the autocrat script by closing independent media, jailing political opponents, and rigging elections. In the meantime, he made Belarus a pawn of Russia.

In June 2006, President George W. Bush issued Executive Order 14038, which froze the assets of the persons "responsible for, or to have participated in, actions or policies that undermine democratic processes or institutions in Belarus." Executive Order 14028 also froze the assets of the persons "responsible for, or to have participated in, human rights abuses related to political repression in Belarus" and the persons who were close to them, such as close family members or that have assisted them.[28] By "persons," the Executive Order means individuals or entities.

The sanctions were imposed after the elections of March 19, 2006, in which Lukashenko won with 83 percent of the votes.[29] The elections were seen as "severely flawed" by European observers[30] and a farce by independent observers.[31] The results were not recognized by Europe or by the US government. But even after the sanctions, and for many years now, Belarus has been an active participant in the international sovereign debt market, issuing $3.3 billion of debt, equivalent to no less than 6 percent of its GDP. The bonds were placed in June 2017 ($1,400 million), in February 2018 ($600 million) and in June 2020 ($1,250 million). The bonds are Reg S or Rule 144A, which means, as I will explain, that they end up in the portfolios of institutional and individual investors of developed economies. The bonds also have ratings by the major credit rating agencies.

After the August 9, 2020, presidential election, which opposition candidate Svetlana Tikhanovskaya claimed was stolen from her,[32] Standard & Poor's changed the outlook of Belarus's debt from neutral to negative, citing "growing risks for the financial stability of the banking system of the republic."[33] However, Standard & Poor's kept Belarus's B rating, which it did not downgrade to CCC until after Russia's invasion of Ukraine. Meeting the criteria set by J.P. Morgan, which include having credit ratings, Belarus sovereign bonds have made it to some emerging market bond indices. By April 2018, Belarus government bonds represented 0.4 percent of the EMBI Global Diversified bond index.[34]

Despite Belarus being a dictatorship since 1996 and the top echelons of its government being sanctioned since 2006, the US government did not prohibit the financing of Belarus until December 2021, and even then, the restriction was limited. Directive 1 under Executive Order 14038 prohibited US persons from "all transactions in, provision of financing for, and other dealings in new debt with a maturity of greater than 90 days issued on or after December 2, 2021, by the Ministry of Finance of the Republic of Belarus or the Development Bank of the Republic of Belarus."[35]

That is, financing Belarus's government at maturities below 90 days was still permitted at the beginning of 2023, which does not look good in light of Belarus's involvement in Russia's war with Ukraine.[36] Trading Belarus's bonds in the secondary market is also permitted. I woke up to that during lunch in Buenos Aires in mid-2022. I was discussing Argentina's outlook with a senior emerging markets portfolio manager of a big investment house, whom I've known for years, when he was interrupted by a call to discuss a Belarus trade. After he hung up, I asked why on earth was he investing in Belarus. His answer was simply, "It is in the index," referring to one of J.P. Morgan's Emerging Market indices.

These examples show that extending sanctions to the issuance and trading of sovereign bonds is common sense. As one seasoned emerging markets investor suggested to me, sanctions should be implemented in a specific order. The issuance of new bonds and stocks should be prohibited first. Thereafter, stocks and bonds should be prohibited from secondary market trading in a second round. This way, the autocrat would not be able to receive new money, and at least initially, sanctions would avoid harming investors who in good faith had bonds and stocks of that country in their portfolios. If the autocrat resorts to indirect ways of placing new bonds, such as Venezuela (see Chapter 2), secondary trading should be prohibited immediately.

Perhaps there is an easier way to put sovereign bonds issued by nondemocratic states off limits to investors than by ad hoc sanctions imposed by executive orders. That way consists in changing the regulations by which these bonds finally make it to the investor's portfolios.

Currently, most of the sovereign bonds issued by democratic and nondemocratic governments alike are documented under the 144A/Reg S or Reg S only formats.

To put it succinctly: "Reg S and Rule 144A bonds are types of bonds allowing the issuer to issue these without the need to register them under the Securities Act of 1933. The two rules are defined as follows: Under the Rule 144A, Qualified Institutional Buyers (QIBs) can trade debt securities without registration and review by the Securities and Exchange Commission (SEC). The Reg S bond type is available for offers and trades of securities outside of the USA to non-US investors."[37]

In the United States, the Securities Exchange Commission (SEC) requires securities offered to individual investors meet disclosure requirements, to ensure that all investors are treated equally and fairly, but registering a new bond issue with the SEC is a lengthy and costly process. Documenting a bond issue under the 144A format allows issuers to do without the lengthy disclosure and registration process as required by the Securities Act of 133 in order to be able to offer the security to US retail investors, and offer the securities instead to institutional investors (Rule 144A) and to non-US investors (Reg S) with lower disclosure requirements. As a result, they can issue securities, bonds in this case, faster, less expensively, and with lesser regular financial data-reporting requirements over the life of the bond as is required for SEC-registered bond issues. A consequence is that individual investors based in the United States end up owning these bonds through mutual funds, which are QIBs under the 144A definitions, among other vehicles.

As an alternative to sanctions implemented through executive orders, I believe the SEC could exclude government bonds from nondemocratic countries, as established by a special law passed for this purpose, from Reg S and Rule 144A and from any other documentation process. For a measure like this to be effective and to avoid undermining the role of the US dollar in the global economy, it should be also adopted by other financial centers like London, Luxembourg, Dublin, Frankfurt, and Zurich.

Whether extending the sanctions to sovereign bond issuance and trading once the top political figures of a regime have been sanctioned is the right thing to do is at least worth a serious debate. After all, the power and legitimacy of autocrats comes from their economic success. As outlined in this book, they most often come to power during economic hardship, in which the traditional parties lose credibility. And they all deliver at least a few years of solid economic expansion of consumption and production, be it due to their own merit, to improved commodity prices, or to the implementation of unsustainable economic policies.

Whatever way they achieve economic success, this book shows that markets have always been on the side of autocrats, oiling the government machinery by which they bought media outlets, expanded surveillance operations, undermined human rights, gained the favor of voters through patronage and clientelism, engrossed their own purses, and financed their political campaigns. Restricting government bond issuance of autocratic countries or of countries that are falling into autocracy would surely harm the population, but it would stain the autocrat's image of success substantially more. By depriving them of funding, they would be forced to slash public spending and/ or to raise taxes, thereby harming their popularity.

What Can Individual Investors, Financial Advisors, and Portfolio Managers Do? A Do-It-Yourself Guide to Implementing DESG

The proposed changes to ESG scores, to bond and equity indices, and to government regulations can take a long time to materialize. In the meantime, individual investors, financial advisors, and portfolio managers have many strategies available to them to add the D of Democracy to ESG. The democracy data required to apply these strategies is publicly available from democracy index providers such as the EIU, Freedom House, and V-Dem. I will frame these DESG or ESG+ strategies for the equity and the fixed income markets in the context of the five most common ESG strategies,[38] which are:

1. **Exclusion.** This strategy consists in the exclusion from the portfolio of specific investments or classes of investments. Common examples include companies in the tobacco, weapons, and pornography industries, and companies that damage the environment. During the apartheid in South Africa, students in the United States pressured their universities to divest stocks of companies doing business in that country.

2. **Positive screening.** This strategy involves selecting a subset of companies from an industry or sector. The portfolio is

modified according to one of the following criteria: (a) best in class: companies that are the best performers according to a desired metric, for instance the apparel companies with the lowest carbon footprint;[39] (b) ESG momentum: increase the weight of companies that have improved their ESG scores, and vice versa; and (c) thematic investment: companies solving one specific ESG issue, such as the environment.

3. **ESG integration.** This strategy adds a layer of ESG criteria into the investment decision process.

4. **Impact investment.** This strategy is about targeting a specific project with a desired social or environmental impact. It is distinct from philanthropy, as there is an expectation of receiving a positive financial return.[40]

5. **Engagement, or active ownership.** This strategy involves actively engaging with the company management and through voting to induce a change in the company policy. To do so requires owning a meaningful proportion of the company shares.

I will relabel these strategies in the context of incorporating the D of Democracy to ESG and propose implementable actions as follows.

DESG Autocratic Exclusion

In this strategy, government bonds, SOE bonds and stocks, and even private company stocks and bonds from nondemocratic countries would be excluded from the DESG portfolio. In Chapter 9, I proposed to define "Nondemocratic" or "Autocratic" countries as those who are in the lowest two categories for at least two democracy indices.

A less restrictive alternative is to exclude only the countries that are highly autocratic from the DESG portfolios. I propose to define those countries that fall into the lowest category for at least two democracy indices as "Highly Autocratic": V-Dem's Closed Autocracy, which encompasses around 16.8 percent of the countries covered; Freedom House's Not Free, which includes 28.7 percent of the countries covered; and EIU's Authoritarian Regimes, which includes 34.1 percent of the countries covered. The different percentages of inclusion of countries in these categories by these democracy indices does not help, but the end result is logical. A rule like this would exclude from the DESG portfolios the stocks and corporate bonds from private companies, sovereign bonds, and SOE stocks and bonds from the worst democracy offender countries such as China, Egypt, Kuwait, Qatar, Saudi Arabia, United Arab Emirates, Kazakhstan, Bahrain, Jordan, Oman, Uzbekistan, Thailand, and Vietnam.

Sovereign Green Bonds, which are in vogue today, should also be considered in a DESG Autocratic Exclusion strategy. The 2021 World Bank-J.P. Morgan report "A New Dawn: Rethinking Sovereign ESG" praises the issuance of sovereign green and "labeled" bonds.[41] Labeled bonds are green, social, and sustainability (GSS) bonds, whose proceeds are earmarked to finance specific green, social, and sustainability projects. In theory, they are highly laudable. In practice, they could be used to greenwash funds for autocratic countries.

The total GSS bond market grew to $2.9 trillion by the end of June 2022, according to a September 2022 report by the Bank of International Settlements (BIS).[42] Sovereign GSS bond issuers started hitting the market later than corporate issuers and supranational issuers, such as the European Investment Bank. Poland and France were the first issuers of green sovereign bonds, as recently as in 2017. But by mid-2022 sovereign GSS issuers increased their share of the total GSS bond market to 7.5 percent, compared to 4.2 percent at the end of 2019. Sovereign green issuance accelerated in 2020–2021, with an average of $88 billion per month from August 2020 until September 2022. As of September 2022, 38 governments had issued GSS bonds and announced a green bond framework, in line with the International Capital Market Association (ICMA) principles, according to the BIS report.[43]

Beware: the sovereign GSS bond market could be used for greenwashing on a grand scale. In Chapter 4, I discussed the case of Türkiye, which issued a Green Bond almost a month before the 2023 presidential elections, and of Poland in Chapter 9. Hungary also issued Green Bonds, EUR 1.5 billion in 2020.[44] More generally, of the 35 countries that had issued GSS bonds by 2021 according to the World Bank–J.P. Morgan report, 11 were Autocratic, as defined in

Chapter 9, and 4 were Highly Autocratic, as defined in this chapter. Taken together, almost one-third of the GSS sovereign bond issuers were nondemocratic governments.

It is important to remember that money is fungible. Even if money earmarked for a green project is not used for other purposes, the fact that the financing for the green project exists frees opportunities in the budget for other government policies. In autocratic countries, such opportunities could include the financing of a repressive police force or a pliant media. Moreover, budgetary frameworks to assure GSS bond investors that the money raised is allocated to its stated purpose are generally weak, including in some countries in the European Union. For instance, proceeds from Green Bonds are usually allocated to finance projects initiated in past years, or to projects that do not look so green, as Hungary's 2020 Green Bond, which financed a diesel-fueled rail operation.[45] In my view, a DESG Autocratic Exclusion strategy should refrain from purchasing labeled sovereign bonds of Autocratic countries. A less restrictive alternative is to omit Green Bonds from Highly Autocratic countries, as defined in this chapter, from DESG portfolios.

In the equity market there is an ETF that helps implement a DESG exclusion strategy:* The Freedom 100 Emerging Markets Index (FRDM), managed by Life + Liberty Indexes.[46] Launched in May 2019, by March 2023 FRDM had nearly $424 million in assets under management (AUM). Its expense ratio is slightly lower than 0.5 percent.

Starting from a universe of stocks from 24 emerging market countries, filtered for their market size and liquidity, eligible countries are assigned weights based on freedom scores. The scores derive from 83 quantitative variables measuring personal and economic freedoms, using data from the Fraser Institute and Cato Institute.[47] This methodology leads Life +Liberty Indexes to exclude the companies of autocratic countries and SOEs, defined as companies with 20 percent or more state ownership. Only then does Life +Liberty

---

* Disclaimer: The mentioning of these products does not represent an offer to buy or a solicitation to sell any security or investment product. They are mentioned only for educational purposes. Also, any comment about past performance does not have any implications on future performance.

Indexes select the 100 securities from the freest emerging markets for the portfolio. The index and the fund are rebalanced annually each January.

As of March 2023, the country weights in FRDM were Taiwan 22.56 percent, South Korea 18.65 percent, Chile 18.01 percent, and Poland 13.08 percent, among its major exposures.[48] In contrast, BlackRock's iShares Core MSCI Emerging Markets ETF (IEMG) invested, at the same time, 29.4 percent in China, 16.03 percent in Taiwan, 14.03 percent in India, 12.32 percent in South Korea, among its major exposures.[49] The most notable difference between FRDM and IEMG arises from FRDM's exclusion of companies domiciled in autocratic countries such as China and Saudi Arabia and its larger allocations to freer countries such as Chile, South Korea, and Taiwan.

I interviewed Perth Tolle, the founder of Life + Liberty Indexes, in January 2023. She told me that Russia was naturally excluded from the ETF at inception given its nondemocratic nature. As a result, FRDM was not negatively affected when Russia invaded Ukraine. More generally, she believes "that countries with stronger rule of law, stronger institutions, and stronger protections for personal and economic freedoms do tend to have faster recoveries and better allocation of capital. They tend to be the safe havens in times of crisis."

Admittedly, it is harder to implement a DESG Autocratic Exclusion strategy in the case of multinational companies domiciled in developed countries. These often source part of their production and have important investments in autocratic countries, or they sell an important part of their production in them. It is difficult, at the moment, to get information about the investments multinational companies make in autocratic countries, except when these make well-publicized acquisitions in some of these countries. One notable example that came to light after Russia's invasion of Ukraine in 2022 was British Petroleum (BP). BP had an almost 20 percent stake in Rosneft, the giant state-controlled oil company.[50] Its divestiture following the invasion cost BP investors $25 billion. Investors in Société Générale, France's third largest bank, lost $3.3 billion after it announced that it would sell its controlling stake in Rosbank.

A positive change would occur if multinational companies domiciled in developed countries were to start reporting their investment positions in Nondemocratic countries and in Highly Autocratic ones;

ESG score providers could also help gather this information. The same applies to supra-national organizations such as the European Union (see Chapter 4) and the World Bank and the IMF (Chapter 7). In the same way as ESG tracks the environmental impact of the companies' supply chains, DESG should add an analysis of the democracy impact of their supply chains. For garment companies, for instance, this should include data on whether they source from forced Uyghurs' labor in Xinjiang, China.

Positive DESG Screening

There are many available alternatives to implement a Positive DESG Screening strategy:

1. **Best in class.** One possible strategy is to assemble portfolios of stocks or sovereign bonds of a determined percentage (e.g., 10 percent, 20 percent) of the most democratic countries as defined by a chosen democracy index, such as the one from the EIU or from Freedom House. This is the type of strategy implemented in the paper written by Xun Lei and Tomasz Wisniewski, mentioned in Chapter 8. In their case, they gave equal weights to the stock indices of the 10 percent more democratic countries, including developed, emerging, frontier, and stand-alone countries. In a best-in-class Positive DESG Screening strategy, the weights would be rebalanced at the end of the year, or whenever the selected democracy index provider releases a new democracy index. The percentage of countries included could change (e.g., 30 percent more democratic countries), and it could include all countries or be restricted, for instance, to Emerging Markets, or to non-developed countries.

2. **DESG momentum.** This strategy could be implemented by overweighting, relative to indices such as the MSCI Emerging Markets stock index, companies located in countries that have improved their democracy ratings during the past year, and underweighting the stocks of companies located in countries whose democracy ratings have deteriorated. In the case of the sovereign bond market, the overweighting and underweighting would be in relation

to any of J.P. Morgan's Emerging Market bond versions or to any other available sovereign bond index. In case the investor or the financial advisor wants to include developed countries, it would be in relationship to the FTSE World Government Bond Index (WGBI) or a similar index.

A nice feature of implementing a DESG momentum strategy in the sovereign bond market is that it would punish wannabe autocrats before it is too late. As it is clear from the multiple country episodes described in the book, democracy dies slowly, mostly in small steps. However, democracy indices keep good track of these steps, and a strategy that punishes countries whose democracy standards are deteriorating would deprive the aspiring autocrats of fresh funds to bankroll their ventures before they become full-fledged autocrats. In the same vein, this strategy would help countries that are improving their democratic standards by providing them with more and cheaper funding.

DESG Integration

To implement a DESG integration strategy, investors, financial advisors, and portfolio managers would have to add an extra layer beyond ESG to their security selection process, based on democracy indices. There is a relatively simple way to do this in the sovereign bond market.

In Chapter 9, I argued that sovereign institutional bond investors tend to use the World Bank's World Governance Indicators (WGI) to measure the G in ESG,[51] and that the WGI had a low correlation with the most commonly used democracy indices. That is, while not totally oblivious to some characteristics of liberal democracies, the WGI is an imperfect indicator of democracy. However, the WGI could be supplemented with a measure of democracy to build DESG scores.

The proposed methodology is similar, but simpler to implement, to the one I proposed for ESG providers earlier in this chapter: to imitate J.P. Morgan's procedure for its ESG corrected indices. The G score provided by ESG providers would be lowered by a predetermined percentage for Nondemocratic countries and by another, higher percentage, for Highly Autocratic countries (in both cases as defined in this book). If the resulting G score is below a preset threshold, the bond would be excluded from the portfolio. In case the investor or the financial advisor does not have access to the G scores, it could directly apply certain overweight and underweight rules to sovereign bonds, depending on whether the country is Democratic, Nondemocratic, or Highly Autocratic.

A similar rule could be applied in the equity market. In the case of equities, human rights considerations are included in the S of ESG. That is where democracy considerations should be integrated. In the equity space, there is an ETF that applies a democracy integration strategy: The Democracy International Fund (DMCY) managed by Democracy Investments.[52] Launched in March 2021, by the end of 2022 its AUM totaled nearly $5 million. As of April 2023, the AUM has more than doubled to over $11 million. The fund's net expense ratio is 0.5 percent. The fund invests in large and mid-capitalization stocks in largely developed countries (85 percent) as well as in emerging markets, but it excludes the United States.

DMCY does not exclude autocratic countries, as is the case of FRDM, but it overweights democracies and underweights authoritarian states.[53] The starting universe of stocks is the Solactive GBS Global Markets ex-US index, which is reweighted using the *Economist*'s Intelligence Unit Democracy Index. The result is the Democracy Investments International Index. For instance, in June 2022 this reweighting took China's weight from about 8 percent in the Solactive GBS Global Markets ex-US index to near 2.5 percent in the Democracy Investments International Index.

I interviewed Julie Cane, CEO and managing partner for Democracy Investments, in December 2022. She told me that during 2022 their ETF had outperformed its benchmark, the Solactive GBS Global Markets ex-US index, and other similar ETFs, such as BlackRock's iShares MSCI ACWI ex US ETF (ACWX), due to its lower exposure to Russia and China. At the time of Russia's invasion of Ukraine, DMCY had already down-weighted Russian equities by 55 percent. The fund then disposed of Russia from the index altogether. In September 2022, DMCY had down-weighted Türkiye and Pakistan 41 percent, UAE 60 percent, and Saudi Arabia 72 percent compared to the benchmark index, among other nondemocratic countries. To compensate, the fund overweighted highly democratic countries such as Japan, Canada, and Taiwan.

Individual investors, financial advisors, and portfolio managers can also check the exposure of different ETFs to autocratic countries on their own thanks to a tool created by the Human Rights Foundation in a joint endeavor with Life + Liberty Indexes. On the Defund Dictators website* investors can check their exposure by entering the name of any US-listed ETF name or ticker that invests in emerging markets, and then choosing among three human rights data sources, Freedom House, Human Rights Foundation, and Fraser and Cato Human Freedom. The tool assigns each ETF a score: the higher the number, the freer the country allocations.

For example, the popular iShares MSCI Emerging Markets ETF (EEM), with more than $20 billion of AUM,[54] had 52 percent of its investments in stocks of countries labeled as Not Free by Freedom House by March 2023. Of these investments, 29 percent were invested in Chinese stocks. EEM had a Defund Dictators score of 4.3. For comparison, another popular emerging markets ETF, the Vanguard FTSE Emerging Markets ETF (VWO), with $83 billion of AUM,[55] had 56 percent of its investments in countries deemed Not Free by Freedom House at the same time. Its Defund Dictators ETF score was even lower, at 3.6.[56] In contrast, FRDM had a Defund Dictators ETF score of 9.

DESG Impact Investment

There are several alternatives to implement a DESG Impact Investment strategy. One is to invest in Green Bonds from companies and countries that excel in their democracy standards. The greater impact would be when the countries issuing them are Emerging Markets or low-income countries, or are from companies domiciled in these types of countries. This would help to overcome a problem of ESG scores, namely that they have an income bias or, put differently, that richer countries tend to have better ESG scores.[57] Emerging Market countries that have issued sovereign Green Bonds such as Chile and Uruguay and that have good democracy standards would be rewarded under such a strategy.

Another democracy strategy that could have an important impact is to invest in sovereign bonds from countries that have just had a

---

* https://defunddictators.org

significant democracy improvement. One example is if and when the current opposition is able to win the presidency in countries such as Hungary, Türkiye, or Venezuela.

DESG Engagement

DESG Engagement strategies would involve shareholder and bondholder activism to prompt companies to include democracy considerations in their strategies and governments to avoid introducing reforms that undermine democracy. In the case of companies' bonds and stocks, investors would engage companies to try to avoid sourcing too much of their products from undemocratic countries, in which elemental human rights are violated.

In the case of sovereign issuers, big investment houses could engage with the issuers to warn them that if they cross certain democratic thresholds, such as the packing of the Supreme Court or of the body that appoints judges, they will not participate in future debt auctions. In my experience, I have seen how big international banks, companies, and investment houses have privileged access to high-ranking government officials. When I organized investor trips to Latin American countries, we could meet with finance ministers and other important cabinet members, opposition leaders, and sometimes even with presidents. The same applies for companies that are about to make important investment decisions. This special access could be used to prompt leaders at least to take small steps to improve human rights conditions in their countries, such as the release of political prisoners.

Final Thoughts

It is by chance, if not destiny, that I am putting the final touches to this book from Oslo, while I am attending the Human Rights Foundation's 2023 Oslo Freedom Forum. The tragic stories of activists subject to human rights violations in different parts of the world are a stark reminder of the importance of making the financial world aware that it may be financing the same autocrats that commit these atrocities.

At the end of the day, countries are independent, and from the outside there are limitations to what we can do to make them avoid undermining their democracy and checks and balances. *But at least we do not want to bankroll them with our money.*

We do not need to wait until a country becomes an autocracy to act, as by then it is usually too late. We know the signals to watch for when a country is in danger of slipping toward autocracy. They are often right in front of our eyes, and they are closely followed by expert democracy and human right watchers. What we need to do is raise awareness of the problem and highlight that we can do something about it.

That is the purpose of this book. Markets facilitated the consolidation of power of autocrats in different parts of the world, but I believe that we have the mechanisms to act on behalf of individual investors, financial advisors, portfolio managers, and other market stakeholders. My proposal is to overhaul ESG investment strategies to include democracy considerations and to add DESG or ESG+ indices to the suite of products that investors can choose from.

In no way do I claim that I have all the answers to the problems raised in this book. It would be sufficient for me to convince readers and market participants that we have a problem, and for this book to start a discussion on how to solve it. My proposal includes practical DESG investment strategies that individual investors, financial advisors, and portfolio managers can start implementing by their own.

KEY TAKEAWAYS OF CHAPTER 10

This chapter:

- Argues that it would be much easier for individual investors, financial advisors, and portfolio managers to avoid investing in autocracies if they had DESG or ESG+ equity and sovereign bond indices, following the rules proposed in Chapter 9 and the one proposed in this chapter. In turn, index providers could benefit if ESG score providers added DESG or ESG+ scores.

- Highlights that regulators also have a job to do, for instance, banning bond and equity issuance first and investing second when sanctioning a country.

- Provides a comprehensive do-it-yourself guide to implementing DESG for individual investors, financial advisors, and portfolio managers. The guide is framed in terms of the most popular ESG strategies: exclusion, positive screening, ESG integration, impact investment, and engagement or active ownership. The guide provides concrete examples, rules, and some ETFs that consider democracy.

- Concludes with the thought that ultimately there is not much that we can do to keep a country from slipping into autocracy. However, we can prevent them from doing so with our money. I believe that overhauling ESG to include democracy in DESG or ESG+ scores and indices is one way to achieve this goal.

ACKNOWLEDGMENTS

Writing a book is at the same time a very lonely endeavor and a collective project. Although the ideas and the errors are mine, I could not have written it without the support and the wisdom of so many people.

I want to mention first those who believed in the project from the very beginning, and who supported me when I was wavering amid a long process to find a publishing agent. They include Moisés Naím, Ana Iparraguirre, and Anna Cohen. The people at the Human Rights Foundation also gave me an important morale boost by inviting me to present my ideas in the Oslo Freedom Forum in 2022 and 2023. These events helped me realize I could have an important idea in my hands and energized me by meeting firsthand with activists suffering under the thumb of autocrats in different parts of the world.

My agent, John Willig, deserves a special mention. He became enthusiastic about the project right away, and with his magic wand, he proposed some tweaks to it that allowed us, in about a month, to land McGraw Hill as a publisher. I also want to thank Judith Newlin, who, at McGraw Hill in 2022, believed in this project and for her superb editing. Her comments helped me to direct the last part of the book in a better direction. I also want to thank Christopher Brown and all the team at McGraw Hill for steering me through the difficult process of publishing my first book in the United States.

Throughout this process that took almost three years, I counted on the support of an amazing team. Ryan McDonough, who used to edit my publications when I was at Bank of America, helped me to get a first and important editorial review. The book significantly improved thanks to his enthusiasm and willingness to go into the detail of each chapter. Miranda Cortizo and Connor Fernandez Quelch were superb research assistants throughout the process. Given my background as an economist, their training in international relations and political science was of great help in navigating the specialized literature. Franco Nuñez also helped with some statistics.

I also want to thank the numerous people who read the whole book or parts of it. Their comments, suggestions, and additions have improved it substantially. They include Ana Lankes, Pablo Eizayaga, Alberto Ades, Patricio Navia, Sebastián Saiegh, Francisco Rodríguez Caballero, Raffaella Tenconi, Florencia Baldi, Erik Berg, and several others who preferred to remain anonymous. Francisco Rodríguez Caballero, José Luis Daza, Francisco Toro, Jorge Piedrahita, and Michael Penfold helped me with the chapter on Venezuela. Of course, all errors remain mine.

Last, but not least, I want to thank my family, who have always supported me and withstood having me busy in my studio so many weekends to finish this project. I want to thank especially my wife, Sofia, my love and my best friend, for her support.

NOTES

PREFACE

1. Steven Levitsky and Daniel Ziblatt, *How Democracies Die* (New York: Crown, 2018), 102.
2. Hugo Alconada Mon, "Vialidad: cómo funcionó la matriz de corrupción que terminó con la condena de Cristina Kirchner y Lázaro Báez," *La Nación*, December 6, 2022, https://www.lanacion.com.ar/politica/vialidad-como-funciono-la-matriz-de-corrupcion-que-termino-con-la-condena-de-cristina-kirchner-y-nid06122022/.
3. Larry Diamond, "Facing Up to the Democratic Recession," *Journal of Democracy* 26, no. 1 (January 2015), 141–55.
4. Marcos Buscaglia, "Democracy is under threat, we must add a D to ESG," *Financial Times*, February 10, 2020, https://www.ft.com/content/61ecdc28-76dd-466a-9ef9-104ad14af7da.
5. Larry Diamond, *The Spirit of Democracy: The Struggle to Build Free Societies Throughout the World* (New York: Holt Paperbacks, 2009).
6. Diamond, *The Spirit of Democracy*, 23.
7. I follow Fareed Zakaria's definitions. See Fareed Zakaria, *The Future of Freedom: Illiberal Democracy at Home and Abroad* (New York: W.W. Norton & Company, 2007), 19.
8. A summary of the 10 points in Diamond, *The Spirit of Democracy*, 22.
9. Gideon Rachman, *The Age of the Strongman* (Bodley Head, 2022).
10. Sergei Guriev and Daniel Treisman, *Spin Dictators: The Changing Face of Tyranny in the 21st Century* (Princeton Oxford: Princeton University Press, 2022).
11. Moisés Naím, *The Revenge of Power* (New York: St. Martin's Press, 2022), xxiii.

CHAPTER 1

1. The outline of this chapter follows my 2021 article: Marcos Buscaglia, "Time for D-Bonds," *RSA Journal* no. 2 (June 2021).

2. Sarah Repucci and Amy Slipowitz, "Democracy Under Lockdown," *Freedom House*, October 2020.

3. Economist Intelligence Unit, "Democracy Index 2020: In Sickness and in Health?," Economist Intelligence Unit, 2020.

4. Reuters Staff, "Vaccine, U.S. Election News Drive Record $76.5 Billion Inflow to EM: IIF," Reuters, December 1, 2020, https://www.reuters.com/article/uk-global-emerging-flows-idUKKBN28B5IH.

5. Tommy Stubbington, "EM Countries Tap 'Red-Hot' Markets in Late-Year Borrowing Spree," *Financial Times*, December 9, 2020, https://www.ft.com/content/37c90fe9-3484-4801-a3ff-ceba669fc521.

6. "Emerging Markets: A 20-Year Perspective," MSCI Barra, accessed August 18, 2022, https://www.msci.com/documents/10199/b0aa2137-8611-48d4-b2f5-90958acf1b8d.

7. Dirk Willer, Ram Bala Chandran, and Kenneth Lam, *Trading Fixed Income and FX in Emerging Markets: A Practitioner's Guide* (New Jersey: John Wiley & Sons, 2020), 3.

8. Willer, Chandran, and Lam, *Trading Fixed Income and FX in Emerging Markets*, 1.

9. Julian E. Barnes and David E. Sanger, "Saudi Crown Prince Is Held Responsible for Khashoggi Killing in U.S. Report," *New York Times*, February 26, 2021, https://www.nytimes.com/2021/02/26/us/politics/jamal-khashoggi-killing-cia-report.html.

10. Matthew Martin, "Saudi Aramco Raises $25.6 Billion in World's Biggest IPO," *Bloomberg*, December 5, 2019, https://www.bloomberg.com/news/articles/2019-12-05/saudi-aramco-raises-25-6-billion-in-world-s-biggest-ipo.

11. "iShares J.P. Morgan USD Emerging Markets Bond ETF," iShares, accessed February 6, 2023, https://www.ishares.com/us/products/239572/ishares-jp-morgan-usd-emerging-markets-bond-etf.

12. "Emerging Markets ETFs Overview," Emerging Markets ETF Channel, accessed February 6, 2023, https://www.etf.com/channels/emerging-markets-etfs#:~:text=Emerging%20Markets%20ETF%20Overview,Equity.

13. William Easterly, *The Tyranny of Experts: Economists, Dictators, and the Forgotten Rights of the Poor* (New York: Perseus Books, 2013), 6.

14. Easterly, *The Tyranny of Experts*, 5.

15. World Bank, "Annual Report 2021: From Crisis to Green, Resilient and Inclusive Recovery," The World Bank, 2021.

16. "Record $269.5bn Green Issuance for 2020: Late Surge Sees Pandemic Year Pip 2019 Total by $3bn," Climate Bonds Initiative, January 24, 2021. https://www.climatebonds.net/2021/01/record-2695bn-green-issuance-2020-late-surge-sees-pandemic-year-pip-2019-total-3bn.

17. Gong Chen, Torsten Ehlers, and Frank Packer, "Sovereigns and Sustainable Bonds: Challenges and New Options," *BIS Quarterly Review*, September 2022, https://www.bis.org/publ/qtrpdf/r_qt2209 .pdf.
18. ICMA, "Green Bond Principles: Voluntary Process Guidelines for Issuing Green Bonds," ICMA, June 2021.
19. Samuel C. Adams and Larry E. Swedroe, *Your Essential Guide to Sustainable Investing: How to Live Your Values and Achieve Your Financial Goals with ESG, SRI, and Impact Investing* (Hampshire: Harriman House, 2022), 78.
20. Steven Levitsky and Daniel Ziblatt, *How Democracies Die* (New York: Crown, 2018), 6.
21. "Freedom in the World," Freedom House, accessed August 17, 2022, https://freedomhouse.org/report/freedom-world.
22. "Democracy in Retreat," Freedom House, accessed August 17, 2022, https://freedomhouse.org/report/freedom-world/2019/democracy -retreat.
23. Freedom House, "Freedom in the World 2023: Marking 50 Years in the Struggle for Democracy," *Freedom House*, March 2023.
24. Economist Intelligence Unit, "Democracy Index 2019: A Year of Democratic Setbacks and Popular Protest," Economist Intelligence Unit, January 2020.
25. Economist Intelligence Unit, "Democracy Index 2020.
26. Economist Intelligence Unit, "Democracy Index 2022: Frontline Democracy and the Battle for Ukraine," Economist Intelligence Unit, 2023.
27. Anna Lührmann, Seraphine F. Maerz, Sandra Grahn, Nazifa Alizada, Lisa Gastaldi, Sebastian Hellmeier, Garry Hindle, and Staffan I. Lindberg, "Autocratization Surges—Resistance Grows: Democracy Report 2020," Varieties of Democracy Institute, 2020, https://v-dem.net/documents/14/dr_2020_dqumD5e.pdf.
28. V-Dem Institute, "Democracy Report 2023: Defiance in the Face of Autocratization," V-Dem Institute, March 2023.

CHAPTER 2
1. Kejal Vyas and Anatoly Kurmanaev, "Goldman Sachs Bought Venezuela's State Oil Company's Bonds Last Week," *Wall Street Journal*, May 28, 2017, https://www.wsj.com/articles/goldman-sachs -bought-venezuelan-oil-co-bonds-last-week-1496020176.
2. Francisco Rodriguez, "Toxic Conflict: Understanding Venezuela's Economic Collapse," *Kellogg Institute for International Studies*, no. 448 (November 2021): 36–37.
3. Caroline Rodda, "BlackRock Reports Full Year 2022 Diluted EPS of $33.97, or $35.36 as adjusted Fourth Quarter 2022 Diluted EPS of

$8.29, or $8.93 as adjusted," January 13, 2023, https://s24.q4cdn.com/856567660/files/doc_financials/2022/Q4/BLK-4Q22-Earnings-Release.pdf.

4. Gold Sachs Asset Management, "Your Performance, Our Priority," https://www.gsam.com/content/gsam/global/en/about-gsam/overview.html.

5. Dirk Willer, Ram Bala Chandran, and Kenneth Lam, *Trading Fixed Income and FX in Emerging Markets: A Practitioner's Guide* (New Jersey: John Wiley & Sons, 2020), 4.

6. Ricardo Hausmann, "The Hunger Bonds," *Project Syndicate*, May 26, 2017, https://www.project-syndicate.org/commentary/maduro-venezuela-hunger-bonds-by-ricardo-hausmann-2017-05.

7. Hausmann, "The Hunger Bonds."

8. Rodriguez, "Toxic Conflict," 36.

9. "Freedom in the World 2017: Venezuela," Freedom House, https://freedomhouse.org/country/venezuela/freedom-world/2017.

10. "Freedom in the World 2017: Venezuela."

11. Francisco Rodriguez, *Scorched Earth: The Political Economy of Venezuela's Collapse, 2012–2022* (Publishing house pending), 111.

12. "Freedom in the World 2017: Venezuela."

13. Rodriguez, *Scorched Earth*.

14. Christopher Sabatini, "The Final Blow to Venezuela's Democracy: What Latin America Can Do About It," *Foreign Affairs*, November 1, 2016, https://www.foreignaffairs.com/articles/venezuela/2016-11-01/final-blow-venezuelas-democracy.

15. Javier Corrales and Michael Penfold, *Dragon in the Tropics: Venezuela and the Legacy of Hugo Chávez* (Washington, DC: Brookings Institution Press, 2015), 200.

16. Carlos De la Torre, *Populisms: A Quick Immersion* (New York, Tibidabo Publishing, 2018), 11.

17. "Freedom in the World 2017: Venezuela."

18. Robin Wigglesworth and Gideon Long, "Why Goldman's Venezuela Bond Trade Sparked Controversy," *Financial Times*, June 1, 2017, https://www.ft.com/content/c2f0fc3c-466b-11e7-8519-9f94ee97d996.

19. Leo Tolstoy, *Anna Karenina* (New York: The Modern Library, 1920), 4.

20. De la Torre, *Populisms*, 61.

21. De la Torre, *Populisms*, 62.

22. Kurt Weyland, "Populism and Authoritarianism," in *Routledge Handbook of Global Populism*, ed Carlos De la Torre, (New York: Routledge, 2020), 324.

23. Corrales and Penfold, *Dragon in the Tropics*, 180.

24. José de Córdoba and Kejal Vyas, "Venezuela Confronts Twilight of Chávez Era," *Wall Street Journal*, December 9, 2012, https://www.wsj .com/articles/SB10001424127887324001104578168283496596560.
25. Madeleine Albright, *Fascism: A Warning* (New York: HarperCollins, 2018), 133.
26. Corrales and Penfold, *Dragon in the Tropics*, 181.
27. "Freedom in the World 2017: Venezuela."
28. John-Paul Rathbone and Andres Schipani, "Oil Price Fall Triggers Fears of Venezuela Default," *Financial Times*, October 16, 2014, https://www.ft.com/content/b7a2ee04-5478-11e4-84c6 -00144feab7de.
29. Pedro Rodriguez, José Morales, and Francisco Monaldi, "Direct Distribution of Oil Revenues in Venezuela: A Viable Alternative?," *Center for Global Development*, no. 306 (September 2012), 1–38.
30. Carmen M. Reinhart and Kenneth Rogoff, "Venezuela's Spectacular Underperformance," Project Syndicate, October 13, 2014, https:// www.project-syndicate.org/commentary/venezuela-economic -underperformance-by-carmen-reinhart-and-kenneth-rogoff-2014 -10.
31. Corrales and Penfold, *Dragon in the Tropic*, 60.
32. Corrales and Penfold, *Dragon in the Tropics*, 60.
33. Anne Applebaum, *Twilight of Democracy: The Seductive Lure of Authoritarianism* (New York: Penguin Random House, 2020), 25–26.
34. Rodriguez, *Scorched Earth*, 23.
35. Francisco Toro, "Chávez, Maduro and the Ascendancy of the Arbitrageur Kleptolobby," *Caracas Chronicles* (blog), February 11, 2016, https://www.caracaschronicles.com/2016/02/11/maduro-and -the-triumph-of-the-arbitrage-lobby/.
36. Rodriguez, *Scorched Earth*, 273.
37. Sabatini, "The Final Blow to Venezuela's Democracy."
38. "Stiglitz se reunió con Chávez y elogió sus planes," *El Universo*, October 12, 2007, https://www.eluniverso.com/2007/10/12/0001 /14/E96A45966AF64B1BB19AA7EA0BD131E5.html/.
39. Rodriguez, "Toxic Conflict," 32.
40. "Freedom in the World 2018: Venezuela," Freedom House, accessed August 18, 2022, https://freedomhouse.org/country/venezuela /freedom-world/2018.
41. Rodriguez, "Toxic Conflict," 38.
42. Rodriguez, *Scorched Earth*, 153.
43. Moisés Naím and Francisco Toro, "Venezuela's Suicide: Lessons from a Failed State," *Foreign Affairs*, November/December 2018, 12, https://www.foreignaffairs.com/articles/south-america/2018-10-15 /venezuelas-suicide.
44. Naím and Toro, "Venezuela's Suicide."

45. Rodriguez, *Scorched Earth*, 15.
46. "Hugo Chávez: Discurso en Aula Magna Universidad de La Habana (1994)," Wiksource, accessed August 19, 2022, https://es.wikisource .org/wiki/Discurso_de_Hugo_Chávez_en_la_Habana_(1994).
47. Michael Coppedge, "Venezuela: Popular Sovereignty Versus Liberal Democracy," *The Helen Kellogg Institute for International Studies*, no. 294 (April 2002): 17–23.
48. Rodriguez, *Scorched Earth*, 2.
49. Coppedge, "Venezuela: Popular Sovereignty Versus Liberal Democracy."
50. Freedom House, *Freedom in the World 1999–2000* (New York: Freedom House, 2000).
51. Albright, *Fascism: A Warning*, 133.
52. Angela Pruitt, "Venezuela's Chávez Charms Wall Street, but Leaves Economic Agenda Unclear," *Wall Street Journal*, June 15, 1999, https://www.wsj.com/articles/SB929387275994216238.
53. Rodriguez, *Scorched Earth*, 18.
54. Willer, Chandran, and Lam, *Trading Fixed Income and FX in Emerging Markets*, 30.
55. Corrales and Penfold, *Dragon in the Tropics*, 81.

CHAPTER 3
1. Asli Kandemir and Cagan Koc, "Turkey Developing Framework for Sovereign ESG Bonds by Year-End," *Bloomberg*, May 19, 2021, https://www.bloomberg.com/news/articles/2021-05-20/turkey -developing-framework-for-sovereign-esg-bonds-by-year-end.
2. The "Shades of Green" methodology grades bonds dark, medium, or light according to their contribution to the environment. See "Green Bonds Mobilising the Debt Capital Markets for a Low-Carbon Transition," Bloomberg Philanthropies OECD, December 2015.
3. Selcan Hacaoglu, "Istanbul Mayor and Potential Erdoğan Challenger Faces Prison," *Bloomberg*, May 28, 2021, https://www.bloomberg.com /news/articles/2021-05-28/istanbul-mayor-and-potential-erdogan -challenger-faces-prison.
4. Ruth Ben-Ghiat, *Strongmen: Mussolini to the Present* (New York: W.W. Norton & Company, 2020), 219.
5. Ben-Ghiat, *Strongmen*, 219.
6. "Turkish Agents Capture Nephew of U.S.-Based Cleric Overseas," *Bloomberg*, May 31, 2021, https://www.bloomberg.com/news/articles /2021-05-31/turkish-agents-capture-nephew-of-us-based-cleric -overseas#xj4y7vzkg.
7. Ayla Jean Yackley, "Mobster Transfixes Turkey with Video Tirade Against Political Elite," *Financial Times*, May 18, 2021, https://www .ft.com/content/a968c2c5-2001-4ae8-9339-58e27bcd7495.

8. Iain Marlow and Isabella Steger, "Investors Are Ignoring a Dangerous Crackdown on Press Freedom," *Bloomberg*, August 4, 2021, https://www.bloomberg.com/news/features/2021-08-04/what-press-freedom-crackdowns-from-u-s-to-china-to-turkey-mean-for-investors.

9. "Turkish Court Acquits Bloomberg Reporters Over 2018 Lira Story," *Bloomberg*, April 29, 2022, https://www.bloomberg.com/news/articles/2022-04-29/turkish-court-acquits-bloomberg-reporters-over-2018-lira-story.

10. "RSF's 2021 "Press Freedom Predators" Gallery—Old Tyrants, Two Women and a European," *Reporters Without Borders*, July 2, 2021, https://rsf.org/en/rsf-s-2021-press-freedom-predators-gallery-old-tyrants-two-women-and-european.

11. "Turkey Using Terrorism Legislation to Gag and Jail Journalists," *Reporters Without Borders*, June 15, 2021, https://rsf.org/en/turkey-using-terrorism-legislation-gag-and-jail-journalists.

12. Kaya Genc, "Erdoğan's Way: The Rise and Rule of Turkey's Islamist Shapeshifter," *Foreign Affairs*, August 12, 2019, https://www.foreignaffairs.com/articles/turkey/2019-08-12/Erdoğans-way.

13. Ugur Yilmaz, "Turkey Policy Shift Pays Off with Record Demand at Bond Sale," *Bloomberg*, January 20, 2021, https://www.bloomberg.com/news/articles/2021-01-20/turkey-policy-shift-pays-off-with-record-demand-at-bond-sale.

14. Zvi Bodie, Alex Kane, and Alan Marcus, *Investments* (New York: McGraw Hill, 2002), 420–421.

15. Jonathan Wheatley, "High Yields Tempt Wary Investors Back into Turkish Debt," *Financial Times*, September 17, 2021, https://www.ft.com/content/6e325c75-93e3-45fe-b08a-da79fd04e501.

16. Soner Cagaptay, *The New Sultan: Erdoğan and the Crisis of Modern Turkey* (London & New York: I.B Tauris & Co. Ltd, 2020), 179.

17. Cagaptay, *The New Sultan*, 178.

18. Sheri Berman, "Islamism, Revolution, and Civil Society," *American Political Science Association* 1, no. 2 (Jun 2003): 257–272.

19. Daron Acemoglu and James Robinson, *The Narrow Corridor: States, Societies, and the Fate of Liberty* (New York: Penguin Press, 2019), 439.

20. Madeleine Albright, *Fascism: A Warning. United States* (New York: HarperCollins, 2019), 138.

21. Cagaptay, *The New Sultan*, 7.

22. Albright, *Fascism: A Warning*, 139.

23. Acemoglu and Robinson, *The Narrow Corridor*, 440.

24. Genc, "Erdoğan's Way."

25. Albright, *Fascism: A Warning*, 140.

26. Genc, "Erdoğan's Way."

27. Cagaptay, *The New Sultan*, 8.

28. Albright, *Fascism: A Warning*, 137.
29. Cagaptay, *The New Sultan*, 83.
30. Genc, "Erdoğan's Way."
31. Cınar Menderes, "From Moderation to De-moderation: Democratic Backsliding of the AKP in Turkey," in *The Politics of Islamism*, ed. J. L. Esposito et al. (New York: Palgrave Macmillan Cham, 2018), 135, https://doi.org/10.1007/978-3-319-62256-9.
32. Bilge Yabanci and Dane Taleski, "Co-opting Religion: How Ruling Populists in Turkey and Macedonia Sacralise the Majority," *Religion, State and Society* 46, no.3 (December 2017), 283–304.
33. Cagaptay, *The New Sultan*, 85.
34. Capital Flows Tracker, "IIF Capital Flows Report—Annual Database," June 2021.
35. Albright, *Fascism: A Warning*, 144.
36. "EMBI Global Diversified," J.P. Morgan, accessed February 10, 2023, https://www.jpmorgan.com/content/dam/jpm/cib/complex/content/markets/composition-docs/pdf-27.pdf.
37. Wheatley, "High Yields Tempt Wary Investors Back into Turkish Debt."
38. Cagaptay, *The New Sultan*, 93.
39. Yabanci and Taleski, "Co-opting Religion."
40. Cagaptay, *The New Sultan*, 94.
41. "Intro to Credit Ratings," S&P Global, accessed 19 August 2022, https://www.spglobal.com/ratings/en/about/intro-to-credit-ratings.
42. Mahir Binici, Michael M. Hutchison, and Evan Weicheng Miao, "Are Credit Rating Agencies Discredited? Measuring Market Price Effects from Agency Sovereign Debt Announcements," *Bank for International Settlements*, 2018; Dirk Willer, *Trading Fixed Income and FX in Emerging Markets: A Practitioner's Guide* (New Jersey: Wiley, 2020), 203–206.
43. Willer, *Trading Fixed Income and FX in Emerging Markets*, 203.
44. Ye Xie and Selcuk Gokoluk, "Turkey Raised to Investment Grade by Moody's on Debt Cuts," *Bloomberg*, May 17, 2013, https://www.bloomberg.com/news/articles/2013-05-16/turkey-raised-to-investment-grade-by-moody-s-on-debt-cuts#xj4y7vzkg.
45. Daniel Dombey, "Fitch Raises Turkey to Investment Grade," *Financial Times*, November 5, 2012, https://www.ft.com/content/9e2c38dc-2742-11e2-9863-00144feabdc0.
46. Xie and Gokoluk, "Turkey Raised to Investment Grade by Moody's on Debt Cuts."
47. Serkan Arslanalp, Dimitris Drakopoulos, Rohit Goel, and Robin Koepke, "Benchmark-Driven Investments in Emerging Market Bond Markets: Taking Stock—Working Paper No. 2020/192," International Monetary Fund, 2020.

48. Alex Sienaert, "Foreign Investment in Local Currency Bonds: Considerations for Emerging Market Public Debt Managers," *World Bank*, 2012.
49. Sienaert, "Foreign Investment in Local Currency Bonds.
50. Cihan Tuğal, *The Fall of the Turkish Model: How the Arab Uprisings Brought Down Islamic Liberalism* (London, New York: Verso), 292.
51. Cagaptay, *The New Sultan*, 131.
52. Kemal Kirişc and Amanda Sloat, "The Rise and Fall of Liberal Democracy in Turkey: Implications for the West," *Brookings*, February 2019.
53. Cagaptay, *The New Sultan*, 108.
54. Dani Rodrik, "Ergenekon and Sledgehammer: Building or Undermining the Rule of Law?," *Turkish Policy* 10, no.1 (June 2011): 99–109.
55. Dov Friedman, "The Causes of the Coup Attempt in Turkey: A History of the Usual Suspects," *War on the Rocks*, July 21, 2016, https://warontherocks.com/2016/07/the-causes-of-the-coup-attempt-in-turkey-a-history-of-the-usual-suspects/.
56. Aslı Aydıntaşbaş, "The Good, the Bad and the Gülenists," *European Council on Foreign Relations*, September 23, 2016, https://ecfr.eu/publication/the_good_the_bad_and_the_gulenists7131/.
57. Dani Rodrik, "Erdoğan Is Not Turkey's Only Problem," *Project Syndicate*, September 11, 2013, https://www.project-syndicate.org/commentary/the-gulenist-subversion-of-turkey-by-dani-rodrik.
58. Halil Karaveli, "Erdoğan's Journey: Conservatism and Authoritarianism in Turkey," *Foreign Affairs*, October 17, 2016, https://www.foreignaffairs.com/articles/turkey/2016-10-17/Erdoğans-journey.
59. Cagaptay, *The New Sultan*, 122.
60. "Sovereign Rating Criteria—Effective from 26 April 2021 to 11 April 2022," Fitch Ratings, accessed February 1, 2023, https://www.fitchratings.com/research/sovereigns/sovereign-rating-criteria-26-04-2021.
61. "How We Rate Sovereigns," S&P Ratings, accessed February 3, 2023, https://www.spglobal.com/ratings/_division-assets/pdfs/021519_howweratesovereigns.pdf.
62. Cagaptay, *The New Sultan*, 135.
63. Kirişc and Sloat, "The Rise and Fall of Liberal Democracy in Turkey."
64. Albright, *Fascism: A Warning*, 150.
65. Cagaptay, *The New Sultan*, 116.
66. Pinar Sevinclidir, "Turkey Crackdown Piles Pressure on Media After Coup Bid," *BBC News*, July 29, 2016, https://www.bbc.com/news/world-middle-east-36916219.

67. "Turkey: Freedom in the World 2018," Freedom House, accessed February 3, 2023, https://freedomhouse.org/country/turkey/freedom-world/2018.
68. Genc, "Erdoğan's Way."
69. Brinley Bruton, "Turkey's President Erdoğan Calls Women Who Work 'Half Persons,'" *NBC News*, June 8, 2016, https://www.nbcnews.com/news/world/turkey-s-president-Erdoğan-calls-women-who-work-half-persons-n586421.
70. Capital Flows Tracker, "IIF Capital Flows Report—Annual Database," *Institute on International Finance*, June 2021.
71. Wheatley, "High Yields Tempt Wary Investors Back into Turkish Debt."
72. "Istanbul Mayor Ekrem İmamoğlu Sentenced to Jail over 'Fools' Insult," *The Guardian*, December 14, 2022, https://www.theguardian.com/world/2022/dec/14/istanbul-mayor-ekrem-imamoglu-sentenced-to-jail-over-fools-insult.
73. Daren Butler, "Turkey Says It Borrowed $2.5 bln in Green Bond Issue," Reuters, April 6, 2023, https://www.nasdaq.com/articles/turkey-says-it-borrowed-$2.5-bln-in-green-bond-issue.
74. "Fiscal Fantasyland: When Will Politicians Wake Up?," *Economist*, May 6, 2023, 16.
75. Beril Akman and Patrick Sykes, "Turkey's Erdogan Adds Energy Bill Discount to Pre-Vote Handouts," *Bloomberg*, April 20, 2023, https://www.bloomberg.com/news/articles/2023-04-20/turkey-s-erdogan-adds-energy-bill-discount-to-pre-vote-handouts?sref=am1wYMj6.

CHAPTER 4
1. "Profile: Lorinc Meszaros," *Forbes*, accessed August 19, 2022, https://www.forbes.com/profile/lorinc-meszaros/?sh=4dc0b8aa4868.
2. Akos Keller-Alant, Tibor Racz, and Krisztian Simon, "In Hungary, Viktor Orban's Favorite Mayor Goes on a Shopping Spree," *DW*, October 25, 2017, https://www.dw.com/en/in-hungary-viktor-orbans-favorite-mayor-goes-on-a-shopping-spree/a-41099347.
3. Paul Lendvai, *Orban: Hungary's Strongman* (New York: Oxford University Press, 2017), 168.
4. Danny Hakim, "A Village Stadium Is a Symbol of Power for Hungary's Premier," *New York Times*, April 3, 2014, https://www.nytimes.com/2014/04/04/business/international/the-village-stadium-a-symbol-of-power-for-hungarys-premier.html; Babett Oroszi, "The Orban Government Spent Billions on Hungarian Football Clubs in Serbia, Romania and Slovakia," *Atlaszo*, December 11, 2018, https://english.atlatszo.hu/2018/12/11/the-orban-government-spent-billions-on-hungarian-football-clubs-in-serbia-romania-and-slovakia/.

5. Lendvai, *Orban: Hungary's Strongman*, 169.
6. CRCB, "New Trends in Corruption Risk and Intensity of Competition in the Hungarian Republic Procurement from January 2015 to April 2020," *CRCB Flash Report*, no 1 (May 2020): 1–57.
7. Lendvai, *Orban: Hungary's Strongman*, 173.
8. "EU Spending and Revenue: Interactive Chart Showing the EU Spending and Revenue for the 2014–2020 Period by Year and by Country," European Commission, accessed August 19, 2022, https://ec.europa.eu/info/strategy/eu-budget/long-term-eu-budget/2014-2020/spending-and-revenue_en.
9. CRCB, "New Trends in Corruption Risk"; OLAF, "The OLAF Report 2015: Sixteenth Report of the European Anti-Fraud Office, 1 January to 31 December 2015," *European Anti-Fraud Office*, no.16: 1–48.
10. Eszter Zalan, "Hungary Heads EU Anti-fraud Investigation List— Again," *EU Observer*, September 11, 2020, https://euobserver.com/justice/149405.
11. Zalan, "Hungary Heads EU Anti-fraud Investigation List."
12. Lendvai, *Orban: Hungary's Strongman*, 16.
13. Rényi Pál Dániel, "The Rise and Fall of the Man Who Created Viktor Orbán's System," *444*, April 22, 2019, https://444.hu/tldr/2019/04/22/the-rise-and-fall-of-the-man-who-created-viktor-orbans-system.
14. Lendvai, *Orban: Hungary's Strongman*, 147.
15. "Lajos Simicska," The Orange Files, accessed April 25, 2023, https://theorangefiles.hu/lajos-simicskakozgep/.
16. Petho András and Szabó András, "Inside the Fall of the Oligarch Who Turned Against Viktor Orban," *Direkt 36*, January 14, 2019, https://www.direkt36.hu/en/feltarul-simicska-bukasanak-titkos-tortenete/.
17. Lendvai, *Orban: Hungary's Strongman*, 146.
18. Andrew Byrne, "Orban Tightens Grip on Hungary's Media," *Financial Times*, August 16, 2016, https://www.ft.com/content/50488256-60af-11e6-ae3f-77baadeb1c93.
19. Reuters Staff, "Orban Loyalists Take Control of Prominent Hungarian News Channel," *Reuters*, August 1, 2018, https://www.reuters.com/article/us-hungary-orban-media/orban-loyalists-take-control-of-prominent-hungarian-news-channel-idUSKBN1KM4VT.
20. Lendvai, *Orban: Hungary's Strongman*, 157.
21. Lendvai, *Orban: Hungary's Strongman*, 158.
22. Byrne, "Orban Tightens Grip on Hungary's Media."
23. Lester Feder and Rebeka Kulcsar, "Meet the Mystery Man Who Is the Power Behind the Throne in Hungary," *BuzzFeed News*, April 4,

2018, https://www.buzzfeednews.com/article/lesterfeder/hungarys
-steve-bannon.

24. Feder and Kulcsar, "Meet the Mystery Man."
25. Lendvai, *Orban: Hungary's Strongman*, 10.
26. "Imre Czirják, "András Lánczi: The Opposition Is at the Level of Joke Parties," *Magyar Idok*, December 21, 2015, https://www.magyaridok
.hu/belfold/lanczi-andras-viccpartok-szinvonalan-all-az-ellenzek
-243952/ (translated with Google Translate).
27. "Freedom in the World 2017: Hungary," Freedom House, accessed August 19, 2022, https://freedomhouse.org/country/hungary
/freedom-world/2017; "Hungary: Klubrádió, the Main Independent Broadcaster, Kicked off the Airwaves," Reporters Without Borders, accessed August 19, 2022, https://rsf.org/es/hungr%C3%ADa
-expulsan-de-las-ondas-klubr%C3%A1di%C3%B3-la-principal
-emisora-independiente.
28. Lendvai, *Orban: Hungary's Strongman*, 118.
29. "Hungary's Leading Independent Radio Station Loses Broadcast License," *France 24*, October 2, 2021, https://www.france24.com
/en/europe/20210210-hungary-s-leading-independent-radio-station
-loses-broadcast-license.
30. Lendvai, *Orban: Hungary's Strongman*, 119.
31. "World Press Freedom Index: Data of Press Freedom Ranking 2021," Reporters Without Borders, accessed August 19, 2022, https://rsf.org
/en/index?year=2021.
32. Andrea Fumarola, "Fidesz and Electoral Reform: How to Safeguard Hungarian Democracy," *LSE*, March 21, 2016, https://
blogs.lse.ac.uk/europpblog/2016/03/21/fidesz-and-electoral-reform-
how-to-safeguard-hungarian-democracy/.
33. Corinne Deloy, "Unsurprisingly Outgoing Prime Minister Viktor Orban Wins the General Election in Hungary," Foundation Robert Schuman, April 6, 2014, https://www.robert-schuman.eu/en/doc/oee
/oee-1493-en.pdf.
34. Bálint Magyar, "The Hungarian Post-Communist Mafia State," *National Research University Higher School of Economics: XVIth International Academic Conference on Economic and Social Development*, April 2015.
35. Larry Diamond, "Democracy's Arc: From Resurgent to Imperiled," *Journal of Democracy*, no. 33 (January 2022):163–179; Steven Levitsky and Daneil Ziblatt, *How Democracies Die* (New York: Crown, 2018), 8–9.
36. Lendvai, *Orban: Hungary's Strongman*, 97.
37. Lendvai, *Orban: Hungary's Strongman*, 103–104.
38. Pieter Cannoot, "Baka v. Hungary: Judicial Independence at Risk in Hungary's New Constitutional Reality" *Strasbourg Observers*, July 12,

2016, https://strasbourgobservers.com/2016/07/12/baka-v-hungary
-judicial-independence-at-risk-in-hungarys-new-constitutional
-reality/.

39. Lendvai, *Orban: Hungary's Strongman*, 104.

40. Paul Lendvai, "The Transformer: Orbán's Evolution and Hungary's Demise," *Foreign Affairs*, August 12, 2019, https://www.foreignaffairs.com/articles/hungary/2019-08-12/transformer.

41. David Frum, "How to Build an Autocracy," *Atlantic*, March 2017, https://www.theatlantic.com/magazine/archive/2017/03/how-to-build-an-autocracy/513872/.

42. Madeleine Albright, *Fascism: A Warning* (New York: HarperCollins, 2019), 179.

43. Barry Eichengreen, *The Populist Temptation: Economic Grievance and Political Reaction in the Modern Era* (New York: Oxford University Press, 2018), 185.

44. "'Stop Brussels': European Commission Responds to Hungarian National Consultation," European Commission, accessed October 30, 2022, https://ec.europa.eu/info/publications/stop-brussels-european-commission-responds-hungarian-national-consultation_en; Cannoot, "Baka v. Hungary."

45. Albright, *Fascism: A Warning*, 172.

46. Ivan Krastev, "Eastern Europe's Illiberal Revolution: The Long Road to Democratic Decline," *Foreign Affairs*, no. 97 (May 2018): 49–56.

47. Rick Noack, "Muslims Threaten Europe's Christian Identity, Hungary's Leader Says," *Washington Post*, September 3, 2015, https://www.washingtonpost.com/news/worldviews/wp/2015/09/03/muslims-threaten-europes-christian-identity-hungarys-leader-says/.

48. Valerie Hopkins, "Viktor Orban Keeps Trianon Treaty Bitterness Alive, 100 Years On," *Financial Times*, June 5, 2020, https://www.ft.com/content/6b785393-bdf8-4974-a17c-4017445fca1b.

49. Albright, *Fascism: A Warning*, 179–180.

50. Krastev, "Eastern Europe's Illiberal Revolution."

51. "Consolidated Version of the Treaty of the European Union," EUR-Lex, accessed August 19, 2022, https://eur-lex.europa.eu/eli/treaty/teu_2012/art_2/oj.

52. Csaba Tóth, "Full Text of Viktor Orbán's Speech at Băile Tuşnad (Tusnádfürdő) of 26 July 2014," *The Budapest Beacon*, July 29, 2014, https://budapestbeacon.com/full-text-of-viktor-orbans-speech-at-baile-tusnad-tusnadfurdo-of-26-july-2014/.

53. "Freedom in the World 2021: Hungary," Freedom House, accessed August 19, 2022, https://freedomhouse.org/country/hungary/freedom-world/2021.

54. Steven Erlanger and Benjamin Novak, "How the E.U. Allowed Hungary to Become an Illiberal Model," *New York Times*, January 3,

2022, https://www.nytimes.com/2022/01/03/world/europe/hungary
-european-union.html.

55. "December Infringements Package: Key Decisions," European Commission, accessed August 19, 2022, https://ec.europa.eu /commission/presscorner/detail/en/inf_21_6201; Benjamin Novak, "Hungary Passes Laws Curtailing Gay Rights and Expanding Executive Power," *New York Times*, December 15, 2020 https://www .nytimes.com/2020/12/15/world/hungary-laws-orban-gay-rights .html.

56. Miranda Cortizo, "The European Union's Response to Internal Democratic Backsliding: Evidence from Hungary and Poland," Universidad de San Andrés, graduate thesis, 2023.

57. "Rule of Law Conditionality Regulation," European Union, accessed March 21, 2023, https://commission.europa.eu/strategy-and-policy /eu-budget/protection-eu-budget/rule-law-conditionality-regulation _en.

58. European Union, "Commission Finds That Hungary Has Not Progressed Enough in Its Reforms and Must Meet Essential Milestones for Its Recovery and Resilience Funds," European Union, accessed March 6, 2023, https://ec.europa.eu/commission /presscorner/detail/en/IP_22_7273.

59. Sigrid Melchior, "Explainer: Europe Cuts off Funds for Hungary— What Is at Stake?," *Investigate Europe*, December 15, 2022, https:// www.investigate-europe.eu/en/2022/explainer-europe-cuts-off -funds-for-hungary-what-is-at-stake/.

60. Melchoir, "Explainer: Europe Cuts off Funds for Hungary."

61. European Union, "Commission Finds That Hungary Has Not Progressed Enough."

62. Paola Tamma, "Hungary Vows to Overhaul Its Judiciary, Hoping to Unlock EU Funds," *Politico*, November 7, 2022, https://www.politico .eu/article/hungary-overhaul-judiciary-unlock-eu-funds/.

63. Will Kenton, "MiFID II," *Investopedia*, September 1, 2021, https:// www.investopedia.com/terms/m/mifid-ii.asp.

64. "Counting the Cost of MiFID II," IHS Markit, accessed August 19, 2022, https://cdn.ihs.com/www/pdf/counting-the-cost-of-mifid-ii .pdf.

65. "Characteristics of Foreign Currency Bonds: Bond Data," ÁKK, accessed August 19, 2022, https://akk.hu/content/path= characteristicseign-currency-bonds.

66. Veronika Gulyas and Lyubov Pronina, "Hungary's Eurobond Plan Suggests EU Dispute Will Drag On," *Bloomberg*, September 13, 2021, https://www.bloomberg.com/news/articles/2021-09-13 /hungary-plans-multi-tranche-bond-sale-to-cover-eu-funding-delay.

67. Robert Tait and Flora Garamvolgyi, "Viktor Orbán Wins Fourth Consecutive Term as Hungary's Prime Minister," *Guardian*, April 3, 2022, https://www.theguardian.com/world/2022/apr/03/viktor-orban -expected-to-win-big-majority-in-hungarian-general-election.

68. Pauline Lutzenkirchen, "Unprecedented Democratic Backsliding in Hungary: Is It Too Late to Turn Around?," *Democratic Erosion*, November 2022.

69. Zsófia Nagy-Vargha, "Orbán: 'We have won a victory so big that you can see it from the moon, but certainly from Brussels,'" Hungary Today, April 4, 2022, https://hungarytoday.hu/orban-election -victory-fidesz-2022-eu-brussels/.

70. Laszlo Balogh, "Hungary Issues FX Benchmark Bonds Worth $3.8 bln, Minister Says," *Reuters*, November 11, 2017, https://www.reuters .com/markets/europe/hungary-has-issued-fx-benchmark-bonds -finance-minister-says-2022-06-09/.

CHAPTER 5

1. Katrin Bennhold, "The Former Chancellor Who Became Putin's Man in Germany," *New York Times*, April 23, 2022, https://www .nytimes.com/2022/04/23/world/europe/schroder-germany-russia -gas-ukraine-war-energy.html.

2. "Former German Chancellor Gerhard Schroeder Becomes Chairman of Russian State-Controlled Nord Stream Pipeline Company Directly After Leaving Office," Alliance for Securing Democracy, accessed on February 1, 2023, https://securingdemocracy.gmfus.org/incident /former-german-chancellor-gerhard-schra%C2%B6der-becomes -chairman-of-russian-state-controlled-nord-stream-pipeline -company-directly-after-leaving-office/.

3. "Who We Are," Nord Stream, accessed February 6, 2023, https:// www.nord-stream.com/about-us/.

4. Pyilip Oldermann, "How Reliant Is Germany—and the Rest of Europe—on Russian Gas?," *Guardian*, July 21, 2022, https://www .theguardian.com/world/2022/jul/21/how-reliant-is-germany-and -europe-russian-gas-nord-stream.

5. Bennhold, "The Former Chancellor Who Became Putin's Man in Germany."

6. "Board of Directors: Matthias Warnig," Rosneft, accessed on February 1, 2023, https://www.rosneft.com/Investors/corporate _governance/Board_of_directors/item/22936/.

7. Karen Dawisha, *Putin's Kleptocracy: Who Owns Russia?* (New York: Simon & Schuster, 2015), 53.

8. Philip Short, *Putin* (New York: Henry Holt and Company, 2022), 95; and Masha Gessen, *The Man Without a Face: The Unlikely Rise of Vladimir Putin* (New York: Penguin Random House LLC, 2012), 63.

9. Catherine Belton, *Putin's People: How the KGB Took Back Russia and Then Took on the West* (London: Harper Collins Publishers, 2020), 29.

10. Gessen, *The Man Without a Face*, 95–99; and Belton, *Putin's People*, 47.

11. Dawisha, *Putin's Kleptocracy*, 54.

12. Dawisha, *Putin's Kleptocracy*, 53.

13. Dawisha, *Putin's Kleptocracy*, 55.

14. Anders Åslund, *Russia's Crony Capitalism: The Path from Market Economy to Kleptocracy* (New Haven: Yale University Press, 2019), 138.

15. Belton, *Putin's People*, 238.

16. Mikhail Khodorkovsky and Martin Sixsmith, *The Russia Conundrum: How the West Fell for Putin's Power Gambit—and How to Fix It* (New York: St. Martin's Press, 2022), 15–16.

17. Khodorkovsky and Sixsmith, *The Russia Conundrum*, 21.

18. Short, *Putin*, 354.

19. Belton, *Putin's People*, 81.

20. Short, *Putin*, 354.

21. Belton, *Putin's People*, 230–232, 281.

22. Khodorkovsky and Sixsmith, *The Russia Conundrum*, 84–89.

23. Short, *Putin*, 355.

24. Dawisha, *Putin's Kleptocracy*, 280.

25. Belton, *Putin's People*, 219.

26. Khodorkovsky and Sixsmith, *The Russia Conundrum*, 93.

27. Khodorkovsky and Sixsmith, *The Russia Conundrum*, 95.

28. Åslund, *Russia's Crony Capitalism*, 101.

29. Belton, *Putin's People*, 234.

30. Khodorkovsky and Sixsmith, *The Russia Conundrum*, 121.

31. Belton, *Putin's People*, 279.

32. Belton, *Putin's People*, 284.

33. Belton, *Putin's People*, 285, and endnote 46 of Chapter 9, 555.

34. Belton, *Putin's People*, 289.

35. Gessen, *The Man Without a Face*, 253.

36. Belton, *Putin's People*, 297.

37. Belton, *Putin's People*, 285.

38. Gregory White and Chip Cummins, "Russia to Form Energy Giant Open to West but Led by Kremlin," *Wall Street Journal*, September 15, 2004, https://www.wsj.com/articles/SB109516016635417245.

39. Belton, *Putin's People*, 286.

40. Erin E. Arvedlund, "Gazprom Merger Plan Collapses," *New York Times*, May 18, 2005, https://www.nytimes.com/2005/05/18/business/worldbusiness/gazprom-merger-plan-collapses.html.

41. Gregory White, "Kremlin Cancels Its Plan to Merge Gazprom, Rosneft," *Wall Street Journal*, May 18, 2005, https://www.wsj.com/articles/SB111634593106435872.

42. Belton, *Putin's People*, 355.
43. Åslund, *Russia's Crony Capitalism*, 119.
44. Joanna Chung, "Bankers to Reap $120m on Rosneft IPO," *Financial Times*, June 27, 2006, https://www.ft.com/content/6d5a6cb8-0603 -11db-9dde-0000779e2340.
45. "Rosneft and BP Complete TNK-BP Sale and Purchase Transaction," British Petroleum, accessed on February 6, 2023, https://www.bp .com/en/global/corporate/news-and-insights/press-releases/rosneft -and-bp-complete-tnk-bp-sale-and-purchase-transaction.html.
46. Åslund, *Russia's Crony Capitalism*, 119.
47. Åslund, *Russia's Crony Capitalism*, 120.
48. Åslund, *Russia's Crony Capitalism*, 120.
49. Åslund, *Russia's Crony Capitalism*, 122.
50. Åslund, *Russia's Crony Capitalism*, 121.
51. Dawisha, *Putin's Kleptocracy*, 323.
52. Dawisha, *Putin's Kleptocracy*, 314.
53. Belton, *Putin's People*, 355.
54. Åslund, *Russia's Crony Capitalism*, 108.
55. Åslund, *Russia's Crony Capitalism*, 114.
56. Åslund, *Russia's Crony Capitalism*, 142.
57. Javier Blas and Jack Farchy, *The World for Sale: Money, Power, and the Traders Who Barter the Earth's Resources* (New York: Oxford University Press, 2021), 212.
58. Blas and Farchy, *The World for Sale*, 215.
59. Belton, *Putin's People*, 321.
60. Dawisha, *Putin's Kleptocracy*, 330-331.
61. Sam Ro, "Jim Grant Makes the Most Contrarian Investment Call in the World," *Business Insider*, May 5, 2014, https://www .businessinsider.com/jim-grant-makes-bull-case-for-gazprom -2014-5.https://www.businessinsider.in/jim-grant-makes-the-most -contrarian-investment-call-in-the-world/articleshow/34705184.cms
62. Dawisha, *Putin's Kleptocracy*, 325.
63. Dawisha, *Putin's Kleptocracy*, 311.
64. Åslund, *Russia's Crony Capitalism*, 115.
65. Kathrin Hille, "Ukraine Bailout Could Derail Putin's Drive to Boost Russian Economy," *Financial Times*, December 18, 2013, https:// www.ft.com/content/3b3db13c-67e3-11e3-a905-00144feabdc0 .https://www.ft.com/content/3b3db13c-67e3-11e3-a905 -00144feabdc0
66. Åslund, *Russia's Crony Capitalism*, 115–117.
67. Åslund, *Russia's Crony Capitalism*, 123.
68. Gabrielle Tétrault-Farber and Olesya Astakhova, "Rosneft Sells Venezuelan Assets to Russia After U.S. Sanctions Ramp Up,"

Reuters, March 28, 2020, https://www.reuters.com/article/us-russia
-rosneft-venezuela-idUSKBN21F0W2.

69. "Average Annual OPEC Crude Oil Price from 1960 to 2022," Statista, accessed on February 6, 2023, https://www.statista.com/statistics/262858/change-in-opec-crude-oil-prices-since-1960/.

70. Belton, *Putin's People*, 230.

71. Timothy Frye, "Russia's Weak Strongman: The Perilous Bargains That Keep Putin in Power," *Foreign Affairs*, April 1, 2021, https://www.foreignaffairs.com/articles/russia-fsu/2021-04-01/vladimir-putin-russias-weak-strongman.

72. Daniel Treisman, Tim Frye, Scott Gehlbach, Arnold Harberger, Brian Richter, Richard Rose, and Jeff, Timmons, "The Popularity of Russian Presidents," University of California, April 2008.

73. Åslund, *Russia's Crony Capitalism*, 26.

74. Short, *Putin*, 313-314.

75. Åslund, *Russia's Crony Capitalism*, 27.

76. Capital Flows Tracker, "IIF Capital Flows Report—Annual Database," Institute on International Finance, June 2021.

77. Capital Flows Tracker, "IIF Capital Flows Report—Annual Database," June 2021.

78. Pivi Munter, "Moody's in Surprise Lift for Russia," *Financial Times*, October 6, 2004, https://www.ft.com/content/7abcf866-17c7-11d9-9ac5-00000e2511c8.

79. Short, *Putin*, 309.

80. Short, *Putin*, 310.

81. Short, *Putin*, 317.

82. Gessen, *The Man Without a Face*, 155.

83. Short, *Putin*, 319.

84. Gessen, *The Man Without a Face*, 163.

85. Gessen, *The Man Without a Face*, 164.

86. Robyn Dixon, "2 Vocal Russian Publications Are Silenced," *LA Times*, April 18, 2001, https://www.latimes.com/archives/la-xpm-2001-apr-18-mn-52403-story.html.

87. Michael McFaul and Kathryn Stoner-Weiss, "The Myth of the Authoritarian Model," *Foreign Affairs* 83, no. 1 (January/February 2008): 68–80.

88. Gessen, *The Man Without a Face*, 27–29.

89. Short, *Putin*, 331.

90. Short, *Putin*, 333.

91. Gessen, *The Man Without a Face*, 181.

92. McFaul and Stoner-Weiss, "The Myth of the Authoritarian Model."

93. McFaul and Stoner-Weiss, "The Myth of the Authoritarian Model."

94. McFaul and Stoner-Weiss, "The Myth of the Authoritarian Model."

95. Dawisha, *Putin's Kleptocracy*, 317.

96. Brian Taylor, "Putin's Rule of the Game," *Foreign Affairs*, April 12, 2021, https://www.foreignaffairs.com/articles/united-states/2021-04 -12/putins-rules-game.

97. Belton, *Putin's People*, 495.

98. AFP, "'One Cold Dude': U.S. Presidents on Putin," *Moscow Times*, June 15, 2021, https://www.themoscowtimes.com/2021/06/15/one -cold-dude-us-presidents-on-putin-a74222.

99. "U.S.-Russia Relations: 'Reset' Fact Sheet," The White House, accessed February 6, 2023, https://obamawhitehouse.archives.gov /the-press-office/us-russia-relations-reset-fact-sheet.

100. Garry Kasparov, *Winter Is Coming: Why Vladimir Putin and the Enemies of the Free World Must Be Stopped* (New York: Public Affairs U.S., 2016), 185.

101. "Freedom in the World 2005: The Annual Survey of Political Rights and Civil Liberties," Freedom House, 2005.

102. Graeme Wearden, "Ukraine Crisis Sends Stock Markets Sliding: Russia's MICEX Tumbles 11%—as It Happened," *The Guardian*, March 3, 2014, https://www.theguardian.com/business/2014/mar /03/ukraine-crisis-hits-stock-markets-as-russia-hikes-interest-rates -business-live.

103. Phillip Inman and Dominic Rushe, "Ukraine Crisis Sends Russian Stock Market Tumbling," *The Guardian*, March 3, 2014, https://www .theguardian.com/world/2014/mar/03/ukraine-crisis-russian-stock -market-falls.

104. Robin Wigglesworth, Chris Flood, Colby Smith, Harriet Agnew, Laurence Fletcher, and Josephine Cumbo, "Investors Are Shocked: How Russia's Attack on Ukraine Roiled Markets," *Financial Times*, February 25, 2022, https://www.ft.com/content/828e786f-fc62-47db -920c-f683211ca853.

105. Jamie Powell and Claire Jones, "Russia's Invasion of Ukraine Rattles Markets," *Financial Times*, February 24, 2022, https://www.ft.com /content/16d25a88-7f9c-4c23-bb80-5456b5c34d80.

106. Bill Browder, *Red Notice: A True Story of High Finance, Murder, and One Man's Fight for Justice* (New York: Simon & Schuster, 2015), Kindle edition.

107. Browder, *Red Notice*.

108. Bill Browder, *Red Notice*.

109. Bill Browder, *Freezing Order: A True Story of Money Laundering, Murder, and Surviving Vladimir Putin's Wrath* (New York: Simon & Schuster, 2022), 17; and Masha Gessen, *The Man Without a Face*, 233–234.

110. Browder, *Freezing Order*, 17–18.

111. Gessen, *The Man Without a Face*, 243.

112. Browder, *Freezing Order*, 18.

113. Browder, *Freezing Order*, 19–20.

114. Browder, *Freezing Order*, 31.

115. Browder, *Freezing Order*, 38.

116. "Permanent Global Magnitsky Act Will Ensure Perpetrators Face Consequences," Freedom House, accessed February 6, https:// freedomhouse.org/article/permanent-global-magnitsky-act-will -ensure-perpetrators-face-consequences.

117. Jacob Lew and Richard Nephew, "The Use and Misuse of Economic Statecraft," *Foreign Affairs*, October 15, 2018, https://www .foreignaffairs.com/articles/world/2018-10-15/use-and-misuse -economic-statecraft.

118. Capital Flows Tracker, "IIF Capital Flows Report—Annual Database," June 2021.

119. "Russian Federation Staff Report for the 2016 Article IV Consultation—Press Release; and Staff Report," *International Monetary Fund*, Country Report 16, no.229 (July 2016), 8.

120. Kenneth Rapoza, "Russia Surprises Euro Bond Market with New Issue, and Europeans Go Nuts," *Forbes*, June 20, 2017, https://www .forbes.com/sites/kenrapoza/2017/06/20/russia-surprises-euro-bond -market-with-new-issue-and-europeans-go-nuts/?sh=1b332bd911a2.

121. "Russian Oligarch Oleg Vladimirovich Deripaska and Associates Indicted for Sanctions Evasion and Obstruction of Justice," The United States Department of Justice, accessed February 6, 2023, https://www.justice.gov/opa/pr/russian-oligarch-oleg-vladimirovich -deripaska-and-associates-indicted-sanctions-evasion-and#:~:text= In%20designating%20Deripaska%2C%20OFAC%20explained,of %20the%20Russian%20Federation%20economy.

122. Alexandra Scaggs, "Rough Days for Russian Debt," *Financial Times*, April 11, 2018, https://www.ft.com/content/c6c03f1c-ea58-3d25 -b7fc-9016cdaa87ee.

123. Oksana Kobzeva and Andrey Ostroukh, "Russia Taps Global Debt Market for First Time in 2020 with Eurobond Deal, Sources Say," *Reuters*, November 12, 2020, https://www.reuters.com/article/us -russia-eurobond-yield-idUSKBN27S13Y.

124. Philip Stafford and Tommy Stubbington, "Investors Struggle to Trade Russian Assets as Sanctions Hit Market Plumbing," *Financial Times*, March 1, 2022, https://www.ft.com/content/ff0f0533-ca8f -4e7b-9cd8-28710dcee5f7.

125. Larry Diamond, "Russia and the Threat to Liberal Democracy: How Vladimir Putin is Making the World Safe for Autocracy," *Atlantic*, December 9, 2016, https://www.theatlantic.com/international /archive/2016/12/russia-liberal-democracy/510011/.

126. Victoria Nuland, "Pinning Down Putin: How a Confident America Should Deal with Russia," *Foreign Affairs*, June 9, 2020, https://www .foreignaffairs.com/articles/russian-federation/2020-06-09/pinning -down-putin.
127. Kasparov, *Winter Is Coming*, xxiii–xxiv.
128. Diamond, "Russia and the Threat to Liberal Democracy."
129. Diamond, "Russia and the Threat to Liberal Democracy"; and Belton, *Putin's People*, 399, 428–430.
130. Financial Times, "Transcript: 'All This Fuss About Spies . . . It Is Not Worth Serious Interstate Relations,'" *Financial Times*, June 27, 2019, https://www.ft.com/content/878d2344-98f0-11e9-9573 -ee5cbb98ed36.
131. Susan Glasser, "Putin the Great: Russia's Imperial Impostor," *Foreign Affairs*, August 12, 2019, https://www.foreignaffairs.comro/articles /russian-federation/2019-08-12/putin-great.

CHAPTER 6

1. Robin Marshall and Zhaoyi Yang, "WGBI Inclusion Confirms China's Arrival on Global Bond Stage," *FTSE Russell*, May 2021.
2. Robin Marshall and Zhaoyi Yang, "Chinese Bond Market: Evolution and Characteristics," *FTSE Russell*, July 2020.
3. "China Government Debt to GDP," Trading Economics, accessed on March 22, 2023, https://tradingeconomics.com/china/government -debt-to-gdp.
4. Eugenio Cerutti and Maurice Obstfeld, "China's Bond Market and Global Financial Market," *International Monetary Fund*, no. 2018/253 (2018).
5. Marshall and Yang, "Chinese Bond Market: Evolution and Characteristics."
6. Dirk Willer, *Trading Fixed Income and FX in Emerging Markets: A Practitioner's Guide* (New Jersey: Wiley, 2020), 47; and Marshall and Yang, "Chinese Bond Market: Evolution and Characteristics."
7. Marshall and Yang, "WGBI Inclusion Confirms China's Arrival on Global Bond Stage."
8. "Fast Track to China Bond Market," Bond Connect, accessed December 26, 2022, https://www.chinabondconnect.com/en/index .html.
9. Susanne Barton and Daniela Sirtori-Cortina, "Dollar's Share of Global Reserves Sinks to Lowest Since 1995," *Bloomberg*, March 31, 2021, https://www.bloomberg.com/news/articles/2021-03-31/dollar -s-share-of-global-reserves-sinks-to-lowest-since-1995.
10. Carmen Reinhart and Kenneth Rogoff, *This Time Is Different: Eight Centuries of Financial Folly* (New Jersey: Princeton University Press, 2009), 27.

11. "WGBI—the Latest Major Index Inclusion for China," HSBC, June 22, 2021, https://www.gbm.hsbc.com/insights/securities-services /wgbi-the-latest-major-index-inclusion-for-china.

12. "FTSE World Government Bond Index (WGBI)," FTSE Russell, accessed November 30, 2022, https://www.yieldbook.com /x/ixFactSheet/factsheet_monthly_wgbi.pdf; Serkan Arslanalp, Dimitris Drakopoulos, Rohit Goel, and Robin Koepke, "Benchmark-Driven Investments in Emerging Market Bond Markets: Taking Stock," *International Monetary Fund*, no. 20/192 (September 2020).

13. David Lubin, *Dance of the Trillions: Developing Countries and Global Finance* (Washington, DC: Brookings Institution Press, 2018), 109–114.

14. Minxin Pei, "China: Totalitarianism's Long Shadow," *Journal of Democracy* 32, no. 2 (April 2021): 5–21.

15. Marshall and Yang, "WGBI Inclusion Confirms China's Arrival on Global Bond Stage."

16. Marshall and Yang, "Chinese Bond Market: Evolution and Characteristics."

17. Elizabeth Economy, *The Third Revolution: Xi Jinping and the New Chinese State* (Oxford University Press, 2018), 95.

18. Minxin Pei, "China: From Tiananmen to Neo-Stalinism," *Journal of Democracy* 31, no. 1 (January 2020): 148–57.

19. Pei, "China: From Tiananmen to Neo-Stalinism."

20. Pei, "China: Totalitarianism's Long Shadow."

21. Larry Diamond, *The Spirit of Democracy: The Struggle to Build Free Societies Throughout the World* (New York: Times Books, 2008), 26.

22. Diamond, *The Spirit of Democracy*, 27.

23. Henry Kissinger, *On China* (New York: Penguin Books, 2011), 444.

24. Kissinger, *On China*, 457.

25. Pei, "China: From Tiananmen to Neo-Stalinism."

26. Julian Gewirtz, "China's Road Not Taken: How the Chinese Communist Party Rewrites History," *Foreign Affairs*, September 29, 2022, https://www.foreignaffairs.com/china/chinas-road-not-taken.

27. Gewirtz, "China's Road Not Taken."

28. Economy, *The Third Revolution*, 3.

29. "Document 9: A China File Translation—How Much Is a Hardline Party Directive Shaping China's Current Political Climate?," China File, November 23, 2013, https://www.chinafile.com/document -9-chinafile-translation; Economy, *The Third Revolution*, 38.

30. Economy, *The Third Revolution*, 10.

31. Pei, "China: From Tiananmen to Neo-Stalinism."

32. Economy, *The Third Revolution*, 18.

33. Economy, *The Third Revolution*, 40.

34. Economy, *The Third Revolution*, 40.

35. Clive Hamilton and Mareike Ohlberg, *Hidden Hand: Exposing How the Chinese Communist Party Is Reshaping the World* (London: Oneworld Publications, 2020), 165.
36. Economy, *The Third Revolution*, 41.
37. Pei, "China: Totalitarianism's Long Shadow."
38. Hamilton and Ohlberg, *Hidden Hand*, 220.
39. Freedom House, *Freedom in the World 2015: The Annual Survey of Political Rights and Civil Liberties* (Maryland: Rowman & Littlefield, 2016), 145.
40. Hamilton and Ohlberg, *Hidden Hand*, 99.
41. Hamilton and Ohlberg, *Hidden Hand*, 101.
42. "International Advisory Council," China Investment Corporation, accessed December 26, 2022, http://www.china-inv.cn/chinainven /Governance/InternationalAdvisoryCouncil.shtml.
43. "About the John L. Thornton China Center," accessed December 26, 2022, https://www.brookings.edu/about-the-china-center/.
44. "About the John L. Thornton China Center."
45. Hamilton and Ohlberg, *Hidden Hand*, 101.
46. Hamilton and Ohlberg, *Hidden Hand*, 101.
47. "About Us," Paulson Institute, accessed December 26, 2022, https:// www.paulsoninstitute.org/about/.
48. Hamilton and Ohlberg, *Hidden Hand*, 102.
49. George Soros, "BlackRock's China Blunder," *Wall Street Journal*, September 6, 2021, https://www.wsj.com/articles/blackrock-larry -fink-china-hkex-sse-authoritarianism-xi-jinping-term-limits -human-rights-ant-didi-global-national-security-11630938728.
50. Consumers' Research, "BlackRock: Backpedaling," Consumers' Research YouTube Channel, accessed March 28, 2022, https://www .youtube.com/watch?v=IaRKQyqCJsw.
51. Consumers' Research, "BlackRock: Backpedaling."
52. Hamilton and Ohlberg, *Hidden Hand*, 110.
53. Post Squawk Box (@SquawkCNBC), "What They Have Is an Autocratic System," Twitter, November 30, 2021, https://twitter .com/SquawkCNBC/status/1465660719756681218?ref_src=twsrc %5Etfw.
54. Human Rights Watch, *Eradicating Ideological Viruses: China's Campaign of Repression Against Xinjiang's Muslims* (New York: Human Rights Watch, 2018).
55. "Joint Declaration on the Question of Hong Kong," Wikisource, accessed February 3, 2023, https://en.wikisource.org/wiki/Sino -British_Joint_Declaration.
56. Michael Davis, "Hong Kong: How Beijing Perfected Repression," *Journal of Democracy* 33, no. 1 (January 2022): 100–15.
57. Davis, "Hong Kong: How Beijing Perfected Repression."

58. Davis, "Hong Kong: How Beijing Perfected Repression."
59. Davis, "Hong Kong: How Beijing Perfected Repression."
60. Hong Kong Monetary Authority, "2020 Annual Report," Hong Kong Monetary Authority, 2021.
61. Nicholas R. Lardy, "The State Strikes Back: The End of Economic Reform in China?," *Peterson Institute for International Economics*, no 7373 (October 2019), x.
62. Lardy, "The State Strikes Back."
63. Lardy, "The State Strikes Back," 20.
64. Hamilton and Ohlberg, *Hidden Hand*, 96.
65. Lardy, "The State Strikes Back," 82.
66. Pei, "China: From Tiananmen to Neo-Stalinism."
67. Hamilton and Ohlberg, *Hidden Hand*, 96.
68. Pei, "China: Totalitarianism's Long Shadow."
69. Hamilton and Ohlberg, *Hidden Hand*, 96.
70. Curtis Milhaupt and Wentong Zheng, "Why Mixed-Ownership Reforms Cannot Fix China's State Sector," Paulson Institute, 2016.
71. Curtis Milhaupt and Wentong Zheng, "Beyond Ownership: State Capitalism and the Chinese Firm," *UF Law Faculty Publications Geo. L.J.*, no. 665 (2015), 672.
72. Timothy Lee, "New Law Bans Government from Buying Tech from Chinese Giants ZTE and Huawei," *Ars Technica*, August 2018, https://arstechnica.com/tech-policy/2018/08/trump-signs-bill -banning-feds-from-using-huawei-zte-technology/.
73. Milhaupt and Zheng, "Beyond Ownership," 684.
74. Milhaupt and Zheng, "Beyond Ownership," 685.
75. Milhaupt and Zheng, "Beyond Ownership," 691.
76. Hamilton and Ohlberg, *Hidden Hand*, 96.
77. Milhaupt and Zheng, "Beyond Ownership," 689.
78. Milhaupt and Zheng, "Beyond Ownership," 690.
79. Milhaupt and Zheng, "Beyond Ownership," 685.
80. Milhaupt and Zheng, "Beyond Ownership," 719.
81. Economy, *The Third Revolution*, 129.
82. Economy, *The Third Revolution*, 133.
83. Milhaupt and Zheng, "Beyond Ownership," 696.
84. Willer, *Trading Fixed Income and FX in Emerging Markets*, 47.
85. Willer, *Trading Fixed Income and FX in Emerging Markets*, 47.
86. "MSCI Emerging Markets Index (USD)," MSCI, accessed February 3, 2023, https://www.msci.com/documents/10199/c0db0a48-01f2 -4ba9-ad01-226fd5678111.
87. "Assets in Global Equity ETFs Linked to MSCI Indexes Reach All-Time High of $707 Billion," MSCI, accessed February 3, 2023, https://www.msci.com/documents/10199/6de39767-c42a-47ba-ab8c -11a6205e397c.

88. "MSCI Inc. Investor Presentation," MSCI, accessed February 3, 2023, https://ir.msci.com/static-files/fcd6be29-5533-4825-8e85 -641663bdcddf.

89. Milhaupt and Zheng, "Beyond Ownership," 691.

90. Tan Jou Teng, "Meet Self-Made Tech Billionaire Wang Xing, Founder of Meituan: After Failed Social Media Networks Based on Facebook and Twitter, He Made Big Bucks with a Groupon-Inspired Shopping Platform," *Style*, May 24, 2021, https://www.scmp .com/magazines/style/luxury/article/3134587/meet-self-made-tech -billionaire-wang-xing-founder-meituan.

91. Reuters staff, "Alibaba Agrees to $266 Million Acquisition Deal with South China Morning Post," *Reuters*, December 13, 2015, https://www.reuters.com/article/us-scmp-group-alibaba -idUSKBN0TX01S20151214.

92. Hamilton and Ohlberg, *Hidden Hand*, 180.

93. Sarah Cook, "Countering Beijing's Media Manipulation," *Journal of Democracy* 33, no. 1 (2022): 122.

94. Jeanny Yu, "China's $1.9 Trillion Stock Rout Has No End in Sight," *Bloomberg*, March 11, 2022, https://www.bloomberg.com/news /articles/2022-03-11/china-s-1-9-trillion-stock-rout-has-no-end-in -sight-tech-watch?.

95. Andrew Browne, "Xi Jinping's Tech Crackdown Ignores Bigger Problems Facing China," *Bloomberg*, August 7, 2021, https:// www.bloomberg.com/news/newsletters/2021-08-07/tech-sector -crackdown-ignores-china-s-bigger-problems-new-economy -saturday.

96. Low De Wei and Olivia Tam, "China's Season of Stock Market Turbulence Continues: A Timeline," *Bloomberg*, August 6, 2021, https://www.bloomberg.com/news/articles/2021-08-06/china-s-wild -summer-of-stock-market-shocks-a-timeline.

97. Ksenia Galouchko and Lisa Pham, "Sell Tech, Buy Green Is Wall Street's Playbook for Trading China," *Bloomberg*, July 30, 2021, https://www.bloomberg.com/news/articles/2021-07-30/sell-tech-buy -green-is-wall-street-s-playbook-for-trading-china?.

98. The Economist Intelligence Unit, "Democracy Index 2021: The China Challenge," *Economist Intelligence Unit*, 2022.

99. Larry Diamond, "Democracy's Arc: From Resurgent to Imperiled," *Journal of Democracy* 33, no. 1 (January 2022): 63–79.

100. Nadège Rolland, "China's Pandemic Power Play," *Journal of Democracy* 31, no. 3 (July 2020): 25–38.

101. Economy, *The Third Revolution*, 186.

102. Rolland, "China's Pandemic Power Play."

103. Economy, *The Third Revolution*, 187.

104. Rolland, "China's Pandemic Power Play."

105. Rana Inboden, "China at the UN: Choking Civil Society," *Journal of Democracy* 32, no. 3 (July 2021): 124.
106. Charles Edel and David O. Shullman, "How China Exports Authoritarianism: Beijing's Money and Technology Is Fueling Repression Worldwide," *Foreign Affairs*, September 2021, 5.
107. Inboden, "China at the UN," 128.
108. Edel and Shullman, "How China Exports Authoritarianism," 5.
109. Cook, "Countering Beijing's Media Manipulation."
110. Cook, "Countering Beijing's Media Manipulation."
111. Sarah Cook, *Beijing's Global Megaphone: The Expansion of Chinese Communist Party Media Influence Since 2017* (Washington: Freedom House, 2021).
112. Economy, *The Third Revolution*, 191.
113. Elizabeth Economy, "Xi Jinping's New World Order: Can China Remake the International System?," *Foreign Affairs*, December 9, 2021, https://www.foreignaffairs.com/china/xi-jinpings-new-world -order.
114. Ros Krasny, "China Overtook U.S. in Foreign Direct Investment, UN Agency Says," *Bloomberg*, January 24, 2021, https://www.bloomberg .com/news/articles/2021-01-25/china-overtook-u-s-in-foreign-direct -investment-un-agency-says?leadSource=uverify%20wall.
115. "Foreign Direct Investment: Inward and Outward Flows and Stock, Annual," UNCTADstat, accessed March 22, 2023, https:// unctadstat.unctad.org/wds/TableViewer/tableView.aspx?ReportId= 96740.
116. "Stock of Chinese Direct Investment in Latin America and the Caribbean Continues to Increase," Economic and Social Policy in Latin America Initiative, accessed December 26, 2022, https://www .brookings.edu/wp-content/uploads/2018/03/global_spotlight_la _chinese_investment_fig1.png.
117. Ding Ding and Fabio Di Vittorio, "Chinese Investment in Latin America: Sectoral Complementarity and the Impact of China's Rebalancing," *International Monetary Fund*, Wo. 2021/160 (2021).
118. Evelyn Simoni, "What Drives Chinese Firms Presence in Latin America? An Empirical Analysis of Chinese Foreign Direct Investment in Latin America," Georgetown University, 2020, 47.
119. Sebastian Horn, Carmen Reinhart, and Christoph Trebesch, "China's Overseas Lending," *Journal of International Economics* 133, no. 3 (November 2021).
120. Horn, Reinhart, and Trebesch, "China's Overseas Lending."
121. "Venezuela 'receives $5bn in finance from China,'" *BBC News*, April 20, 2015, https://www.bbc.com/news/world-latin-america -32381250.
122. Horn, Reinhart, and Trebesch, "China's Overseas Lending."

CHAPTER 7

1. Carlos De la Torre, *Populisms: A Quick Immersion* (New York: Tibidabo, 2019), 14.
2. See Rudiger Dornbusch and Sebastian Edwards, *The Macroeconomics of Populism in Latin America* (Chicago: University of Chicago Press, 1991).
3. Kenneth Roberts and Steven Levitsky, eds., *The Resurgence of the Latin American Left* (Baltimore: Johns Hopkins University Press, 2011), 25.
4. Arturo Sarukhan, "America Must Not Ignore Mexico's Democratic Decay," *Foreign Affairs*, February 18, 2022, https://www .foreignaffairs.com/articles/central-america-caribbean/2022-02-18 /america-must-not-ignore-mexicos-democratic-decay.
5. "Las Fuerzas Armadas de Bolivia le pidieron la renuncia a Evo Morales," *Infobae*, September 5, 2022, https://www.infobae.com /america/america-latina/2019/11/10/las-ffaa-de-bolivia-le-pidieron -la-renuncia-a-evo-morales/ (translated with Google Translate and own edits).
6. Raul Madrid, "Bolivia: Origins and Policies of the Movimiento al Socialismo," in *The Resurgence of the Latin American Left*, ed. Steven Levitsky and Kenneth M. Roberts (Baltimore: The Johns Hopkins University Press, 2011).
7. Kurt Weyland, "How Populism Corrodes Latin American Parties," *Journal of Democracy* 32, no. 4 (October 2021): 42–55.
8. Abigail Bengwayan-Anongos et al., *The Indigenous World 2022* (Copenhagen: Eks-Skolens Grafisk Design & Tryk, 2022).
9. Laurence Blair and Dan Collyns, "Evo Morales: Indigenous Leader Who Changed Bolivia but Stayed Too Long," *The Guardian*, November 15, 2019, https://www.theguardian.com/world/2019/nov /15/evo-morales-indigenous-leader-who-changed-bolivia-but-stayed -too-long.
10. Madrid, "Bolivia: Origins and Policies of the Movimiento al Socialismo," 252–253.
11. A. Carlos and L. Quiroga, "Bolivia coloca primer bono global en casi un siglo," Reuters, October 23, 2012, https://www.reuters.com/article /latinoamerica-economia-bolivia-bono-idLTASIE89L08E20121022 (translated with Google Translate and own edits).
12. Madrid, "Bolivia: Origins and Policies of the Movimiento al Socialismo," 253.
13. "Democracy Index 2010: Democracy in Retreat," Economist Intelligence Unit, 2010.
14. "Bolivia dice 'No' en referendo a otra reelección de Evo Morales," *BBC News Mundo*, February 24, 2016, https://www.bbc.com /mundo/noticias/2016/02/160223_bolivia_evo_morales_referendo _resultado_ep.

15. Fabrice Lehoucq, "Bolivia's Citizen Revolt," *Journal of Democracy* 31, no. 3 (July 2020): 130–144.
16. Blair and Collyns, "Evo Morales."
17. "Freedom in the World 2018: Bolivia," Freedom House, accessed September 5, 2022, https://freedomhouse.org/country/bolivia/freedom-world/2018.
18. "2018 Corruption Perceptions Index," Transparency International, accessed on March 27, 2023, https://www.transparency.org/en/cpi/2018.
19. Marcelo Claure, "La importancia de la emisión de bonos soberanos en el 2017," *EC Noticias*, 2017, https://medios.economiayfinanzas.gob.bo/MH/documentos/2017/Periodico-No-4-interactivo.pdf.
20. Lehoucq, "Bolivia's Citizen Revolt."
21. OAS, "Electoral Integrity Analysis General Elections in the Plurinational State of Bolivia," *Organization of American States*, October 2019, 8.
22. John Curiel and Jack R. Williams, "Analysis of the 2019 Bolivia Election," Center for Economic and Policy Research, February 2020.
23. Frances Jenner, "Excessive Police Violence in Protests Cause Deaths and Thousands of Injuries," *Latin America Reports*, November 27, 2019, https://latinamericareports.com/excessive-police-violence-protests-deaths-injuries/3917/.
24. X. Velasco, Calla Hummel, Sam Handlin, and Amy Erica Smith, "Latin America Erupts: When Does Competitive Authoritarianism Take Root?," *Journal of Democracy* 32, no. 3 (July 2021): 63–77.
25. "Variable Graph: Liberal Democracy Index—Bolivia," V-Dem, accessed September 20, 2022, https://v-dem.net/data_analysis/VariableGraph/.
26. Alexander Saeedy, "Bolivia Bonds Tank with Foreign Reserves at Lowest in over 20 Years," *MarketWatch*, March 28, 2023, https://www.marketscreener.com/news/latest/Bolivia-Bonds-Tank-With-Foreign-Reserves-at-Lowest-in-Over-20-Years--43359967/
27. Reuters Staff, "UPDATE 1-Ecuador launches $2 bln 10-yr bond at 7.95 pct -IFR," Reuters, June 17, 2014, https://www.reuters.com/article/ecuador-debt-idUKL2N0OY1FG20140617.
28. Boris Korby and Christine Jenkins, "Ecuador Sells $2 Billion in Return to Bond Market," *Bloomberg*, June 17, 2014, https://www.bloomberg.com/news/articles/2014-06-17/ecuador-plans-bond-market-return-today-five-years-after-default#xj4y7vzkg.
29. Carmen Reinhart and Kenneth Rogoff, *This Time Is Different: Eight Centuries of Financial Folly* (New Jersey: Princeton University Press, 2009).
30. Max Seitz, "Los países que más 'defaults' han tenido en la historia (y no son Grecia ni Argentina)," *BBC News Mundo*, June 29, 2015,

https://www.bbc.com/mundo/noticias/2015/06/150629_economia
_grecia_mayores_deudores_default_ms.

31. Jonathan Eaton and Mark Gersovitz, "Debt with Potential Repudiation: Theoretical and Empirical Analysis," *Review of Economic Studies* 48, no. 2 (1981): 289–309.

32. Arturo C. Porzecanski, "When Bad Things Happen to Good Sovereign Debt Contracts: The Case of Ecuador," *Law and Contemporary Problems* 73, no. 4 (2010): 251–271, 258.

33. Porzecanski, "When Bad Things Happen to Good Sovereign Debt Contracts," 261, 265.

34. Roberts and Levitsky, *The Resurgence of the Latin American Left*, 260, 271.

35. Felipe Burbano and Carlos de la Torre, *El Populismo en el Ecuador* (Virginia: ILDIS, 1989), 72.

36. Roberts and Levitsky, *The Resurgence of the Latin American Left*, 271.

37. Roberts and Levitsky, 272; "Freedom in the World 2021: Ecuador," Freedom House, accessed September 5, 2022, https://freedomhouse.org/country/ecuador/freedom-world/2021.

38. De la Torre, *Populisms: A Quick Immersion*, 120.

39. Ley Organica de Comunicación (Ecuador: Asamblea Naciónal, 2013) (translated with Google Translate and own edits).

40. José Miguel Vivanco, "Correa's Clamp on the Media," *Human Rights Watch*, July 11, 2016, https://www.hrw.org/news/2016/07/11/correas-clamp-media.

41. Irene Caselli, "Ecuador's Rafael Correa Under Fire for Media Laws," *BBC News*, February 2, 2012, https://www.bbc.com/news/world-latin-america-16806224.

42. De la Torre, *Populisms: A Quick Immersion*, 124.

43. "Correa le quita pauta oficial a medios privados," *El Cronista*, July 29, 2012, https://www.cronista.com/interNaciónales/Correa-le-quita-pauta-oficial-a-medios-privados-20120729-0011.html (translated with Google Translate and own edits).

44. De la Torre, *Populisms: A Quick Immersion*, 121.

45. Vivanco, "Correa's Clamp on the Media."

46. Soraya Constante, "La autocensura es ley en la prensa de Ecuador," *El País*, July 3, 2014, https://elpais.com/interNaciónal/2014/07/02/actualidad/1404333934_595067.html.

47. "An Assault on Democracy," *New York Times*, January 23, 2012, https://www.nytimes.com/2012/01/24/opinion/an-assault-on-democracy.html.

48. Editorial Board, "Ahmedinejad Trip to Ecuador: A Meeting of International Pariahs," *Washington Post*, January 11, 2012, https://www.washingtonpost.com/opinions/ahmedinejad-trip-to-ecuador-a-meeting-of-international-pariahs/2012/01/11/gIQAobzwrP_story.html.

49. John Polga-Hecimovich and Francisco Sánchez, "Latin America Erupts: Ecuador's Return to the Past," *Journal of Democracy* 32, no. 3 (July 2021): 5–18, 11.
50. Carolina Silva-Portero, "Chronicle of an Amendment Foretold: Eliminating Presidential Term Limits in Ecuador," *Constitutionnet*, January 20, 2016. https://constitutionnet.org/news/chronicle-amendment-foretold-eliminating-presidential-term-limits-ecuador.
51. "Miles marchan en Ecuador contra políticas de Rafael Correa," *BBC News Mundo*, March 20, 2015, https://www.bbc.com/mundo/ultimas_noticias/2015/03/150319_ultnot_ecuador_protesta_opositora_lav.
52. Richard Lapper, *Beef, Bible and Bullets: Brazil in the Age of Bolsonaro* (Manchester: Manchester University Press, 2021).
53. Gideon Rachman, *The Age of the Strongman: How the Cult of the Leader Threatens Democracy Around the World* (New York: Other Press, 2022), 159.
54. Yasmeen Serhan, "Trump Endorses His Legacy," *Atlantic*, October 28, 2021, https://www.theatlantic.com/international/archive/2021/10/donald-trump-jair-bolsonaro/620504/.
55. Fabrício H. Chagas Bastos, "Political Realignment in Brazil: Jair Bolsonaro and the Right Turn", *Revista de Estudios Sociales*, 69 | 2019, 92-100.
56. Gideon Rachman, *The Age of the Strongman: How the Cult of the Leader Threatens Democracy Around the World* (New York: Other Press, 2022), 161.
57. Bryan Harris, Andres Schipani, and Carolina Unzelte, "Brazil's Bolsonaro Keeps It in the Family," *Financial Times*, May 6, 2019, https://www.ft.com/content/2fad23d2-6cdf-11e9-80c7-60ee53e6681d.
58. Luis Barrucho, "Brazilian Vote-Pledge Stirs Memories of Military Rule," BBC News, April 21, 2016, https://www.bbc.com/news/world-latin-america-36093338.
59. Harris, Schipani, and Carolin Unzelte, "Brazil's Bolsonaro Keeps It in the Family."
60. Gideon Rachman, *The Age of the Strongman: How the Cult of the Leader Threatens Democracy Around the World* (New York: Other Press, 2022), 161.
61. Moisés Naím, "The Dictator's New Playbook: Why Democracy Is Losing the Fight," *Foreign Affairs*, February 22, 2022, https://www.moisesnaim.com/my-columns/2022/3/8/the-dictators-new-playbook-why-democracy-is-losing-the-fight.
62. Moisés Naím, *The Revenge of Power* (New York: St. Martin's Publishing Group, 2022), 242.
63. "'Gripezinha': el día que Bolsonaro se burló del coronavirus en una conferencia oficial," *La Nación*, July 7, 2020,

https://www.laNación.com.ar/el-mundo/gripezinha-dia-bolsonaro
-se-burlo-del-coronavirus-nid2392758/ (translated with Google
Translate and own edits).

64. "Mortality Analyses," Johns Hopkins University & Medicine,
accessed September 5, 2022, https://coronavirus.jhu.edu/data
/mortality.

65. Oliver Stuenkel, "Bolsonaro Fans the Flames: Brazil's Government
Still Has One Faction That Can Douse Them," *Foreign Affairs*,
August 30, 2019, https://www.foreignaffairs.com/articles/americas
/2019-08-30/bolsonaro-fans-flames.

66. Gideon Rachman, *The Age of the Strongman: How the Cult of the Leader
Threatens Democracy Around the World* (New York: Other Press, 2022),
124.

67. Flavia Bellieni Zimmermann, "El proyecto autoritario de Bolsonaro:
reflexiones sobre la agonizante democracia brasileña," *Open
Democracy*, February 16, 2021, https://www.opendemocracy.net/es
/proyecto-autoritario-bolsonaro-pandemia-reflecciones-agonizante
-democracia-brasilena/.

68. Daniel Carvalho, "Yo soy la Constitución, dice Bolsonaro mientras
defiende la democracia y la libertad un día después del golpe mili-
tar," *Folha de S.Paulo*, Abril 20, 2020, https://www1.folha.uol.com
.br/poder/2020/04/democracia-e-liberdade-acima-de-tudo-diz
-bolsonaro-apos-participar-de-ato-pro-golpe.shtml (translated with
Google Translate and own edits).

69. Zimmermann, "El proyecto autoritario de Bolsonaro."

70. Daniel Carvalho and Simone Preissler Iglesias, "Bolsonaro Calls
Ambassadors to Cast Doubt on Electoral System," *Bloomberg*, July
19, 2022, https://www.bloomberg.com/news/articles/2022-07-18
/bolsonaro-calls-ambassadors-to-cast-doubt-on-electoral-system.

71. "Brasil: la Corte ratificó el voto electrónico, que Bolsonaro quiere
cambiar," *El Cronista*, August 2, 2021, https://www.cronista.com
/interNaciónales/brasil-la-corte-suprema-ratifico-el-voto-electronico
-que-bolsonaro-quiere-cambiar/.

72. Oliver Stuenkel, "Bolsonaro's Failed Reelection Bid Is Certain to
Inspire Others Like Him," *Carnegie Endowment for International
Peace*, November 8, 2022, https://carnegieendowment.org/2022/11
/08/bolsonaro-s-failed-reelection-bid-is-certain-to-inspire-others
-like-him-pub-88357.

73. Charles Newbery, "Guedes: Finance Minister of the Year,
LatinFinance, March 23, 2020, https://www.latinfinance.com
/magazine/2020/q1/guedes-finance-minister-of-the-year.

74. "Relatório Mensal da Dívida (RMD)," Tesouro Naciónal Transparente,
accessed September 5, 2022, https://www.tesourotransparente.gov.br
/publicacoes/relatorio-mensal-da-divida-rmd/2022/5.

75. This comes from a private conversation with Di Marco. Her book is: Laura Di Marco, *Cristina Fernández: La Verdadera Historia* (Argentina: Editorial Sudamericana, 2014); Martín Rodríguez Yebra, "El mensaje de Cristina Kirchner: cómo apoyar a Putin sin decirlo," *La Nación*, February 28, 2022, https://www.laNación.com .ar/politica/el-mensaje-de-cristina-kirchner-como-apoyar-a-putin -sin-decirlo-nid28022022/; "Elisa Carrió: 'Cristina Kirchner trabaja para Sputnik,'" *La Nación*, June 4, 2021, https://www.laNación .com.ar/politica/elisa-carrio-cristina-kirchner-trabaja-para-sputnik -nid03062021/.

76. Mariana Zuvic, *El Origen: La Intimidad del Nacimiento de la Corrupción Kirchnerista en Santa Cruz* (Argentina: Editorial Sudamericana, 2018), 11–12 (translated with Google Translate and own edits).

77. Zuvic, *El Origen*, 83, 86.

78. Zuvic, *El Origen*, 84–85, 98–99.

79. Zuvic, *El Origen*, 112.

80. Luis Majul, *El Dueño: La historia secreta de Néstor Kirchner, el hombre que maneja los negocios públicos y privados de la Argentina* (Buenos Aires: Editorial Planeta, 2009), 27 (translated with Google Translate and own edits).

81. Mariela Arias, "Retornaron al país los fondos de Santa Cruz," *La Nación*, March 3, 2006, https://www.laNación.com.ar/politica /retornaron-al-pais-los-fondos-de-santa-cruz-nid785506/.

82. "Néstor Kirchner tras un discurso y sin saber que lo filmaban: 'Tengo 600 millones de pesos,'" YouTube, accessed March 5, 2023, https:// www.youtube.com/watch?v=lvkuCkgNjck (translated with Google Translate and own edits).

83. "Solo quedan USD 10.000 de los fondos de Santa Cruz," *Infobae*, February 9, 2018, https://www.infobae.com/politica/2018/02/09 /solo-quedan-usd-10-000-de-los-fondos-de-santa-cruz/.

84. "Argentina Will Pay in Advance IMF Debt," *MercoPress*, December 16, 2005, https://en.mercopress.com/2005/12/16/argentina-will-pay -in-advance-imf-debt.

85. Ceferino Reato, *Doce Noches 2001: El fracaso de la alianza, el golpe peronista y el origen del Kirchnerismo* (Argentina: Editorial Sudamericana, 2015), 298.

86. Reato, *Doce Noches 2001*, 389.

87. Majul, *El Dueño*, 13.

88. Majul, *El Dueño*, 19.

89. Hugo Alconada Mon, *La Piñata* (Buenos Aires: Editorial Planeta, 2015), 43.

90. Arias, "La verdadera historia de la toma del banco de Santa Cruz."

91. "Qué decía el informe de Vialidad que motivó la denuncia de Iguacel a Cristina Kirchner," *Perfil*, August 23, 2022, https://www.perfil.com /noticias/politica/obra-publica-que-decia-el-informe-de-vialidad -que-motivo-la-denuncia-de-iguacel-a-cristina-kirchner.phtml.

92. "El abandono de las obras y el plan 'limpiar todo,' el fin de la operación," *El Tribuno*, August 2, 2022, https://www.eltribuno.com/salta /nota/2022-8-2-0-0-0-el-abandono-de-las-obras-y-el-plan-limpiar -todo-el-fin-de-la-operacion.

93. Zuvic, *El Origen*, 173–174.

94. Zuvic, *El Origen*, 173.

95. "Dams in Santa Cruz River," Represas Patagonia, accessed September 5, 2022, https://represaspatagonia.com.ar/index.php/en/.

96. "El Calafate: los terrenos de la polémica, con plan de obras," *La Nación*, November 12, 2012, https://www.laNación.com.ar /politica/el-calafate-los-terrenos-de-la-polemica-con-plan-de-obras -nid1525744/.

97. Alconada Mon, *La Piñata*, 44.

98. Alconada Mon, *La Piñata*, 45.

99. Alconada Mon, *La Piñata*, 482.

100. Majul, *El Dueño*, 189.

101. Majul, *El Dueño*, 191.

102. Alconada Mon, *La Piñata*, 47.

103. Majul, *El Dueño*, 60.

104. "Quienes Somos," Casino Club, http://www.casino-club.com.ar /quienessomos.html.

105. Alconada Mon, *La Piñata*, 251.

106. Alconada Mon, *La Piñata*, 253; Hugo Alconada Mon, "Cristóbal López no pagó a la AFIP $ 8000 millones durante el kirchnerismo," *La Nación*, March 13, 2016, https://www.laNación.com.ar /politica/cristobal-López-no-pago-a-la-afip-8000-millones-durante -el-kirchnerismo-nid1879369/; Hugo Alconada Mon, "La deuda de Cristóbal López con el fisco no deja de crecer y ya supera los $8200 millones," *La Nación*, December 30, 2018.

107. Majul, *El Dueño*, 117.

108. Majul, *El Dueño*, 133.

109. Majul, *El Dueño*, 382.

110. Majul, *El Dueño*, 381.

111. Majul, *El Dueño*, 150.

112. Alconada Mon, *La Piñata*, 214.

113. Manuel Tarricone, "Diez preguntas y respuestas sobre la integración del Consejo de la Magistratura y lo que puede pasar en los próximos días," *Chequeado*, April 6, 2022, https://chequeado.com/el-explicador /diez-preguntas-y-respuestas-sobre-la-integracion-del-consejo-de-la -magistratura-y-lo-que-puede-pasar-en-los-proximos-dias/.

114. Tarricone, "Diez preguntas y respuestas sobre la integración del Consejo de la Magistratura."

115. Mariano Espina, "El Frente de Todos pierde la mayoría en el Senado," *Bloomberg Linea*, December 2, 2021, https://www.bloomberglinea.com/2021/11/15/el-frente-de-todos-pierde-la-mayoria-en-el-senado/.

116. Martín Angulo," En el Consejo de la Magistratura analizan dictar un reglamento especial para después del 15 de abril," *Infobae*, March 31, 2022, https://www.infobae.com/politica/2022/03/31/en-el-consejo-de-la-magistratura-analizan-dictar-un-reglamento-especial-para-despues-del-15-de-abril/.

117. "Consejo de la Magistratura: unas cacerolas frente a Tribunales y la teoría animal de los 'palomapájaros' de Cristina Kirchner," *Clarín*, April 20, 2022, https://www.Clarín.com/politica/consejo-magistratura-vivo-repercusiones-maniobra-oficialismo-senado-minuto-minuto_0 (translated with Google Translate and own edits).

118. Alconada Mon, *La Piñata*, 215.

119. Majul, *El Dueño*, 129.

120. "'Nisman se suicidó, espero que Luciani no haga algo así': la frase de Alberto Fernández que desató una nueva tormenta," *Perfil*, August 24, 2022, https://www.perfil.com/noticias/politica/definiciones-alberto-fernandez-tn-nisman-se-suicido-espero-fiscal-luciani-no-haga-algo-asi.phtml.

121. "Deuda: por qué es engañosa la forma en la que el Presidente mostró el ahorro por el acuerdo en C5N," *Chequeado*, August 5, 2020, https://chequeado.com/hilando-fino/deuda-por-que-es-enganosa-la-forma-en-la-que-el-presidente-mostro-el-ahorro-por-el-acuerdo-en-c5n/.

122. Marcos Buscaglia, "El plan contra la inflación dejará efectos significativos en la economía real y la política," *La Nación*, October 7, 2018, https://www.laNación.com.ar/economia/el-plan-inflacion-dejara-efectos-significativos-economia-nid2179121/.

123. "Total IMF Credit Outstanding Movement from March 01, 2023 to April 03, 2023," International Monetary Fund, accessed April 4, 2023.

124. "IBRD Statement of Loans—Historical Data," World Bank, accessed April 4, 2023, https://finances.worldbank.org/Loans-and-Credits/IBRD-Statement-Of-Loans-Historical-Data/zucq-nrc3.

CHAPTER 8

1. Chris Flood, Colby Smith, Harriet Agnew, Josephine Cumbo, Laurence Fletcher, and Robin Wigglesworth, "'Investors Are Shocked': How Russia's Attack on Ukraine Roiled Markets," *Financial Times*, February 25, 2022, https://www.ft.com/content/828e786f-fc62-47db-920c-f683211ca853.

2. Selcuk Gokoluk and Srinivasan Sivabalan, "BlackRock Is Among Russia Bond Holders Tangled in $15 Billion Rout," *Bloomberg*, February 25, 2022, https://www.bloomberg.com/news/articles/2022-02-25/blackrock-among-russia-bond-holders-tangled-in-15-billion-rout.

3. Hazel Bradford, "Russian Invasion of Ukraine Has European Investors on Alert," *Pension and Investment*, February 24, 2022, https://www.pionline.com/international/russian-invasion-ukraine-has-european-investors-alert.

4. Daniel Thomas, "Norway's $1.3tn Oil Fund to Sell out of Russia," *Financial Times*, February 27, 2022, https://www.ft.com/content/475838e4-a430-4c08-bd18-24f14beb4a9e.

5. Eric Platt, "Moody's Warns Russia Could Lose Investment-Grade Credit Rating," *Financial Times*, February 25, 2022. https://www.ft.com/content/93554a7e-f974-49fc-85ba-c111d253b002.

6. Angela Cullen, "Moody's Cuts Russia's Rating Deeper into Junk Territory to CA," *Bloomberg*, March 6, 2022, https://www.bloomberg.com/news/articles/2022-03-06/moody-s-cuts-russia-s-rating-deeper-into-junk-territory-to-ca.

7. Will Daniel, "BlackRock Funds Just Lost $17 Billion Due to Russian Exposure. That's Just the Tip of the Iceberg, as Western Banks Are Owed $121 Billion by Russian Entities," *Fortune*, March 11, 2022, https://fortune.com/2022/03/11/blackrock-banks-lose-billions-tip-iceberg-russia-ukraine/.

8. Flood et al., "'Investors Are Shocked.'"

9. Adrienne Klasa, Laurence Fletcher, Josephine Cumbo, and Tommy Stubbington, "Investors Face Deep Losses on $170bn in Russian Assets," *Financial Times*, March 4, 2022, https://www.ft.com/content/dca77dfb-f5a8-4e99-a53f-a2778d115410.

10. John Caparusso and Bryan Hardy, "Russia's Pre-war Position in the International Banking System," *BIS Quarterly Review*, June 2022.

11. Lisa Abramowicz, "Everyone Plays Venezuela's Hunger Games," *Bloomberg*, March 31, 2017, https://www.bloomberg.com/opinion/articles/2017-05-31/goldman-sachs-is-just-part-of-venezuela-s-hunger-bonds-crowd?leadSource=uverify%20wall.

12. Abramowicz, "Everyone Plays Venezuela's Hunger Games."

13. Maria Elena Vizcaino and Nicolle Yapur, "Defaulted Venezuela Bonds Are Luring Buyers Betting on U.S. Deal," *Bloomberg*, March 18, 2022, https://www.bloomberg.com/news/articles/2022-03-18/defaulted-venezuela-bonds-are-luring-buyers-betting-on-u-s-deal?leadSource=uverify%20wall.

14. Laurie Chen, "Former Chinese President Hu Jintao Removed from Congress," *Japan Times*, October 23, 2022, https://www.japantimes.co.jp/news/2022/10/23/world/politics-diplomacy-world/hu-jintao-china-congress-removed/.

15. "China Stocks Crumble in US as Worry Over Xi Spurs Record Selloff," *Bloomberg*, October 24, 2022, https://www.bloomberg .com/news/articles/2022-10-24/alibaba-jd-com-tumble-in-us-as-xi -asserts-full-control-in-china?leadSource=uverify%20wall.

16. Sofia Horta e Costa, Tania Chen, and Rebecca Choong Wilkins, "Xi's $6 Trillion Rout Shows China Markets Serve the Party First," *Bloomberg*, October 27, 2022, https://www.bloomberg.com/news /articles/2022-10-27/xi-s-6-trillion-rout-shows-china-markets-serve -the-party-first?leadSource=uverify%20wall.

17. "The Biggest Growth Opportunity in the History of Capitalism," McKinsey & Co, accessed November 23, 2022, https://emqqetf.com/.

18. Madeleine Albright, *Fascism: A Warning* (New York: HarperCollins, 2019), 177.

19. "Jarosław Kaczyński: Fue un choque de civilizaciones. Si alguien se cree polaco, debe estar del lado que defiende los valores tradiciona- les," *WPolityce*, July 19, 2020, https://wpolityce.pl/polityka/509968 -jaroslaw-kaczynski-to-bylo-starcie-cywilizacyjne.

20. Wojciech Sadurski, "How Democracy Dies (in Poland): A Case Study of Anti-Constitutional Populist Backsliding," *Legal Studies Research Paper—Sydney Law School* 18, no. 1 (January 2018).

21. Henry Foy, "Poland Should Buy up Foreign Banks Says Deputy PM," *Financial Times*, June 19, 2016, https://www.ft.com/content /57b26cae-348c-11e6-ad39-3fee5ffe5b5b.

22. "Poland's Government Wants to Take Control of Banking," *Economist*, August 9, 2018, https://www.economist.com/europe/2018 /08/09/polands-government-wants-to-take-control-of-banking.

23. "Poland's Government Wants to Take Control of Banking."

24. Marton Varju and Mónika Papp, "Sectorial Special Taxes in Hungary as Instruments of a Populist Fiscal Policy: A Legal Analysis," *Review of Central and East European Law*, 2022.

25. "Central Europe's Media-Capturing Epidemic," Reporting Democracy, accessed November 23, 2022, https://balkaninsight.com /2021/03/16/central-europes-media-capture-epidemic/.

26. "Egypt: Owners of Largest Dairy Production Co. Allegedly Unlawfully Imprisoned and Accused of Terrorism After Refusing to Hand over Shares to Military," Business & Human Rights Resources Centre, March 7, 2022, https://www.business-humanrights.org /en/latest-news/egypt-founders-of-egypts-largest-dairy-production -company-allegedly-unlawfully-improisonned-and-accused-of -terrorism-after-refusing-to-hand-over-shares-to-military/.

27. "Struggle over Egypt's Juhayna Behind Arrest of Founder, Son— Amnesty," Reuters, September 27, 2021, https://www.reuters.com /world/middle-east/struggle-over-egypts-juhayna-behind-arrest -founder-son-amnesty-2021-09-27/.

28. "Egypt: Owners of Largest Dairy Production Co. Allegedly Unlawfully Imprisoned."

29. "Why Egypt Isn't Open for Business: Despite Pro-business Talk, the Army Grabs Whatever It Wants," *Economist*, April 21, 2022, https://www.economist.com/middle-east-and-africa/2022/04/21/why-egypt-isnt-open-for-business.

30. "Why Egypt Isn't Open for Business."

31. Consumers' Research, "BlackRock: Backpedaling," Consumers' Research YouTube Channel, accessed March 28, 2022, https://www.youtube.com/watch?v=IaRKQyqCJsw.

32. See, for instance, a survey of papers in Larry Swedroe and Samuel Adams, *Your Essential Guide to Sustainable Investment* (Hampshire Harriman House, 2022).

33. Xun Lei and Tomasz Wisniewski, "Democracy and Stock Market Returns," *Social Science Research Network*, June 2018.

34. "The Polity Project," Center for Systematic Peace, accessed November 23, 2022, https://www.systemicpeace.org/polityproject.html.

35. Lei and Wisniewski, "Democracy and Stock Market Returns."

36. Federico Sturzenegger and Jeromin Zettelmeyer, "Haircuts: Estimating Investor Losses in Sovereign Debt Restructurings, 1998–2005," *Journal of International Money and Finance* 27, issue 5 (2008): 780–805.

37. David Lubin, *Dance of the Trillions: Developing Countries and Global Finance*, (Washington, DC: Brookings, 2018).

38. Douglass North and Barry Weingast, "Constitutions and Commitment: The Evolution of Institutions Governing Public Choice in Seventeenth Century England," *Journal of Economic History* 49, no. 4 (December 1989): 803–832.

39. Sebastian Saeigh, "Do Countries Have a Democratic Advantage? Political Institutions, Multilateral Agencies, and Sovereign Borrowing," *Comparative Political Studies* 20, no. 10 (2005).

40. Candence Archer, Glen Biglaiser, and Karl DeRouen, "Sovereign Bonds and the Democratic Advantage: Does Regime Type Affect Credit Rating Agency Ratings in the Developing World?," *International Organization* 61, no.2 (Spring 2007): 341–365.

41. Emily Beaulieu, Gary Cox, and Sebastian Saeigh, "Sovereign Debt and Regime Type: Reconsidering the Democratic Advantage," *International Organization* 66 (2012): 709–738.

42. Daron Acemoglu, Suresh Naidu, Pascual Restrepo, and James Robinson, "Democracy Does Cause Growth," *Journal of Political Economy* 127, no. 1 (February 2019).

43. Acemoglu et al., "Democracy Does Cause Growth."

44. Ding Gang, "Why the West Has Been Nervously Forecasting When China's Economy Will Overtake US," *Global Times*, September 7, 2022, https://www.globaltimes.cn/page/202209/1274841.shtml.

45. Ruchir Sharma, "China's Economy Will Not Overtake US Until 2060, If Ever," *Financial Times*, October 24, 2022, https://www.ft.com/content/cff42bc4-f9e3-4f51-985a-86518934afbe.

46. Michael Massing, "Does Democracy Avert Famine?," *New York Times*, March 1, 2003, https://www.nytimes.com/2003/03/01/arts/does-democracy-avert-famine.html.

47. Daniel Deudney and G. John Ikenberry, "The Myth of the Autocratic Revival: Why Liberal Democracy Will Prevail," *Foreign Affairs*, January 1, 2009, https://www.foreignaffairs.com/articles/china/2009-01-01/myth-autocratic-revival

48. Daron Acemoglu and James A. Robinson, *Why Nations Fail: The Origins of Power, Prosperity and Poverty* (London: Profile Books, 2013).

49. John Gerring, Philip Bond, William Barndt, and Carola Moreno, "Democracy and Economic Growth: A Historical Perspective," *World Politics* 57 (April 2005), 323–364.

50. Acemoglu et al., "Democracy Does Cause Growth."

51. Luis Martinez, "How Much Should We Trust the Dictator's GDP Growth Estimates?," *Journal of Political Economy* 130, no. 10 (October 2022).

52. Acemoglu et al., "Democracy Does Cause Growth."

53. Elias Papaioannou and Gregorios Siourounis, "Democratization and Growth," London Business School Economics Working Paper, July 2004.

54. Manuel Funke, Moritz Schularick, and Christoph Trebesch, "Populist Leaders and the Economy," *ECONtribute*, no. 36 (October 2020).

55. Rudiger Dornbusch and Sebastian Edwards, *The Macroeconomics of Populism in Latin America* (Chicago: Chicago University Press, 1991), 223–262.

56. Daron Acemoglu, Simon Johnson, and James Robinson, "Institutions as a Fundamental Cause of Long-Run Growth," in *Handbook of Economic Growth* (Amsterdam: Elsevier, 2005), 385–472.

57. Funke, Schularick, and Trebesch, "Populist Leaders and the Economy."

58. Ida Nesset, Ingrid Bøgeberg, Frode Kjærland, and Lars Molden, "How Underlying Dimensions of Political Risk Affect Excess Return in Emerging and Developed Markets," *Journal of Emerging Market Finance* 18, no. 1 (2019).

59. Heikki Lehkonen and Kari Heimonen, "Democracy, Political Risks and Stock Market Performance," *SSRN Electronic Journal*, November 2012.
60. Pablo Riveroll and James Barrineau, "Argentinian Markets Tumble as Political Uncertainty Returns," *Schroders*, August 13, 2019, https://www.schroders.com/en-us/us/individual/insights/argentinian-markets-tumble-as-political-uncertainty-returns/.
61. Lehkonen and Heimonen, "Democracy, Political Risks and Stock Market Performance."
62. René Stulz, "The Limits of Financial Globalization," *National Bureau of Economic Research*, no. 11070 (January 2005).
63. Stulz, "The Limits of Financial Globalization."
64. Rafael La Porta, Florencio Lopez-deSilanes, Andrei Shleifer, and Robert Vishny, "Investor Protection: Origins, Consequences and Reform," *National Bureau of Economic Research*, no. 7428 (July 1999).
65. Stulz, "The Limits of Financial Globalization."

CHAPTER 9

1. Samuel C. Adams and Larry E. Swedroe, *Your Essential Guide to Sustainable Investing: How to Live Your Values and Achieve Your Financial Goals with ESG, SRI, and Impact Investing* (Hampshire: Harriman House, 2022), 15.
2. "A Broken Idea: ESG Investing," *Economist*, Special Report, July 2022, 4.
3. Adams and Swedroe, *Your Essential Guide to Sustainable Investing*, 78.
4. Adams and Swedroe, *Your Essential Guide to Sustainable Investing*, 33.
5. Adams and Swedroe, *Your Essential Guide to Sustainable Investing*, 32.
6. Adams and Swedroe, *Your Essential Guide to Sustainable Investing*, 15.
7. Adams and Swedroe, *Your Essential Guide to Sustainable Investing*, 4.
8. Adams and Swedroe, *Your Essential Guide to Sustainable Investing*, 14–15.
9. "ESG: The Letters That Won't Save the Planet," *Economist*, July 2022, 8.
10. John Crider, "How Does Tesla Get a Worse ESG Score Than 2 Oil Companies?," *CleanTechnica*, May 11, 2022, https://cleantechnica.com/2022/05/11/how-does-tesla-get-a-worse-esg-score-than-2-oil-companies/.
11. Tariq Fancy, "The Secret Diary of a 'Sustainable Investor'—Part 1," *Medium*, August 20, 2021, https://medium.com/@sosofancy/the-secret-diary-of-a-sustainable-investor-part-1-70b6987fa139.
12. "Aswath Damodaran," Wikipedia, accessed February 6, 2023, https://en.wikipedia.org/wiki/Aswath_Damodaran.

13. Bradford Cornell and Aswath Damodaran, "Valuing ESG: Doing Good or Sounding Good?," NYU Stern School of Business, March 2020.
14. "ESG: The Letters That Won't Save the Planet," 9.
15. Cornell and Damodaran, "Valuing ESG: Doing Good or Sounding Good?," 2.
16. "A Broken Idea: ESG Investing," 9.
17. Florian Berg, Julian F. Kölbel, and Roberto Rigobon, "Aggregate Confusion: The Divergence of ESG Ratings," *Review of Finance* 26, no. 6 (November 2022): 1315–1344, 2.
18. Ľuboš Pástor, Robert F. Stambaugh, and Lucian A. Taylor, "Sustainable Investing in Equilibrium," *Journal of Financial Economics* 142, no.2 (November 2021): 550–571.
19. Becky O'Connor, *The ESG Investing Handbook: Insights and Developments in Environmental, Social and Governance Investment* (Hampshire: Harriman House, 2022), 265.
20. Adams and Swedroe, *Your Essential Guide to Sustainable Investing*, 89.
21. Adams and Swedroe, *Your Essential Guide to Sustainable Investing*, 89.
22. "SEC Charges BNY Mellon Investment Adviser for Misstatements and Omissions Concerning ESG Considerations," U.S. Securities and Exchange Commission, accessed September 4, 2023, https://www.sec.gov/news/press-release/2022-86.
23. Tim Quinson, "The SEC War on Greenwashing Has Begun", *Bloomberg*, June 15, 2022, https://www.bloomberg.com/news/articles/2022-06-15/the-sec-s-war-against-greenwashing-and-esg-misuse-has-begun.
24. "A Broken Idea: ESG Investing," 3.
25. "A Broken Idea: ESG Investing," 10.
26. "International Sustainability Standards Board," IFRS, accessed February 6, 2023, https://www.ifrs.org/groups/international-sustainability-standards-board/.
27. O'Connor, *The ESG Investing Handbook*, 216–219.
28. Brendan McDermid, "Russia Will Be Excluded from All JPMorgan Fixed Income Indexes," Reuters, March 7, 2022, https://www.reuters.com/business/finance/russia-will-be-excluded-all-jpmorgan-fixed-income-indexes-statement-2022-03-07/.
29. J.P. Morgan, "J.P. Morgan ESG EMBI Global Diversified Index. Methodology and Factsheet," J.P. Morgan, May 2021.
30. Kate Allen, "Poland Returns to Debt Market to Bolster Green Credentials," *Financial Times*, February 28, 2019, https://www.ft.com/content/bb722b42-3b66-11e9-b856-5404d3811663.
31. McDermid, "Russia Will be Excluded from All JPMorgan Fixed Income Indexes."

32. Ross Kerber and Tommy Wilkes, "How Russia's War Blindsided the World of ESG Investing," Reuters, July 1, 2022, https://www.reuters .com/business/how-russias-war-blindsided-world-esg-investing -2022-07-01/.

33. Ross Kerber, "How Russia's War Blindsided the World of ESG Investing," *Japan Times*, July 3, 2022, https://www .japantimes.co.jp/news/2022/07/03/business/financial-markets/russia -war-esg-investing/.

34. S&P Global, "S&P Global ESG Scores Methodology," S&P Global, 2022.

35. "RepRisk Methodology Overview," RepRisk, accessed February 6, 2023, https://www.reprisk.com/news-research/resources /methodology.

36. "MSCI ESG Rating Methodology," MSCI, accessed February 3, 2023, https://www.msci.com/esg-and-climate-methodologies.

37. "ESG Risk Ratings Methodology," Sustainalytics, accessed February 3, 2023, https://connect.sustainalytics.com/esg-risk-ratings -methodology.

38. Berg, Kölbel, and Rigobon, "Aggregate Confusion."

39. "One Planet Sovereign Wealth Funds: Integrating Climate Change Risk and Investing in the Smooth Transition to a Low Emissions Economy," One Planet SWF Network, accessed February 6, 2023, https://oneplanetswfs.org/.

40. Anna Georgieva, James Allen, Justin Sloggett, Kris Douma, Matt Orsagh, and Sofia Bartholdy, *Guidance and Case Studies for ESG Integration: Equities and Fixed Income* (New York: CFA Institute, 2018).

41. Iain Marlow and Isabella Steger, "Investors Are Ignoring a Dangerous Crackdown on Press Freedom," *Bloomberg*, August 4, 2021, https://www.bloomberg.com/news/features/2021-08-04/what -press-freedom-crackdowns-from-u-s-to-china-to-Turkey-mean-for -investors.

42. Gina Gambetta and Dominic Webb, "Industriens Pension Sells Myanmar and Belarus Govvies as Pension Funds Continue Human Rights Push," *Responsible Investor*, May 27, 2021, https://www .responsible-investor.com/industriens-pension-sells-myanmar-and -belarus-govvies-as-pension-funds-continue-human-rights-push/.

43. Richard Wike, Katie Simmons, Bruce Stokes, and Janell Fetterolf, "Globally, Broad Support for Representative and Direct Democracy: But Many Also Endorse Nondemocratic Alternatives," *Pew Research Center*, October 16, 2017, https://www.pewresearch.org/global /2017/10/16/globally-broad-support-for-representative-and-direct -democracy/.

44. Gerardo L. Munck and Jay Verkuilen, "Conceptualizing and Measuring Democracy: Evaluating Alternative Indices," *SAGE Journals* 35, no.1 (2002): 9.
45. "Democracy Index 2022," Economist Intelligence Unit, February 2023.
46. Freedom House, "Freedom in the World 2023: Marking 50 Years in the Struggle for Democracy," Freedom House, 2023.
47. V-Dem Institute, "Democracy Report 2023: Defiance in the Face of Autocratization," V-Dem Institute, 2023.
48. Michael Coppedge, John Gerring, Carl Henrik Knutsen, Staffan I. Lindberg, Jan Teorell, Kyle L. Marquardt, Juraj Medzihorsky, Daniel Pemstein, Nazifa Alizada, Lisa Gastaldi, Garry Hindle, Josefine Pernes, Johannes von Römer, Eitan Tzelgov, Yi-ting Wang, and Steven Wilson, "V-Dem Methodology v12," Varieties of Democracy (V-Dem), 2022.
49. Munck and Verkuilen, "Conceptualizing and Measuring Democracy," 28.
50. Munck and Verkuilen, "Conceptualizing and Measuring Democracy," 29.
51. "IEDGE—Índice Riesgo País," IEDGE Business School, accessed February 6, 2023, https://www.iedge.eu/aurelio-garcia-indices -riesgo-pais.
52. MSCI, "MSCI Emerging Markets Index (USD)," MSCI, 2023.

CHAPTER 10

1. "Index Composition: J.P. Morgan," J.P. Morgan, accessed January 23, 2023, https://www.jpmorgan.com/insights/research/index-research /composition-docs.
2. "ESG Investing: Momentum Moves Mainstream," J.P. Morgan, accessed January 23, 2023, https://www.jpmorgan.com/insights /research/build-back-better-esg-investing.
3. J.P. Morgan, "J.P. Morgan ESG CEMBI Broad Diversified Custom Maturity Index," J.P. Morgan, March 2023.
4. "J.P. Morgan ESG CEMBI Broad Diversified Custom Maturity Index," March 2023.
5. "J.P. Morgan ESG CEMBI Broad Diversified Custom Maturity Index," March 2023.
6. "MSCI ESG Indexes Factsheet," MSCI, 2023.
7. "Emerging Markets ETF Overview," Emerging Markets ETF Channel, accessed January 23, 2023, https://www.etf.com/channels /emerging-markets-etfs.
8. "iShares J.P. Morgan USD Emerging Markets Bond ETF," BlackRock, accessed January 23, 2023, https://www.blackrock.com /cl/productos/239572/ishares-jp-morgan-usd-emerging-markets -bond-etf.

9. "Emerging Markets ETF Overview," January 23, 2023.

10. "VWO: Vanguard FTSE Emerging Markets ETF," Vanguard, accessed January 23, 2023, https://investor.vanguard.com/investment -products/etfs/profile/vwo.

11. Jianli Yang and Alvaro Piaggio, "It's Time We Give Corporations a Human Rights Scorecard," *Globe Post*, March 9, 2022, https:// theglobepost.com/2022/03/01/corporations-human-rights/.

12. Kevin Phillips, *1775: A Good Year for Revolution* (New York: Penguin Books, 2013), 96.

13. Barry Eichengreen, "What Money Can't Buy: The Limits of Economic Power," *Foreign Affairs*, June 21, 2022, https://www .foreignaffairs.com/articles/united-states/2022-06-21/what-money -cant-buy-economic-power.

14. Jacob Lew and Richard Nephew, "The Use and Misuse of Economic Statecraft," *Foreign Affairs*, October 15, 2018, https://www .foreignaffairs.com/articles/world/2018-10-15/use-and-misuse -economic-statecraft.

15. Daniel Drezner, "The United States of Sanctions: The Use and Abuse of Economic Coercion," *Foreign Affairs*, August 24, 2021, https:// www.foreignaffairs.com/articles/united-states/2021-08-24/united -states-sanctions.

16. Drezner, "The United States of Sanctions."

17. The Department of the Treasury, "The Treasury 2021 Sanctions Review," The Department of the Treasury of the United States, October 2021.

18. Justyna Gudzowska and John Prendergast, "Can Sanctions Be Smart? The Costs and Benefits of Economic Coercion," *Foreign Affairs*, February 22, 2022, https://www.foreignaffairs.com/articles/world /2022-02-22/can-sanctions-be-smart.

19. Lew and Nephew, "The Use and Misuse of Economic Statecraft."

20. Drezner, "The United States of Sanctions."

21. Lew and Nephew, "The Use and Misuse of Economic Statecraft."

22. Eichengreen, "What Money Can't Buy: The Limits of Economic Power."

23. Drezner, "The United States of Sanctions."

24. Office of Foreign Assets Control, "Directive 1 Under Executive Order of April 15, 2021 Blocking Property with Respect to Specified Harmful Foreign Activities of the Government of the Russian Federation," The Department of the Treasury of the United States, April 2021.

25. Office of Foreign Assets Control, "Directive 1A Under Executive Order 14024: Prohibitions Related to Certain Sovereign Debt of the Russian Federation," The Department of the Treasury of the United States, February 2022.

26. Andrew Wilson, *Belarus: The Last European Dictatorship* (London: Yale University Press, 2021), 256.

27. Maryia Sadouskaya-Komlach, "Belarus Goes Its Own Way: Thanks for the Advice, but This Movement Knows What It's Doing," *Foreign Affairs*, August 18, 2020, https://www.foreignaffairs.com/articles/belarus/2020-08-18/belarus-goes-its-own-way.

28. The Department of the Treasury, "Executive Order Blocking Property of Certain Persons Undermining Democratic Processes or Institutions in Belarus," The Department of the Treasury of the United States, June 2006.

29. Wilson, *Belarus: The Last European Dictatorship*, 218.

30. European Parliament, "Belarus Election: Severely Flawed According to Election Monitors," *European Parliament*, March 2006.

31. "Belarus Election Labeled 'A Farce,'" CBS News, March 20, 2006, https://www.cbsnews.com/news/belarus-election-labeled-a-farce/.

32. Andrew Roth and Yan Auseyushklin, "Belarus Opposition Candidate Rejects Election Result After Night of Protests," *Guardian*, August 11, 2020, https://www.theguardian.com/world/2020/aug/10/belarus-opposition-candidate-rejects-election-result-protests-svetlana-tikhanovskaya-lukashenko.

33. Russian News Agency, "S&P Changed Outlook for Belarus' Sovereign Credit Rating to Negative," Russian News Agency, September 12, 2020, https://tass.com/economy/1200123.

34. "J.P. Morgan ESG CEMBI Broad Diversified Custom Maturity Index," March 2023.

35. Office of Foreign Assets Control, "Directive 1 Under Executive Order 14038," The Department of the Treasury of the United States, (December 2021).

36. Wilson Center, "The Role of Belarus in the Russia-Ukraine Conflict: From Guarantor of Security to a Source of Instability," streamed July 2022 at Wilson Center, https://www.wilsoncenter.org/event/role-belarus-russia-ukraine-conflict-guarantor-security-source-instability.

37. Clearstream Spotlight, "Reg S & Rule 144A Securities Remain Key Component of the Issuers Financing Toolkit," Clearstream—Deutsche Börse Group, July 2020.

38. Rakhi Kumar, Natasha Dayaramani, and James D. Rocha, "Understanding and Comprehending ESG Terminology: A Practical Framework for Identifying the ESG Strategy That Is Right for You," State Street Global Advisors, 2018.

39. Marta Domínguez-Jiménez and Alexander Lehmann, "Accounting for Climate Policies in Europe's Sovereign Debt Market," *Policy Contribution* 10, no.21 (April 2021).

40. Domínguez-Jiménez and Lehmann, "Accounting for Climate Policies in Europe's Sovereign Debt Market."
41. Ekaterina M. Gratcheva, Bryan Gurhy, Teal Emery, Dieter Wang, Luis Oganes, Jarrad K. Linzie, Lydia Harvey, Katherine Marney, Jessica Murray, and Rupert Rink, "A New Dawn: Rethinking Sovereign ESG," J.P. Morgan and World Bank, 2021.
42. Gong Chen, Torsten Ehlers, and Frank Packer, "Sovereigns and Sustainable Bonds: Challenges and New Options," *BIS Quarterly Review*, September 2022.
43. Chen, Ehlers, and Packer, "Sovereigns and Sustainable Bonds."
44. Domínguez-Jiménez and Lehmann, "Accounting for Climate Policies in Europe's Sovereign Debt Market."
45. Domínguez-Jiménez and Lehmann, "Accounting for Climate Policies in Europe's Sovereign Debt Market."
46. "Freedom-Weighted. Emerging Markets Equity," Freedom ETFs, accessed January 23, 2023, https://freedometfs.com/.
47. Morningstar, "FRDM: Freedom 100 Emerging Markets ETF Factsheet," Morningstar, 2023.
48. FRDM, "Freedom y 100 Emerging Markets ETF," *The Freedom 100 Emerging Markets*, March 2023.
49. "iShares Core MSCI Emerging Markets ETF: Fact Sheet," iShares by BlackRock, March 2023.
50. Angelo Calvello and Elisabetta Basilico, "Three Ways to Assess Your Portfolio's Exposure to Autocratic Regimes," IMD, July 19, 2022, https://www.imd.org/ibyimd/finance/three-ways-to-assess-your-portfolios-exposure-to-autocratic-regimes/.
51. Gratcheva et al., "A New Dawn: Rethinking Sovereign ESG."
52. "DMCY: Democracy International Fund ETF," Democracy Investments, accessed January 23, 2023, https://www.democracyinvestments.com/fund.
53. "Democracy Investment Management Factsheet: The Democracy International Fund ETF," DMCY, accessed January 23, 2023. https://www.democracyinvestments.com/fund.
54. iShares, "iShares MSCI Emerging Markets ETF Factsheet," iShares, 2023.
55. "VWO: Vanguard FTSE Emerging Markets ETF," accessed January 23, 2023.
56. "Defund Dictators Portfolio," Defund Dictators, accessed January 23, 2023, https://defunddictators.org/#/portfolio?etfs=%7B%22etf%22:%22EEM%22,%22weight%22:0.5%7D&etfs=%7B%22etf%22:%22VWO%22,%22weight%22:0.5%7D&methodology=FREEDOM_HOUSE.
57. Gratcheva et al., "A New Dawn: Rethinking Sovereign ESG."

INDEX

Page numbers followed by *n* refer to notes.

ABOUT THE AUTHOR

Marcos Buscaglia is an economist, former Wall Street analyst, and Emerging Markets expert. He has more than 30 years experience doing research on the economies of Emerging Market countries and advising Wall Street companies.

For five years he was the head of the Latin America economics team at Bank of America Merrill Lynch in New York. In 2015, he was number one in the Institutional Investor rankings in the Latin America economics and Argentina categories. He also served as chief economist for Latin America at Citibank in New York and chief economist for the Southern Cone countries at Citibank, based in Buenos Aires. Previously, he was the Dean of Graduate Business Programs at the University of San Andrés, and a professor at IAE Business School, Universidad Austral. He taught International Finance at different universities in Latin America.

In addition to *Beyond the ESG Portfolio*, he has published two books in Spanish, and several papers. Marcos is regularly featured in international media, including the BBC, *Bloomberg*, Reuters, *Financial Times*, the *Wall Street Journal*, *El País* (Spain), *El Mercurio* (Chile), and *Folha* (Brazil). He has a biweekly column in *La Nación*'s Sunday edition in Argentina. He is also emerging as a leading voice on the theme of financial markets and democracy, with publications on this topic in the *Financial Times* and the *RSA Journal*. He has been a panelist on this subject in the Oslo Freedom Forum in 2022 and 2023.

Marcos holds a PhD in economics from the University of Pennsylvania, where he was a Fulbright scholar. He has a graduate degree in economics from Universidad Torcuato Di Tella and a degree in economics (summa cum laude) from the Catholic University of Argentina. He is married and has four children.